The year is 1909 and two-year-old 7790 is sitting on the Ann Arbor station wye.
Schramm Collection

Special 109

WHEN EASTERN MICHIGAN RODE THE RAILS III

TRANSIT ACROSS MICHIGAN BY INTERURBAN, TRAIN, BUS

Jack E Schramm

BY

Jack E. Schramm

William H. Henning

Richard R. Andrews

INTERURBAN PRESS • GLENDALE, CALIFORNIA

This book has been endorsed by the Michigan Sesquicentennial Commission as a Sesquicentennial project.

WHEN EASTERN MICHIGAN RODE THE RAILS, Book III

Published by:
INTERURBAN PRESS
P. O. Box 6444
Glendale, CA 91205

Manufactured in the United States of America

FIRST PRINTING: Summer 1988

Library of Congress Cataloging-in-Publication Data
(Revised for vol. 3)

Schramm, Jack E.
    When Eastern Michigan rode the rails.

    (Interurbans special; 94, 105, 109)
    Vols. 1-2 have variant series title: Special.
    Vol. 2 by: Jack E. Schramm, William H. Henning.
    Includes bibliographies and indexes.
    Contents: [1] [without special title] — 2. The rapid railway and Detroit-Port Huron by rail-ship-bus — 3. Transit across Michigan by interurban, train, bus.
    1. Street-railroads—Michigan—History. I. Henning, William H. II. Andrews, Richard R. III. Title. IV. Series: Interurbans special; 94, etc.

TF724.M5S37   1984   385'.5   84-19180
ISBN 0-916374-65-3 (v. 1)

TABLE OF CONTENTS

ACKNOWLEDGEMENTS

OUR THANKS to the many newspaper editors and reporters who documented the building, operation, and, in many cases, the demise of the various types of public transportation in southeastern Michigan. Through the years The Detroit United Railway daily mounted these articles into large scrapbooks. Fortunately, we were able to obtain over 40 volumes of these scrapbooks covering almost all the years from 1894 to 1931.

This saved valuable time in historical research since few company records have been located. Upon completion of this four-volume series on interurbans, the scrapbooks will be placed in the Bentley Historical Library at the University of Michigan in Ann Arbor.

When quotations from other than Detroit newspapers are used, the city, town or village in which they were published is identified. Lengthy articles have been abstracted or condensed for the most important data.

For in-depth material on Ann Arbor, we were fortunate to obtain a copy of *History of Public Transit in Ann Arbor* compiled by the AATA. This publication contains articles clipped from the local newspapers, covering the years from 1888 to 1969.

To add human interest stories and operational experiences, two books provided interesting excerpts. They were *Ann's Amazing Arbor* by Alger Buell Crandell, and *Northville, The First Hundred Years* by Jack W. Hoffman.

To complete this volume with its wide diversity of subjects, we must acknowledge the assistance of the following rail, traction, boat and bus enthusiasts:

Donald Baut
Sam Breck
Gordon Bugbee
George Cutler
Bernard Drouillard
Frank Frazen
H. M. Hildebrandt
John Hoschek

Norman Krentel
Rod Lenderink
Donald S. Moore
Ray Radway
Robert Radway
John Stewart
Allan R. Treppa
Clarence Woodard

Thanks also to the many helpful libraries, historical societies, museums and friends who provided pictures and a story or two.

The indexing was again done by Joseph Oldenburg, Detroit Public Library.

This was Michigan Avenue in 1908 at Burrell switch, 3½ miles east of Ypsilanti.   *Hildebrandt Collection*

PREFACE

DETROIT HAS ALWAYS BEEN the major population and commercial center of Michigan. Commerce moved in and out along five major arteries. Our two earlier volumes featured the routes along Woodward, Grand River and Gratiot avenues. This volume covers the development and usage of public transit along the Michigan Avenue corridor west from the metropolis. It includes not only the interurban itself, but its interaction with the railroads and their steamboats, and the buses which appeared later along with the automobile.

Peak travel by public carrier was reached about the time of World War I, when extensive service was provided by interurban, train and boat. Business and commerce flourished in the area, and the state of Michigan became an industrial leader.

Today, what little surface public transit remains is furnished by only two weekday Amtrak trains between Detroit and Chicago, with a third train on weekends. Bus lines are rapidly curtailing service. Highways have taken over, and the automobile reigns supreme.

In 1880 the Dearborn Hotel offered food and a place of rest for the weary traveler. It was located at the corner of Michigan Avenue and Center Street (now Monroe Boulevard). In front is a three-seat horse-drawn surrey.
Dearborn Historical Commission

The tollgate at Inkster Road and Michigan on the Detroit & Saline Plank Road. The collector is probably taking the toll from the buggy driver. The large building next to the tollhouse was Wietoff's Tavern. Toll roads, never a large profit maker, suffered a sharp drop in revenue after the coming of the interurban.
Dearborn Historical Commission

The original Michigan Central depot in Ypsilanti. The locomotive *Reliable* was built in 1872.
Stoner Collection

Car 7297 of the Rapid Railway loads passengers in Ypsilanti in this 1911 view. It was equipped with third-rail shoes for operation over Michigan Railway lines beyond Jackson.
Maguire Collection

These two photos appeared in a November 1925 article in *Bus Transportation* magazine on early motor coach operation in Michigan. Both buses appear to be built on Reo chassis.

Detroit Public Library

BACKGROUND

LAKE ERIE'S first steamboat, *Walk-in-the-Water*, was launched in 1818 to compete with the sailing ships. For the next six years the Fulton-Livingston steamboat syndicate had exclusive navigation rights in New York State waters. This contract retarded development of shipping service until 1824 when the U.S. Supreme Court struck down the New York legislature's grant to the syndicate.

On October 25, 1825, the Erie Canal opened, which offered shippers an easier and cheaper way to move heavy and bulky cargo. Barges built specifically for the canal carried passengers and merchandise from the Hudson River to lakes Erie and Ontario. Travel time was reduced to only 5½ days from Detroit to New York. "Before the war (1812), it took at least two months," noted a contemporary newspaper.

By 1831 service had improved greatly. Daily sailings were scheduled from each end of the lake with a week needed for the steamboat's round trip, due in part to stopping at each port along the south shore of the lake. By 1834, two daily sailings were listed, and two years later the number had reached three. The year 1838 saw almost 50 ships on Lake Erie, as well as a ship owners organization called the Combination that set rates and schedules for both passengers and freight.

With the opening of the Erie Canal, the availability of cheap land in what was then considered the "West" (especially Michigan) and lower shipping rates for farm products through the Erie Canal, brought settlers into Michigan Territory in ever-increasing numbers. Merchants received their orders from the East quicker, allowing them to sell the latest products. Cheap land attracted both speculators and settlers taking advantage of the 1820 Congressional Land Act that permitted settlers to purchase 80 acres for $1.25 an acre. In 1831 the Detroit office sold 217,943 acres, and by the time Michigan applied for statehood in 1836, more than 4,000,000 acres had been sold. Farmers in the territory could now ship their harvest to the New York market for just $8 a ton, where previously it had been $100 a ton.

Travel by Land

The first recorded road in the Michigan Territory was a narrow path used to take mail to Detroit from Cincinnati. The mail was delivered by horseback, which meant the "post road," as it was called, was little more than a bridle path. During the War of 1812 troops from Ohio brought supplies to Detroit in wagons after the military improved the road. The route was from Port Lawrence (Toledo) through Monroe, Trenton (Dixie Highway) and along the Detroit River (West Jefferson) to Detroit.

The first surveyed road was authorized by Congress on December 15, 1815, and called the "Pontiac Road" along what today is Woodward Avenue. In 1822 a road from Ohio to Detroit was authorized, followed by the "Chicago Road" on March 3, 1825. The Chicago Road followed an old Indian trail named Sauk-Fox Trail to the shore of Lake Michigan, along what is now U.S. Highway 12. Included in this authorization were roads to Saginaw, Fort Gratiot (Port Huron) and Sandusky, Ohio. On July 4, 1832, Congress provided for a road northwest out of Detroit along present-day Grand River Avenue.

Transportation was now sorely needed to handle the influx of settlers into the Detroit area. The first public stage line was advertised in Detroit's newspapers in June 1822. It met the steamboats in Detroit and continued to Mt. Clemens, probably along the shoreline of the Detroit River and Lake St. Clair. In 1827 stage service to Ohio was inaugurated, and by the early 1830's there were post stages carrying mail and passengers to Ypsilanti, Ann Arbor and Tecumseh.

By April 1832, the stage network included a line to Sandusky, Ohio, via Monroe, and Maumee, Ohio, leaving Detroit daily. Another line ran from Detroit to St. Joseph passing through Ypsilanti, Saline, Clinton, Jonesville, White Pigeon, Mottville and Niles, leaving at 7 a.m. daily during the summer and three times weekly during the winter. A line to Ann Arbor was scheduled three times weekly through Pekin, Plymouth and Panama. The Pontiac line left daily with a branch going three times weekly to Rochester, Stoney Creek and Romeo. A line to Mt. Clemens was also scheduled three times weekly along what is now Gratiot. All these routes also carried mail.

May 30, 1834, was the start of a new stage line offering coach service across the state to St. Joseph on the eastern shore of Lake Michigan. From there a steamship took passemgers across the lake to Chicago. The trip was supposed to take less than five days. The 1837 Mac Cabe's *Detroit Directory* advertised three daily departures by the Western Stage Company at Woodward and Jefferson. One trip was to Chicago in 4½ days with stops at Ypsilanti, Tecumseh, Jonesville, White Pigeon, Niles and Michigan City. The other two went to Kalamazoo in 2 days and Sandusky, Ohio, in 2½ days. It was not unitl 1873, after the expansion of railroads, the last scheduled stagecoaches left Detroit.

The Railroads Arrive

The next form of land transportation to appear was the railroad. The first routes planned were to operate from ports on the east side of Michigan across the state to navigable rivers on the west side. From New York west to Michigan, travel by ship was still considered best. Railroads began laying track into the state's interior, opening communication and ease of travel for passengers and freight to the port cities. The Territory and later the State of Michigan encouraged railroad construction, realizing what the development of the railroads could mean to the economy of the country.

The first railroad in the Midwest, the Erie& Kalamazoo (E&K), was planned from Port Lawrence (Toledo] to the Kalamazoo River. The E&K began operation to Adrian in the fall of 1836, using horse power and wooden rails. Soon other east-west lines were started in Michigan.

In 1837 Michigan became the 26th state and began a program of major improvements. One major item in the program was for the state to build and operate three railroads across the lower peninsula. To accomplish this, the Detroit & St. Joseph Railroad, which was building a line from Detroit to Ypsilanti, was purchased by the state which subsequently completed and operated the line as far as Kalamazoo—140 miles. This line later was to become the Michigan Central Railroad (MCRR).

Michigan Southern Railroad laid out a line from Monroe on Lake Erie to New Buffalo on Lake Michigan. First, the state purchased the short River Raisin & Lake Erie Railroad near Monroe. Then a 65-mile line was built from Monroe to Hillsdale.

The third line across the state was to be named the Michigan Northern. It was graded only for a short distance out of Port Huron before the project ceased.

Nearly bankrupt in 1846, the state decided it had enough of owning and operating railroads and sold its interests to private owners. The sales agreement included provisions that the roads had to be completed across the state. The Michigan Southern and Michigan Central eventually were completed, but not in the manner the state had planned. There was a great deal of maneuvering and infighting, and both lines terminated in Chicago which was destined to become the main railroad center of the Midwest.

Toll Roads are Tried

With the threat of a Canadian invasion diminishing, the military roads ceased being maintained and rapidly deteriorated. The few early railroads did not serve many rural areas. The state was unwilling to invest money in building a network of highways, leaving individual communities to finance and control their own roads. A new answer was sought.

In 1845 the state legislature passed an act authorizing toll roads. Since state money was not involved, 60-year franchises were available to those wishing to invest in building and operating such a road. Toll roads were built in many parts of the state, with the greatest network in southeastern Michigan radiating from Detroit. Here the former military roads became toll roads with a few new routes added, including Jefferson Avenue to Grosse Pointe.

The Interurban Era

Horse-drawn streetcars first appeared on Detroit's streets in 1863, soon to be followed by lines in other cities and towns. While car lines improved the movement of people and aided the growth of the cities, they were limited by the use of horse power. The car lines remained short and travel was slow. Then in 1886 early experimental electric lines were built in some Detroit suburbs. By 1892 the electric streetcar became a reality in Detroit with the city's first major conversion from horse power. In 1895 the changeover to electricity was complete, and Detroit's area and population both grew rapidly.

By 1895 many Michigan towns were served by a streetcar system and most were electrified. Promoters now saw a new means of moving people and merchandise between cities and towns, by building an electric line connecting communities, often along the original toll road right-of-way. Success in 1891 with the steam-powered "Ypsi-Ann" between Ypsilanti and Ann Arbor, started promoters considering this form of investment.

Early passenger cars, called *interurbans*, were not much larger than the city cars, but in time grew in size, comfort and speed. Freight operations were started, carrying many items including milk, which was brought fresh daily from farms to the city.

This volume covers Michigan's two largest interurban operations. First the Detroit United Railway organized December 31, 1900, consolidating all the Detroit city railway companies into a single company. Later the DUR gained control of all interurban lines entering Detroit (see Family Tree, chapter 3), and the rail lines in Windsor, Ontario, Canada. The second company, Michigan United Railways (later Michigan Railway), controlled the lines west of Jackson to Lake Michigan and north to Lansing and beyond. It also controlled the line from Flint to Saginaw and Bay City (see volume 1: *When Eastern Michigan Rode the Rails*).

Both companies flourished until the 1920's when the newest modes of transportation, the automobile and the motor bus, came into their own. By the mid-1930's, the last interurban ran in Michigan and the last streetcar operated over Detroit streets on April 8, 1956.

The Highway Network

The Motor Age was actually started by bicycle enthusiasts, who, at the turn of the century, were numerous enough to become a powerful political force. Led by Horatio Earle and Edward Hines, a drive for year-round hard surface roads in Michigan culminated in 1905 with the creation of the office of State Highway Commissioner. This act empowered the state improve roads, and county road commissions were soon established. Earle became the state's first highway commissioner, and Hines became chairman of the Wayne County Road Commission.

In 1909, two roads were scheduled to be paved: Woodward from Six to Seven Mile roads and Michigan from Livernois to Miller Road. By a vote of two of the three commissioners (John S. Haggerty and Edward Hines) it was decided to pave Woodward with concrete and Michigan with brick to compare costs and durability. In August 1909, the nation's first mile of concrete highway was laid. Since concrete proved to be cheaper, the use of brick for paving was dropped by Wayne County in 1911.

During the first years of the century there were few automobiles, but this was soon to be changed. As their number increased and tax revenues from license fees and gasoline taxes mushroomed, demands for better roads increased. Federal funds were now becoming available for interstate and certain local roads.

Today there is an extensive network of expressways throughout Michigan. All are freeways, though there has been an occasional promotion to build toll roads. The remaining vestigal passenger rail service is confined to the Amtrak lines from Detroit to Chicago, Port Huron to Chicago and Grand Rapids to Chicago.

The only surviving cross-lake passenger and auto service is across Lake Michigan from Ludington, Michigan, to Kewaunee, Wisconsin. This service is normally provided by #41, *City of Midland*, an ex-Pere Marquette (rail) carferry now operated by the Michigan-Wisconsin Transportation Company.

Bus service has greatly diminished, in Russell's *Official Motor Coach Guide for Michigan* of June 5, 1929, there were listed 68 bus companies serving 775 towns. In Russell's National Edition for December 1986, there are only 15 Michigan bus companies with 133 bus stations.

Michigan Avenue in Dearborn, showing four modes of transportation: interurban, horse and buggy, bicycle and the newest on the scene, the motor car.
Moore Collection

11

This series of photos graphically illustrates the rapid changes in Michigan highways with the coming of the automobile. First, Miller Road and Michigan Ave. are shown on April 22, 1910.
Dearborn Historical Commission

Taken just west of Miller Road, this April 26, 1921, photo shows the first narrow pavement of Michigan Ave. and an early Ford Model T. The vacant interurban track was a sign of what was to come.
Dearborn Historical Commission

Twenty Years of Change

Michigan and Miller Road just five years later on May 18, 1926. The interurban line is now double-tracked and moved to the center. Note the early Detroit Motorbus and DSR bus, both serving the new Ford Rouge Plant.
Dearborn Historical Commission

By late 1927, Michigan Avenue was put under the recently elevated Pere Marquette Railroad tracks near Miller Road. The DJ&C was living out its last few days in this September 1, 1929, view, which shows a DSR Peter Witt car enroute to Schaefer Road and the Ford Rouge. In another three years the track area would be paved over.

William Bradley

13

This 1907 photo shows car 26 competing with horsepower in downtown Ypsilanti. In later years this car was renumbered 7768; in 1925 it became a trailer and in 1930 a camp car for track construction crews.

Schramm Collection

1
BUILDING THE YPSI-ANN

IN THE SUMMER OF 1890 one of those useful but unpopular promoters dropped off the train at Ypsilanti and began to get a franchise for a street railway between Ann Arbor and Ypsilanti. He got some people of those towns interested after a lot of urging, and what seemed big stories of the traffic to be developed. For instance, he claimed that 500 people a day would ride between the towns.

"After we had ascertained that the Michigan Central (Railroad) was only carrying 40 people a day between Ann Arbor and Ypsilanti it seemed impossible. But he had us telegraph to the eight or ten interurban roads then in operation in the United States to verify his rosy dream. To our surprise we learned they were building up a large communication between towns which were near each other, when they could offer frequent service and low fares.

"To our further surprise, we afterwards found the promoter's estimate was below the number that was daily carried, for over 600 a day availed themselves of the convenience not long after the road was in operations, instead of the 40 who took Michigan Central. This was mainly because the service was every hour and a half, while the fare one way was ten cents instead of twenty-five cents on the steam railroad.

"It was greatly helped by the simple fact that, while Ann Arbor had 3,000 boys and not enough girls, Ypsilanti had a 1,000 girls at the Normal College (Eastern Michigan University) and not enough boys. The street railway helped restore the equilibrium on Friday evenings, Saturdays and Sundays."

The above recollection was delivered at the annual meeting of the Michigan Historical Society in 1905 by

An early photo of the "Ypsi-Ann." Too bad it isn't in color, with its cardinal red locomotive and canary yellow trailers!
Stoner Collection

Junius Beal, and was titled *The Beginnings of Interurbans*, first published in *The Michigan Letter* in 1907. Beal's remarks are often quoted and help greatly to explain the early interurban mania which gripped Michigan and many other states.

The Promoter Arrives

When Charles D. Haines alighted from the train that day in 1890, he already had a franchise, relatively speaking, in his hip pocket. Because the neighboring city of Ann Arbor approved a franchise for a street railway, Ypsilanti wanted the same. On October 16, 1889, a letter was sent to Haines Brothers of Kinderhook, N.Y., contractors for both steam and street railways. The city wanted to know if the Haines Company would be interested in building a street railway in Ypsilanti.

The response was favorable, and while the brothers did not plan to travel west any more that year, Haines "decided to build a car line in Ypsilanti provided the franchise is given us at an early date." This reply was reported in the *Ypsilantian* on November 14, 1889, along with the city's response. The newspaper noted that the city council on November 4, by unanimous vote, passed an ordinance which ". . . granted and vested in Charles D. Haines, Elmer T. Haines and Andrew Haines, of Kinderhook, New York . . . to locate, establish, construct and maintain street railways upon the streets within the city of Ypsilanti . . ."

Upon his arrival in Ypsilanti, Haines quickly determined that the community itself would be unable to support a local streetcar system. He proposed a 7½-mile line from downtown Ypsilanti to the Ann Arbor city limits. At a meeting on August 9, the townships of

Ann Arbor, Pittsfield and Ypsilanti announced their approval of the proposed road passing through their townships. This endorsement stimulated the road's supporters to begin obtaining the needed right-of-way on South Ypsilanti (Packard) Road.

By August 21, the *Ypsilantian* reported the last section of right-of-way had been obtained. On August 30, 1890, the Ann Arbor & Ypsilanti Street Railway (AAYSRy) was incorporated (locally referred to as the *Ypsi-Ann*) with a capital stock of $100,000. The stockholders were Charles D. Haines of Kinderhook, N.Y., John Milton of New York City and W. L. Marquardt of Ypsilanti.

A committee was appointed to consider the route within the city of Ypsilanti, and the committee's report was received on October 6. The route approved, as reported in the *Ypsilantian* on October 9, was "from the Michigan Central track on Cross Street, to Washington Street then by a loop line up Washington to Congress Street (Michigan) and return, and finally out Cross to Ann Arbor Road (Packard) and city limits. The route thus touched the passenger station, the high school, and Normal School, the two business centers of the city, four churches, and (reach) within one block of two other churches and the Business College (Cleary) and Opera House."

The contract to build and equip the AAYSRy was given to Judson Kingsley, of New York State, who in turn sub-contracted to the Donovan Morgan Company of St. Louis, Missouri. Beal continued: "At first it was thought to run the cars with naptha motors, but a type of Porter enclosed steam motor, so successful in the woods (hauling logs) was determined upon as safest and most reliable. Consequently, the first equip-

16

ment consisted of one Porter Motor for $3,750, with a headlight costing $50, and brakes $275. The two passenger cars were $1,000 each. When it got to running, the expenses were $35 per day.

"It might be added that there were no salaries for the president, secretary or treasurer. The cost to build the road was $45,000 with $20,000 in addition being spent the following year since the original roadbed had been frozen when first constructed."

On October 17, AAYSRy was reorganized. At the meeting of stockholders, Junius Beal was chosen president with Henry Glover as vice-prisident, Joseph Jacobs as secretary and Daniel Quirk, treasurer.

Construction of the AAYSRy began on October 22, 1890, in Ypsilanti, when a gang of 35 to 50 men began burying ties on Washington Street at the Congress Street terminal. By dusk they had completed the line to the city limits.

On November 17, the railway asked the Ann Arbor common council for permission to enter the city. On December 2, council received a petition signed by 70 residents who were opposed to having the steam operation on their streets. The petition was filed and council on December 15, agreed to wait to see what could be worked out between the Ypsi-Ann and the Ann Arbor Street Railway Company, the franchised street railway operator in Ann Arbor.

By December 19, finishing touches were being given all along the line, although the rolling stock had not arrived. On December 26, a dark red steam locomotive and two canary yellow trail cars were delivered.

A trial run was made January 2, 1891; included were Henry Glover and Charles Haines. The run was from Ypsilanti to the eastern Ann Arbor city limits. The first official trip was run on January 3, 1891, with the return from Ann Arbor to Ypsilanti recounted by Beal:

The first official trip of the motor was an eventful one. The members of the common council and newpapermen of the two cities were invited for a ride. They went out on the electric car to the Ann Arbor city limits where transfers were made to the steam motor. Fortunately it did not jump the track on the excursion trip and it only set fire to one barn! But that was soon put out and the party safely landed in Ypsilanti. Not wishing to run any more risks, they were all returned home on the Michigan Central night train, declaring the road a success because no one was killed or maimed for life.

On January 9, 1891, regular service began. Trips were made regularly after that and 600 passengers a day were carried. Beal in his paper recalled something of the everyday operation: "In the country it ran on the highway, consequently, horses, cows and chickens were occasionally offered up as sacrifices. Whether they were sometimes very old and driven on the track

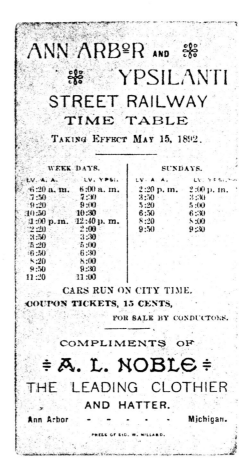

A. L. Noble Clothiers published this early Ypsi-Ann timetable to promote business and bring customers to its store. The schedule went into effect May 1892 and is possibly the earliest interurban timetable published in Michigan.
Schramm Collection

purposely or not by the owner, the road never had a suit, but always settled for the livestock. This kept the good will of the farmers and they would turn out in the night or storm to help boost the motor on the track. The farmers and their families had a rate made for them by books giving 17 rides for a dollar."

By January 12, the *Washtenaw Evening News* reported the Ypsi-Ann and Ann Arbor Street Railway Company had reached an agreement that their cars would meet at the Ann Arbor city limits to transfer passengers. It was agreed that this arrangement would terminate in the spring. Thereafter, the cars of the Ypsi-Ann would be taken downtown by the Ann Arbor Street Railway Company. Furthermore, the Ypsi-Ann guaranteed the Ann Arbor Street Railway four dollars a day with one and one-half cents per passenger, and one cent per passenger after five dollars had been collected.

The Two Companies Combine

A few days later Charles Haines sold his interests in the AAYSRy to Henry Glover for $45,000. Glover then was mayor of Ypsilanti, having made his fortune in dress stays and pasteboard boxes. Because the Ann Arbor lines did not extend to the city limits, Glover now purchased that company and extended the line. On January 26, 1891, the Ypsi-Ann owners purchased the Ann Arbor Street Railway Company for $84,000. Possession took place on January 31; however, it was decided to operate them as two separate companies.

On February 18, 1892, the Ann Arbor council awarded a franchise to the AAYSRy for operation along the portion of Packard Road annexed by Ann Arbor in 1891. The franchise allowed for either steam, animal or electrical motive power, but at a speed not to exceed six miles per hour.

The AAYSRY motor cars continued to terminate at the Ann Arbor city limits until the Ypsi-Ann was electrified, in the fall of 1896, when, as Beal noted, "the old steam dummy being so uncertain it was decided to change." At a stockholders' meeting on July 31, 1896, agreement on how to combine the Ypsi-Ann and the Ann Arbor city operations was reached. The stockholders received an equal amount of bonds they held, plus $40,000 in newly issued bonds.

The next day the Ann Arbor & Ypsilanti Electric Railway (AAYERY) was formed with John Winter as president, H.P. Glover, vice-president and J.E. Beal secretary. On August 18, 1896, a new 30-year franchise was granted in place of an amended franchise from the city of Ypsilanti. No route was stated, but the franchise provided for the continual use of the present tracks with the provision that they be replaced within six years with girder rail or its equal.

Any future track would have to be approved by Ypsilanti common council prior to being laid. The fare was fixed at five cents for trips within the city limits, except after 10:00 p.m. or on special cars run for the accommodation of public meetings and entertainment; then a double fare could be charged.

This ordinance was accepted to replace the former Haines Brothers franchise. On August 20, 1896, the Ann Arbor & Ypsilanti Electric Railway was incorporated.

Trials with electric cars began on November 20, 1896. The *Free Press* on November 25, 1896, noted "Arrangements were all made for running regular electric cars between this city (Ypsilanti) and Ann Arbor, today (November 24), and a second trial trip was to have been made last evening, when the burning out of a dynamo at the powerhouse prevented this, causing a delay of about two days. On the first trial the distance from Ann Arbor Court House to the car barn in this city was made in 22 minutes. The new company will run a car hourly. To passengers a most pleasant feature in the change from steam to electric power lies in the fact that the cars run through to the Court House, the annoyance and delay of transferring at the Ann Arbor corporation line not being necessary."

Regular service commenced November 26, 1896, making the Ypsi-Ann a true interurban, although not the first in the area. The Wyandotte and Detroit River Railway connecting Detroit with Wyandotte had started as a steam line on June 1, 1892, but was converted to electricity by November 24, 1892, becoming the area's first electric interurban, followed by the Rapid Railway on July 14, 1895, and the Detroit to Royal Oak service on Oakland Railway which started February 8, 1896.

The cost of conversion to electric power was $25,000 with the current purchased from the Ann Arbor Electric Company at the rate of $2.50 per day per car. The Ann Arbor Electric Company was another of Beal's enterprises, thus explaining the low rate. The daily cost of operation was $60 and the average daily income $100, apparently a good investment, althought the tiny Ann Arbor city system never did pay its own way.

Detroit's Street Railways

By 1892 there were two steam dummy operations on Detroit's east side. These were small locomotives disguised to look like streetcars, so as not to frighten the horses which still dominated the streets. The East Detroit and Grosse Pointe line went out Mack Avenue while the Jefferson Avenue Railway followed Jefferson; both terminated in Grosse Pointe. Detroit's main streetcar system was still a horsecar operation with two electric operations limited to the suburbs. The Highland Park Railway ran out Woodward Avenue from Grand Boulevard to the village of Highland Park. The Detroit, River Rouge & Dearborn Railway went by way of West Fort Street from Dearborn Avenue, across the Rouge River to a suburban community named Oakwood.

During 1892-3 four city lines were converted to electricity. Three were Jefferson, Mack and Woodward (from downtown to Grand Boulevard) operated by the Detroit Citizens' Street Railway, now under new management. The Fort Wayne & Belle Isle Railway also electrified its single crosstown line.

Michigan Avenue however, remained a horsecar line which threatened to make through electric operation from Dearborn into downtown difficult. The Rapid Railway operated for several months in 1895 on outer Gratiot Avenue while the city portion was still a horsecar line, forcing passengers to change cars at the city limits. However, assurances were made that Gratiot would be electrified shortly after the Rapid Railway completed its line. (See *When Eastern Michigan Rode the Rails, Book Two*.)

New owners purchased Detroit's city lines during 1894-5. R.T. Wilson of New York, in partnership with

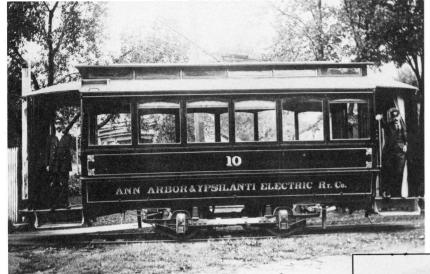

It is believed this was the type of car purchased for the Ypsi-Ann route upon its electrification. This view of car 10 was probably taken shortly after arrival.
Stoner Collection

Large and ungainly, Number 1 may have been homemade; at least the flat-front windows made it look that way. The enclosed front headlight came from a steam locomotive. The car may have been used for the heavy weekend college crowd.

Company Files

Tom Johnson, proceeded to electrify the balance of the city system and consolidate the various companies. Johnson was named president, with Jere Hutchins becoming vice-president and acting general manager. On August 13, 1895, the first electrics went into service on the Michigan line, and by August 21, cars began operating to Livernois Avenue, then the western city limits.

Detroit's Mayor Hazen Pingree had persuaded the Everett-Pack syndicate to build his own brainchild, the famous Pingree "three-cent lines." Pingree gave them franchises on certain streets and even agreed to have the city maintain the roadway in return for low fares. On July 8, 1895, the Detroit Railway began operating with Pingree proudly acting as motorman on the lead car. By July 29, 1896, however, the company was in trouble. It was reorganized as the Detroit Electric Railway, and by January 4, 1897, the officers of the Detroit Citizen's Street Railway were in complete charge.

The Detroit Entry

During the early years of the Ypsi-Ann, other promoters were pressing for construction of a line between Detroit and Ypsilanti. As early as February 18, 1892, the Township of Dearborn awarded a 30-year franchise to the Detroit & Dearborn Street Railway Company. The route was from the township's eastern boundary westward to St. Joseph's Retreat (Outer Drive). Motive power could be either steam dummy or electric.

A time limit for construction of one year was imposed, but failure to obtain the Detroit & Saline Plank Road Company's permission to use its right-of-way doomed the project. The plank road stockholders wanted to sell their interests, but their price was too high.

The townships of Springwells and Dearborn, located immediately west of Livernois, gave franchises in 1894 to a new company, the City and Suburban Traction Company. This firm also planned to build a 7½-mile line as far as St. Josephs Retreat.

Newspapers were reporting that the Detroit and Saline Plank Road Company now wanted $30,000 for its franchise. And agreement with the plank road company was not reached, as reported in the *Free Press*, on January 23, 1895, and the franchise was annulled due to the delay.

The *Journal of Detroit's Common Council* on April 9, 1895, noted that the plank road company was collecting tolls inside Detroit as far as Fifth Street. Within the next few years the city purchased toll road grants outright. One irony was that tolls were still collected on portions of the road being maintained by the city.

On March 5, 1895, the township of Springwells issued a grant to the Detroit Railway for a line up Livernois Avenue and out Michigan Avenue. This allowed a connection with DR's Dix Avenue city line and provided for an all-electric operation into downtown Detroit.

Additional grants were requested from the townships of Dearborn and Nankin, and it was reported that the Detroit Railway planned to build to Ypsilanti. Pack had acquired the plank road franchise which extended out Michigan Avenue to the community of Wayne, and the line was constructed out Michigan to Springwells' western limits (Greenfield Road).

However, because the franchise called for a single fare and the township officials refused to amend it, the new track never was put into operation. The *Journal* reported that the Detroit Railway's request for an additional fare within the township would result in a double fare to go downtown. This extra charge was the practice of all companies serving the suburbs. Detroit never had streetcar zone fares, and to be eligible for the lower basic fares many suburban communities were eager to be annexed to Detroit.

After the takeover of the Detroit Railway by the Citizens' Railway, one of its first acts was to remove any duplicate or unused trackage such as the Springwells line. On Sunday, May 9, 1897, the track from the Five Mile House located 1½ miles west of Livernois on Michigan, to the western end at Greenfield Road was removed. A work force of 500 men removed the rails which were then used to double-track Fort Street from the city limits to Woodmere Cemetery in Detroit.

On May 11, the *Tribune* reported the Springwells' township board ordered the township's road commission to hire men to remove the balance of the track between Five Mile House and Livernois. The commission refused, fearing a lawsuit from the Citizens' Company. By May 14, an agreement had been reached to operate the remaining Detroit Railway track on Michigan and the Citizens' track could now be connected. Residents were finally willing to pay the additional fare to have service. The justice hearing the case was quoted as saying: "had they so agreed last fall the entire line would now be operating."

The western terminus of the line at Five Mile House became known as Addison 'Y' and remained the end of the city line and beginning of the interurban track until the city of Detroit's purchase in 1922.

By Rail to Dearborn

In the mind of Daniel L. Quirk, ex-president and general manager of the Detroit, Hillsdale & Southwestern Railroad, president of the Ypsilanti 1st National Bank and official of the Ypsi-Ann, an electric line to Detroit was imperative. He invited engineer J.D. Hawks and investor S.F. Angus to a meeting on October 12, 1897. His persuasivenesss convinced Hawks and Angus to be the builders of the electric line.

On November 2, 1897, Hawks and Angus filed incorporation papers for the Detroit, Ypsilanti and Ann Arbor Railway (DY&AA) with capital stock of $25,000. They started acquiring the franchises needed for the right-of-way from Addision 'Y' along Michigan Avenue to Ypsilanti to connect with the Ypsi-Ann.

By the 19th of the month the two men purchased the franchise rights for $1, the same amount noted in both original franchises given by the township of Dearborn to the Detroit & Dearborn Street Railway Company on February 18, 1892 and the City & Suburban Traction Company on March 23,1894. This exchange of money was a bit unusual.

Money, of course, had been a problem for other groups considering building a line on Michigan in the township. The *Free Press* on November 24, 1897, in reporting the meeting to obtain the franchise, noted that the Dearborn township board had first demanded a $5,000 cash guarantee that the road would be completed by January 24. After failing to reach an agreement, the board recessed and later met and agreed on a $2,000 guarantee.

However, the township had to file a $25,000 bond for the company's protection against any previous franchise. The completion date, according to the *Journal*, was also moved back to April 5, 1898.

The three remaining townships granted franchises to agent Thomas D. Kearney. Nankin did so on April 16, 1895; Canton on March 26, 1895; and Van Buren on April 5, 1895, all of which required completion within five years. On December 12, 1897, the three franchises were assigned to the DY&AA. The remaining township was Ypsilanti, which on July 25, 1896, awarded a franchise to Henry Glover, Robert W. Hemphill, Oliver H. Lau and John Winter; on January 8, 1898, this franchise was assigned to the DY&AA. Lau and Winter now turned their attention to building the Flint line (see Book 1 of *When Eastern Michigan Rode the Rails*). Meanwhile, Glover and Hemphill began obtaining franchises for a line from Ypsilanti to Saline.

With all the needed franchises in hand, construction of the line began. The first portion from Addison 'Y' to Dearborn, a three-mile section, was quickly completed.

The *News* on December 24, 1897, reported the arrival in Dearborn of the first car to operate from Detroit. The car that left from the front of the post office on Fort Street at 2:30 p.m. was Superintendent Dupont's private car, number 88. This car had originally been one of the first electrics used on Jefferson Avenue in 1892. The party on board included Hawks, Angus, Hutchins and Dupont.

A temporary traffic agreement was reached on December 24, and replaced by a new one on July 25, 1898. The agreement allowed the Citizens' crews to receive the DY&AA cars at Addison 'Y' and operate the cars on the Michigan line track downtown, looping on Griswold, Atwater, Woodward and Michigan. The Citizens' agreed to pay the DY&AA 1¾ cents per passenger mile to cover interest, repairs and depreciation while on DY&AA tracks. The charge for a trailer was ½ cent per passenger mile. The DY&AA was to pay the Citizens' the same rates for the operation on its tracks of borrowed Citizens' four-wheel cars or trailers. The charge for fares within Detroit was 5 cents.

Power cost extra. The Citizens' agreed to furnish the necessary 550-volt power at Addison 'Y' and DY&AA would pay the Citizens' two cents per mile for each 8-wheel car mile and one cent per mile for a 4-wheel car or trailer.

In quoting DY&AA secretary John A. Leslie, the *Journal* on March 15, 1898, noted "the cars were to be 45 feet long, furnished with comfortable seats and toilets and every other. convenience." It was not until June 17, 1898, that the *Tribune* reported two new cars had arrived in the city; they were painted green, 43'11" in length, 8'9" wide, and 12'2" in height. It was reported that they made a trial run down Woodward Avenue the previous day.

Building to Ypsilanti

Progress the following year in the construction of the line was reported in the newspapers. The *Journal*, on March 15, mentioned that ties and rails were being distributed along the route, and the laying of track should begin by April 1. The building of the powerhouse in Ypsilanti also was under way. The DY&AA continued purchasing Citizens' power until its own powerhouses were finished. The Citizens, at this time, had surplus capacity, due to consolidation of the former systems, each having had it own power plant.

By April 24, 1898, the line was reported in the *Tribune* as operating to the village of Inkster, a distance of 14 miles from Detroit. "The progress of the construction being so fast the cars will probably enter the Village of Wayne tomorrow and Ypsilanti by the end the week."

However, there were problems along the way. In Wayne, when the company petitioned for a route through the village, a dispute erupted. While everyone wanted the line, nobody wanted it running in front of

A track gang spikes down the rails on Michigan Avenue near Center Street (Monroe Boulevard) in Dearborn. You are looking west in this December 1897, view.
Dearborn Historical Commission

The first car into Dearborn on December 24, 1897, was Dupont's private car, 88. The chimneys in the background beyond the car were part of the Commandant's House, now the home of the Dearborn Historical Museum. The location is Michigan and Center Street.
Dearborn Historical Commission

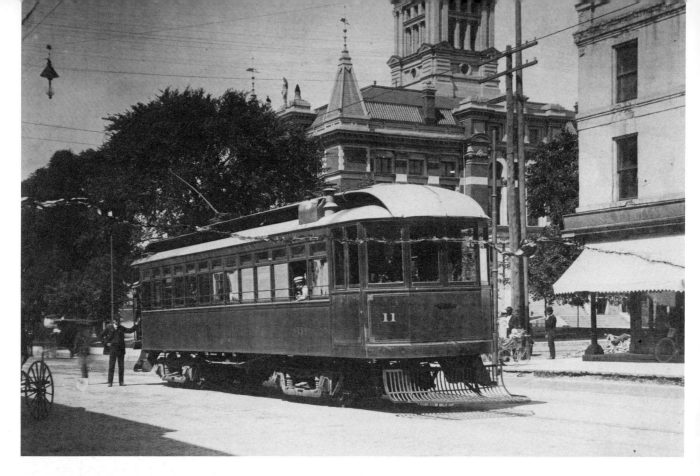

This cracked plate shows car 11 in an early view at Main and Huron in Ann Arbor. The county courthouse is in the background. In later years the company operated the *Cupid Special*, transporting students traveling late at night between the University of Michigan and the present Eastern Michigan University.

their home. The original request was for an alignment along Main Street (Michigan), which at this time was a tree-lined residential street and the location of a number of churches. The village council settled on an alternate route to go south on Hastings (Wayne Road), turning west on Park (Jones Street) four blocks, then north one block back to Main, deftly avoiding the residence or business of any council member. But this route raised even more protests, and after a long debate the council on April 11, 1898, voted to have the route remain on Main Street through the village. When the first cars arrived, they turned back at Elizabeth Street and returned to Detroit until the line was completed beyond Wayne.

West of Wayne the line was built along the side of the highway after the townships of Canton and Van Buren threatened injunctions. Township officials discovered the company had begun construction in the center of the roadway. It was noted that the road was 3 to 4 rods wide (3 rods equal 49½ feet and 4 rods equal 66 feet), and with the necessary power poles only 15 feet of roadway remained. Thus, if the tracks were placed in the center, there would be inadequate roadway on either side.

On June 10, 1898, newspapers were reporting the line completed to Ypsilanti. There, connections were made with the Ypsi-Ann which had been purchased May 11, 1896, by the DY&AA. The *Ann Arbor Democrat* reported that regular operations began June 12, with 30-minute service from Detroit to Wayne, and a 90-minute headway from Wayne to Ann Arbor.

In the *Railroad Gazette* of December 28, 1898, a short article on the DY&AA noted that after the franchises had been secured, the Westinghouse Company took over the engineering work on the Detroit to Ann Arbor line. The route was 42 miles in length, with DC power coming from two identical powerhouses built 20 miles apart in Dearborn and Ypsilanti.

The rolling stock consisted of 10 cars, each equipped with two trolley poles and Westinghouse air brakes. They were built by the Barney & Smith Car Company, and had four 50 h.p. Westinghouse motors. They had a partially enclosed front platform for the motorman, leaving part of the platform open for passengers to board or alight. The cars were in service by October 5, 1898, as evidenced by newspaper reports of car #5 impounded by a deputy sheriff.

It seems the company refused to pay a $10 fine for

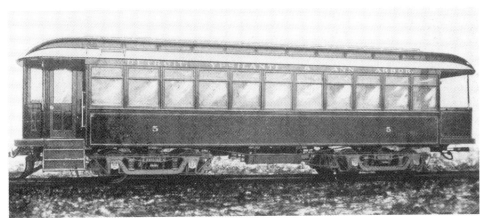

The first large cars for DY&AA were ten from Barney & Smith, each equipped with four 50-h.p. Westinghouse motors. In 1906 cars 1-3 were spliced with 30-32 and later renumbered 7772-7774. Car 4 became 7785 and in 1926 was converted into a trailer. Cars 5 and 6 became 7786 and 7787 and in 1906 became freight motors. Cars 7-10 were renumbered 407-410 as express cars, later becoming 7800-7803.
Schramm Collection

failure to lay planks on its roadway. The court imposed the fine, and, as usually happened after impounding a car, the fine was rapidly paid.

Detroit's *City Manual* of 1898-9 published the following about the DY&AA:

> Cars start from the waiting room, 111 Griswold Street and run down Griswold Street to Atwater Street, to Woodward Avenue, to Michigan Avenue and out Michigan Avenue to West Detroit, Dearborn, Wayne, Denton, Sheldon's, Ypsilanti and Ann Arbor—a distance of 39 miles is traversed in about two hours. Commencing at 6:30 a.m. the cars run every half-hour until 7:00 p.m., and then every hour until the last car leaves Detroit at 11:00 p.m. The last car leaves Ann Arbor at 11:15 p.m.
>
> The fare to Ann Arbor is 50 cents one-way, $1 round trip; to Ypsilanti 40 cents one-way, 80 cents round trip; to Wayne 25 cents one-way, 40 cents round trip; to Dearborn 15 cents one-way, 25 cents round trip. Thousand mile books of tickets are sold for $10, thus making the rate to Ann Arbor 40 cents.
>
> The cars of this line connect with the Wayne, Plymouth and Northville Railway at Wayne.

The 1900 manual, in addition, listed the officials of the DY&AA: President & General Manager J.D. Hawks; Secretary F.A. Hinchman; Superintendent W. Hemphill, Jr.; Treasurer S.F. Angus; Manager F.E. Merrill.

The February 3, 1900, *Street Railway Journal* reported that the 1899 financial results of the DY&AA were sufficient to give the stockholders a substantial dividend. Local passengers averaged only 200 a day for the year over the entire 42-mile line, while 4000 commuters were carried per day. In September 1899, the average fare per passenger was 15.9 cents.

Extending to Jackson

The success of the line to Ann Arbor stimulated plans to extend the route to Jackson. Already another group was planning to build a competing line from Jackson to Detroit. This group was led by William A. Boland, owner of the Jackson Street Railway. The Boland line figured in the later Ann Arbor franchise and construction fights, as we shall soon see.

Problems among the bondholders were reported in the *Journal* on July 19, 1901. There was disagreement between the majority and minority interests within the DY&AA. When the problem occurred two years earlier, the minority stockholders transferred their interests, one-tenth of the property, to James Parmalee, of Summit, N.J., who was secretary of a trust company. Because Parmalee was not a Michigan resident, he would have certain rights in a United States District Court over which Judge Swan presided.

Before the transfer to Parmalee, the company executed a $600,000 mortgage to build the road. Later, a consolidated first mortgage of $1,000,000 was made and $600,000 was received to pay off the first mortgage. Of the rest, $100,000 was reserved to buy the Detroit & Saline Plank Road Company, although it was later claimed that John Russell had purchased it for only $19,000 paid out of DY&AA funds.

Parmalee's attorney had stopped the issuing of consolidated bonds the previous year. A board composed of Hawks, Angus and their friends made an agreement with the Detroit, Ypsilanti, Ann Arbor & Jackson Railway (DYAA&J) which had been organized January 22, 1901, with a capital of $2,600,000 and a bond issue of a like amount. The board wanted Parmalee to transfer the stock in the DY&AA to the new company for bonds of equal par value. In other words, Parmalee was asked to exchange $400,000 in stock in a profit-making company that might have made as much as 20%, for bonds paying 5%.

The dispute was settled and the DYAA&J was incorporated on January 23, 1901. The necessary franchises were ready for the extension from Ann Arbor to Jackson.

Ann Arbor approved a franchise on December 22, 1900, providing for an extension from Main and Huron streets west on Huron and Jackson Avenue to the Western city limits. The DYAA&J could cross the Toledo, Ann Arbor & North Michigan Railroad tracks at grade on Huron Street if approved by the state railroad commissioner. If not approved, a bridge would carry both the electric line and street traffic over the railroad. The franchise also provided that the railroad and electric railway company would pay for the bridge, and all adjoining property damages.

The towns and townships west to Jackson all approved franchises, either along private rights-of-way, beside the Michigan Central Railroad tracks or, in a few cases, on public streets such as on Page Avenue approaching Jackson. It seems one lesson learned too late for the DYAA&J was that even though street running was cheap and convenient, future political wrangles could have been avoided by building more routes on private right-of-way.

In Jackson, Boland was already operating the city lines. Hawks-Angus wanted two routes in Jackson: one on Cooper Street for a planned route north towards Lansing, and on Franklin Street goind southwest toward Concord and Homer. There were to be three loops in the city. The ordinances covered 21 streets and offered 5 cent fares or six rides for 25 cents. The *Tribune*, on September 11, 1901, said Hawks-Angus planned to extend the lines to both Lansing and Coldwater. On September 17, the mayor vetoed a franchise proposal, but on October 1, 1901, the *Free Press* reported that the franchise was approved by a vote of 12 to 3. The route entering the city was to be on Chapin Street.

On June 30, 1902, the franchise was amended to allow for use of workingman's tickets between 6 and 7 a.m. and 5:15 to 6:15 p.m., at the rate of eight tickets for 25 cents. This followed the pattern set in Detroit of using discount fares during rush hours. Also included was a provision that the interurban line could not be sold to a steam road, and if sold to another electric, both railways must be kept in operation.

Four years later, August 6, 1906, the franchise was again amended to include an unusual provision: street sprinkling was required four times a day between April 15 and October 15 each year on the main streets, and on secondary streets at least three times a day. Failure to do this could result in fines of $10 to $50.

Battling for the Streets

There were two disputes between the Hawks-Angus and Boland groups over rights-of-way which took place in Ann Arbor. The first regarded franchise rights to build on certain streets and the second concerned crossing the tracks of the Ann Arbor Railroad.

The *Tribune* reported on August 21, 1901, that DYAA&J wanted to locate its turning 'Y' at the corner of Huron and Main streets, but residents complained. A compromise was reached when it was agreed to locate the 'Y' in front of the waiting room on Huron Street, about a half a block west of Main Street. This meant that the car being turned would use the railway property by turning in and backing out onto Huron Street.

However, Boland held the franchise for Huron Street including this particular block, which meant that the 'Y' would interfere with his operation. Work had begun that morning on the 'Y', but a court order stopped it.

The *Free Press* on September 4, 1901, reported that the Ann Arbor city council failed to negotiate a compromise between Hawks-Angus and Boland. In fact, Boland's forces were in court attempting to prove Hawks-Angus had no franchise in Ann Arbor. The following day the *News* mentioned that the court had agreed the Hawk-Angus group had no right to operate on Huron Street.

Today (a Detroit paper) said, on September 10, the judge had prohibited Boland from interferring with the

Men Who Built the DYAA&J

SAMUEL FLOYD ANGUS

- Born Monroe County, Ohio
- Married Dorothy Hood of Milan, Ohio
- Died Feb. 6, 1908. Age 52

Prior to moving to Detroit, he was a book agent traveling through Ohio. He entered the life insurance field and moved to Detroit as the local agent for the Home Life Insurance Company and National Life Insurance Company.

While in the insurance business, he, along with J.D. Hawks, Henry A. Haigh and associates formed the Toledo, Fremont & Norwalk Railway (first car Sept. 5, 1900; sold line to Lake Shore Electric September 1901).

Angus and Hawks owned the Grand Rapids, Grand Haven & Muskegon Railway besides the DJ&C and the Lansing city lines.

Angus was owner of the Detroit Baseball Club from 1901 to 1903. This well-liked man belonged to over eight social clubs.

JAMES DUDLEY HAWKS

- Born Oct. 13, 1847, Buffalo, N.Y.
- Graduated from University of Michigan 1870
- Married Caroline A. Cooke of Buffalo, Oct. 7, 1875
- Died Sept. 21, 1921

First job in the engineering office of the Lake Shore & Michigan Southern Railroad.

1875-78. Division engineer of the Lake Shore's Erie Division.

1881. Superintendent of construction of N.Y. West Shore & Buffalo Railroad.

1884-92. Chief engineer of Michigan Central Railroad.

1892-93. Manager of Detroit Citizens' Street Railway.

1893-1920. General Manager of Detroit & Mackinac Railroad.

Associated with S. F. Angus in various electric railway projects.

Hawks-Angus group building west of Ashley Street, a block west of Main Street in Ann Arbor. The article noted the Hawks-Angus group had the track complete from Ann Arbor to Jackson and ballasting would be finished within a week. A gap of 1½ miles in Ann Arbor was all that remained to complete a Detroit to Jackson route. In this case the Hawks-Angus group received a favorable decision on September 19, allowing them to build their line west beyond Ashley to the city limits.

The second contention was also reported in the *Tribune* on August 6, 1901, when Angus and Hawks were in town to look over the proposed Ann Arbor Railroad grade separation with Ann Arbor city officials. The railroad would pay 40%, Hawks-Angus 30% and Boland 30%. Urged on by the railroad, State Railroad Commissioner Osborne had decided on the need for a grade separation.

Hawks-Angus and Boland continued to argue over the track on Huron Street. The *Free Press* on September 13, described how the Ann Arbor Railroad joined in the strife by placing a locomotive on its Huron street crossing. A second locomotive was sent to do the switching so the first could remain in place. The entire track was laid except where the locomotive was parked and the one block on Huron between Ashley and Main, for which Boland had the injunction. About ten days later, the engine was joined by a full crew and caboose to guard the crossing. Evidently the Ann Arbor Railroad did not want the electric line crossing its rails until the dispute was resolved.

By November 7, 1901, the matter was still unsettled, and Hawks-Angus agreed to pay their portion of $30,000 for the grade separation. The Ann Arbor Railroad offered $32,000, which left $18,000 for Boland or the city of Ann Arbor to pay. The *Free Press* on Febrary 10, 1902, announced that the injunction prohibiting the crossing of the Ann Arbor Railroad was lifted. The *Jackson Daily Citizen* on January 28, 1902, reported that Railroad Commissioner Osborne had granted Hawks-Angus a temporary grade crossing pending final settlement of the grade separation problem.

Soon after, the Hawks-Angus line was completed and passengers were able to ride from Detroit to Jackson without change of cars. The grade corssing problem eventually was settled by the Ann Arbor Railroad when it raised the level of its tracks through Ann Arbor passing over Huron Street.

On to Jackson

Local newspapers followed the progress of constructing the Jackson extension with great interest; often the stories were repeated in the major Detroit papers. The *Free Press* noted that the first car went from Ann Arbor to Chelsea and returned on August 22,

1901, "All went well and two cars will begin service tomorrow to Chelsea. Since the matter of crossing the railroad is unsettled, the cars will start three blocks (west) from Main Street."

The *Free Press* further stated on September 29, 1901, that Hawks-Angus had a large group of laborers building the line from Jackson south to Vandercook Lake. "Boland was to have built this line; however, when the railroad commissioner insisted on a bridge over the Michigan Central tracks, Boland let the option die. Hawks-Angus quietly picked up the rights-of-way and built the line. Their line is laid directly ahead of Boland's Francis Street line."

The first Hawks-Angus car reached Grass Lake from Ann Arbor on December 8, 1901, and the *Free Press* continued "that cars will leave each half hour," The *Ann Arbor Argus* said regular service between Grass Lake and Ann Arbor began December 15.

Finally came the big day: the *Tribune* reported the first Ann Arbor to Jackson car arrived on January 18, at noon. Hawks-Angus had won the race with Boland in completing the line. The Ann Arbor-Jackson trip took one hour and 45 minutes. Service began with two medium-size cars. The through passengers from Detroit had to transfer at the Ann Arbor Railroad tracks until the crossing was complete. To turn the seven new large cars purchased for the Detroit-Jackson run, a 'Y' was installed on the Sibley Lot in Ann Arbor.

On April 22, 1902, the first cars ran through from Detroit to Jackson. An interlocker had been completed to allow the cars to cross the Ann Arbor Railroad tracks at grade. The schedule called for hourly service from Detroit to Jackson, and each alternate car reaching Ann Arbor at the quarter before the hour would return to Detroit.

Ypsilanti to Saline

At the time of the formation of the DYAA&J, part of the new funding was to purchase the Ypsilanti & Saline Electric Railway Company (Y&SE). After selling their Michigan Avenue franchises to Hawks-Angus, Hemphill and Glover obtained the needed documents to build a line from Ypsilanti to Saline.

The route was built along the side of the Chicago Road (later U.S. Highway 12) starting at the tracks of the DY&AA at Congress and Washington in Ypsilanti. The city of Ypsilanti granted a franchise on February 25, 1899, followed by the townships between there and Saline: Ypsilanti on April 22, 1898, Pittsfield on April 27, 1898, and York on March 4, 1899. Saline awarded a franchise on February 20, 1899, for operation on Chicago, Adrian, Henry, Ann Arbor and Monroe streets. On May 17, 1899, Hempill and Glover incorporated the Y&SE. All the franchises were then transferred to the Y&SE on May 20, 1899.

Car 4 was the first into Jackson, on January 18, 1902, thus heralding completion of the line from Detroit to Jackson. Hawks & Angus planned to expand the line southwest to Coldwater and north to Lansing.

Schramm Collection

This early photo shows the car running along Michigan Avenue in its original paint scheme with the various cities served lettered on the front.
Wayne Historical Society

This short ten-mile line was in operation by September 2, 1899. There is little information to be found on its early operation. It is thought that the power was purchased from the new Ypsilanti powerhouse of the DY&AA, and that rolling stock probably was purchased or leased from them as well. It is also probable that the small single-truck cars used for the first electric operation on the Ypsi-Ann were used here. These cars would have been surplus when the Ypsi-Ann became part of the DYAA in 1898.

Through the years there was talk of extending the Saline line another 25 miles to Adrian where it could connect with the Toledo & Western Railway, and offer a more direct route to Chicago. For years the dream of interurban builders in Michigan was to connect Detroit and Chicago. However, being located along the Chicago Road led to the branch line's early abandonment, when the State of Michigan wanted to use that route to build a second paved Detroit to Chicago highway.

The interurban car is standing in front of the Saline waiting room (on the right). A wye on the hill to the station proved to be troublesome to larger cars trying to back up, so smaller cars were assigned to this line. Many of the same buildings in this photo are still standing as of September 1987. ***Woodard Collection***

All franchises were transferred to the DYAA&J On March 25, 1901. In addition to these rights, Hawks-Angus purchased the property of the Detroit & Saline Plank Road Company on January 16, 1904. The price was $6,306.55 and a release from all indebtedness.

Articles were written about the DYAA&J in the *Street Railway Journal* on October 4, 1902, and the *Street Railway Review* on September 20, 1902. These articles revealed that rolling stock included 33 closed cars averaging 52 feet in length, seating 56, including a 12-foot smoking section. The non-smoking sections were 32 feet long and finished in oak. There were four open cars, which may have been former Ann Arbor city cars.

The DYAA&J was not operated in divisions as was the Rapid Railway from Detroit to Port Huron. Here crews made the entire run from Jackson to Detroit and return. There were usually 70 motormen and conductors on the payroll. All runs of less then eight hours were call "extra," and men holding these were given first chance to cover a regular run when it was open, in case the run-holder was off.

The cars were scheduled at hourly intervals from 6 a.m. to 9 p.m. between Detroit and Jackson. From Detroit to Ann Arbor, service was every half hour between 6:15 a.m. and 10:45 p.m.

Fares charged were usually paid with 100-mile ticket books which cost 1¼ cents per mile. Thousand-mile ticket books cost one cent per mile and were good only between Ann Arbor and Detroit. For payment of fares on the cars, a duplex ticket was sold which showed mileposts instead of the normal station names on the ticket. Fares paid on the cars was at the rate of 1½ cent per mile.

Cars in regular service on the typical day included 13 interurban, four Ann Arbor local cars, four freight cars and one construction car.

Movements of cars were controlled from a central dispatcher located in Ypsilanti using a private telephone system.

Normally the powerhouse, with this load, ran five 250 kw. units. When the extension to Jackson was built, the line was converted from d.c. to a.c. power, which had been used successfully on the Rapid Railway. The Ypsilanti powerhouse was enlarged, and all apparatus from the Dearborn powerhouse, except a direct current generator, was moved there. The born facility was converted to a substation and car house.

Substations were located in Wayne, Ann Arbor, Lima Center, Francisco, Michigan Center and Saline. All equipment was Westinghouse and each substation was equipped with three 200 kw. oil-cooled transformers, two 250 kw. rotary converters with a switchboard of six panels, two alternating current machine panels, two direct current machine panels and two feeder panels. All overhead wire was copper except between

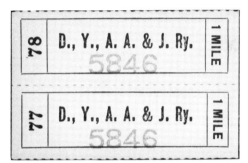

Michigan Center and Jackson, where aluminum was tested.

The substations were built of brick, iron and tile with a combined waiting room and freight room. Exceptions were Ann Arbor where business was large enough to require a separate building, and Dearborn, because the location of the old powerhouse was not convenient for passengers.

The Ypsi-Ann's first car house and yard was built by September 1892. It was located in Ypsilanti on Harriet Street between Washington and Adams streets. When the DY&AA took over the Ypsi-Ann, the car house was replaced by a new larger facility a few blocks away on the north side of Michigan Avenue just east of the Huron River.

Car houses of brick and steel were constructed in Dearborn (six-car capacity) and Ypsilanti (18 cars). The Jackson (four cars) and Ann Arbor (six cars) car houses were built of corrugated iron. General repair facilities were located in Ypsilanti.

Limited stop service began between Detroit and Jackson on November 28, 1904. The cars carried a blue sign during the day and displayed a blue light at night, running every two hours from 6:45 a.m. until 8:45 p.m. The locals were now scheduled every hour

from Detroit to Ann Arbor and every two hours from there to Jackson, eliminating the 30-minute service between Detroit and Ann Arbor. The fare for the limited was an additional 5 cents to 20 cents.

On August 18, 1905, newspapers reported car #4 had been rebuilt with steel sides, the first of the cars the DYAA&J planned to rebuild. Then on February 2, 1906, multiple-unit controlled cars were placed in service; these included both passenger and freight equipment.

M.E. Cooley's *Appraisal of the DUR System as of January 1, 1915*, reported the existence of two bridges on the line; one near Ypsilanti across the Huron River, the other at Michigan Center over the Michigan Central Railroad. Both bridges were obtained as surplus from the Michigan Central which was actively double tracking and replacing its bridges with wider spans.

The bridge at Ypsilanti was a nine panel Pratt through truss 130'-6" in length, fabricated by Detroit Bridge and Iron Works in 1878 for the Detroit, Lansing and Northern Railroad.

The bridge new Michican Center was the same type, built in 1883 for the MCRR and located east of Ann Arbor. In 1900 it was sold to the interuban and moved to its new location.

With longer runs came the need for larger and heavier cars. Here is a builder's photo of 27, a Barney & Smith product, later to become 7769. The open rear platforms were a Michigan trademark for many years. By 1905 cars like No. 29 were rebuilt with steel sides—some had rear platforms enclosed—and were given a bright brown paint job for limited service.

Ferriss Collection.

To handle an increase in passenger traffic, company shops would take two small older cars and make one larger car. Car 30 is an example of this 1906 remodeling procedure.

Schramm Collection.

Late in 1904 new cars 23-32 arrived from the builder for service as the *Blue Racer Limited*. Passengers on this new high-speed service were charged a premium of up to 70 cents. The local passengers objected to both the extra fare and the delays to the regular scheduled local cars.

Moore Collection.

DUR freight motor 83 behind passenger car 24 at Duffield switch in Dearborn. The 83 was one of four freight motors, numbered 80-83, purchased in 1902 from ACF. All were assigned to the Flint Division.

Schramm Collection.

DETROIT, JACKSON & CHICAGO RAILWAY.

In effect February 1, 1907.   Subject to change without notice..   Light figures a. m. Dark figures p. m.

Mls.	STATIONS	Limited Trains	WEST BOUND—DETROIT TO JACKSON	Local Trains
0	Detroit, Wtg.Rm Lv	6 45 8 45 10 45 12 45 2 45 4 45 6 45	6 00 6 55 7 55 8 55 9 55 10 55 11 55 12 55 1 55 2 55 3 55 4 55 5 55 6 55 7 55 8 55 9 55 10 55	
10	Dearborn		6 17 6 45 7 45 8 45 9 45 10 45 11 45 12 45 1 45 2 45 3 45 4 45 5 45 6 45 7 45 8 45 9 45 10 45 11 33	
13	Wayne		6 37 7 09 8 09 9 09 10 09 11 09 12 09 1 09 2 09 3 09 4 09 5 09 6 09 7 09 8 09 9 09 10 09 11 09 11 53	
30	Ypsilanti	5 30 8 09 10 09 12 09 2 09 4 09 6 09 8 09	5 45 6 45 7 45 8 45 9 45 10 45 11 45 12 45 1 45 2 45 3 45 4 45 5 45 6 45 7 45 8 45 9 45 10 45 11 45 12 20	
39	Ann Arbor	5 51 8 30 10 30 12 30 2 30 4 30 6 30 8 30	6 15 7 15 8 15 9 15 10 15 11 15 12 15 1 15 2 15 3 15 4 15 5 15 6 15 7 15 8 15 9 15 10 15 11 15 12 45	
50	Lima Center		7 41 9 41 11 41 1 41 3 41 5 41 7 41 9 41 11 37	
53	Chelsea	6 20 8 58 10 58 12 58 2 58 4 58 6 58 8 58	7 50 9 50 11 50 1 50 3 50 5 50 7 50 9 50 11 56	
60	Francisco		8 05 10 05 12 05 2 05 4 05 6 05 8 05 10 05	
65	Grass Lake	6 44 9 18 11 18 1 18 3 18 5 18 7 18 9 18	8 15 10 15 12 15 2 15 4 15 6 15 8 15 10 15 12 04	
68	Leoni		8 21 10 21 12 21 2 21 4 21 6 21 8 21 10 21 12 09	
71	Mich. Center		8 29 10 29 12 29 2 29 4 29 6 29 8 29 10 29 12 15	
76	Jackson, WtgRmAr	7 15 9 45 11 45 1 45 3 45 5 45 7 45 9 45	8 45 10 45 12 45 2 45 4 45 6 45 8 45 10 45 12 30	

Mls.	STATIONS	Limited Trains	EAST BOUND—JACKSON TO DETROIT	Local Trains
0	Jackson, Wt'g Rm. Lv	6 45 8 45 10 45 12 45 2 45 4 45 6 45	5 45 7 45 9 45 11 45 1 45 3 45 5 45	7 45 9 45 11 15
5	Mich. Center		6 00 8 00 10 00 12 00 2 00 4 00 6 00	8 00 10 00 11 27
8	Leoni		6 07 8 07 10 07 12 07 2 07 4 07 6 07	8 07 10 07 11 32
11	Grass Lake	7 10 9 10 11 10 1 10 3 10 5 10 7 10	6 20 8 20 10 20 12 20 2 20 4 20 6 20	8 20 10 20 11 39
16	Francisco		6 24 8 24 10 24 12 24 2 24 4 24 6 24	8 24 10 24 11 49
23	Chelsea	7 29 9 29 11 29 1 29 3 29 5 29 7 29	6 39 8 39 10 39 12 39 2 39 4 39 6 39	8 39 10 39 11 59
26	Lima Center	7 37 9 37 11 37 1 37 3 37 5 37 7 37	6 48 8 48 10 48 12 48 2 48 4 48 6 48	8 48 10 48 12 07
37	Ann Arbor	8 00 10 00 12 00 2 00 4 00 6 00 8 00	6 15 7 15 8 15 9 15 10 15 11 15 12 15 1 15 2 15 3 15 4 15 5 15 6 15 7 15 8 15	9 15 10 15 12 30
46	Ypsilanti	8 20 10 20 12 20 2 20 4 20 6 20 8 20	5 45 6 45 7 45 8 45 9 45 10 45 11 45 12 45 1 45 2 45 3 45 4 45 5 45 6 45 7 45 8 45	9 45 10 45 12 50
58	Wayne		6 19 7 19 7 50 8 19 9 19 10 19 11 19 12 19 1 19 2 19 3 19 4 19 5 19 6 19 7 19 8 19 9 19 10 19 12 19	
66	Dearborn		5 40 6 10 6 40 7 40 8 10 8 40 9 40 10 40 11 40 12 40 1 40 2 40 3 40 4 40 5 40 6 40 7 40 8 40 9 40 10 40 12 40	
76	Detroit, Wtg. Rm. Ar	9 35 11 35 1 35 3 35 5 35 7 35 9 35	6 23 6 53 7 23 8 23 8 53 9 23 10 23 11 23 12 23 1 23 2 23 3 23 4 23 5 23 6 23 7 23 8 23 9 23 10 23 11 23 1 23	

NOTE.—In addition to the regular cars and the Detroit-Jackson limiteds, cars will leave Detroit Waiting Room for Wayne as follows: 6:25, 7:25, 8:25, 9:25, 10:25 and 11:25 a. m., and 12:25, 1:25, 2:25, 3:25, 4:25, 5:25 and 6:25 p. m. Making half-hourly service between Detroit and Wayne, from 6:25 a. m. to 6:25 p. m.

NOTE.—In addition to the regular cars and Detroit-Jackson limiteds, cars will leave Wayne for Detroit as follows: 6:50, 7:50, 8:50, 9:50, 10:50 and 11:50 a. m., and 12:50, 1:50, 2:50, 3:50, 4:50, 5:50, 6:50 and 7:50 p. m. Making half-hourly service between Wayne and Detroit from 6:19 a. m. until 8:19 p. m. Main line limiteds connect at Ypsilanti both East and West with cars for Saline.

This early photo of the Detroit, Plymouth and Northville car could have been taken near Wayne or Northville. In both places the line crossed arms of the Rouge River.

2

COMPETING LINES

IT WAS LIKE A HOMECOMING when William A. Boland returned to Jackson in the spring of 1897. He was negotiating for the Jackson Street Railway, a small operation consisting of ten motor cars, eight trailers and seven miles of track. Congressman John B. Corliss, the largest stockholder, was ready to dump his debt-riddled company to this man from Boston and New York who had grown up in the Jackson area.

The *Free Press* on April 7, 1897, and May 25, 1897, briefly mentioned their meetings while awaiting the results of Boland's offer to the bondholders. By June 26, the bondholders had rejected the Boland offer, and the company that night was placed in receivership under the watchful eye of William A. Foote.

William A. Boland, the Jackson native, was a financier and promoter of electric properties, including streetcar lines since 1888 starting with a line connecting Cambridge to Boston. In the New York City area he helped R.T. Wilson (onetime owner of the Detroit Citizens' Street Railway) develop the Nassau Electric Railroad in Brooklyn. Following this, Boland purchased the New York, Westchester & Connecticut Traction Company and People's Traction Co. which were absorbed by the Metropolitan Street Railway.

On September 13, 1900, Boland outbid Hawks-Angus at auction and purchased the Jackson lines from the receiver, Foote. He then formed the Jackson & Suburban Traction Co. on September 27, 1900, which took over the Jackson Street Railway and began to expand eastward to Grass Lake and Wolf Lake. Taking shape in his mind was a plan to build one of the longest car lines in the country—a line that would stretch from

Very few interurban systems faced the competition's track across the road from their own. It did occur in a four-mile section east of Jackson along Page Avenue.

Schramm Collection

An eastbound Boland car has stopped on the bridge over the MCRR tracks east of Michigan Center. Why the passengers are all standing around is not known. One possibility was the car had jumped the tracks; it may even have been the formal opening of the line on June 29, 1901. Note the DYAA&J bridge in the background.

Schramm Collection

Jackson east to Detroit, and west to Chicago under the name Detroit & Chicago Traction Company.

At this point, Boland and W.A. Foote of the Jackson Electric Light Company combined forces to construct electric traction lines in south central Michigan. Previously Boland helped find funding for Foote's electric light company which eventually became the nucleus for what is now the Consumer's Power Company.

Early electric power companies were formed to provide power mainly for street lighting. Electrical home appliances were in the future, and the demand for power was relatively low. The Jackson Electric Light Company soon was supplying power to the Jackson Street Railway Company which became its largest customer. So when the traction company became delinquent in paying its power bills, Foote was appointed receiver for the railway company until purchased by Boland.

Boland Begins to Build

The Boland syndicate obtained a franchise from the city of Ann Arbor on December 21, 1900, from the western city limits along Miller Avenue, Ashley, Huron, Fifth Avenue, Beakes Street to Broadway, crossing the Michigan Central on an iron bridge. The route continued along the center of Broadway to the eastern city limits. Also called for was a bridge, if required, over the Ann Arbor Railroad.

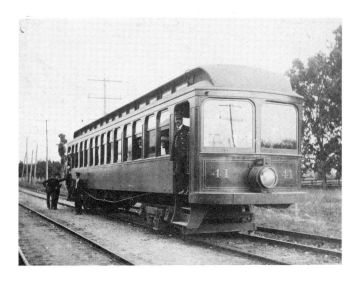

The first large cars purchased by Boland were these two-front-window units, which cost $13,400 each. Seven cars came equipped with smoking compartments and lavatories.

Schramm Collection

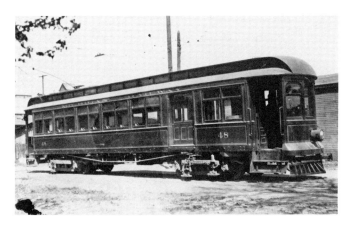

Cars such as 48, originally purchased by the Jackson-Battle Creek Traction Company, were assigned the Grass Lake run during 1914-1918.

Stoner Collection

We have seen, in the previous chapter, the furious competition in Ann Arbor between Boland and the Hawks-Angus Syndicate. The fight continued, from the Ann Arbor Railroad tracks westward, as the two companies each built its own line.

Boland received his original franchises from the townships of Scio on October 29, 1900, Lima on August 12, 1901, Sylvan on November 15, 1900, and Grass Lake on September 24, 1900, along with the villages of Dexter on October 7, 1901, Chelsea on October 17, 1900, and Grass Lake on September 14, 1900.

Unlike the Hawks-Angus Syndicate, Boland began

building from the west heading toward Ann Arbor. The *Journal* on April 19, 1901, reported several workmen laying the track through the main street of Grass Lake, while a much larger force was grading a roadbed for the Hawks-Angus Syndicate a quarter mile away. It was also noted that Boland was able to hire most of the laborers which were scarce, while Hawks was not able to get all the men he wanted. On the other hand, Hawks had it fixed so Boland could not get any rail. The article concluded with the dry observation that "the parties on each side deny the story."

On April 25, 1901, the *Free Press* mentioned rumors of an impending merger, noting that operations on the Hawks-Angus extension had slowed lately, and that they did not have a complete right-of-way between Jackson and Ann Arbor. Further hampering efforts was the fact that the legislature was not able to pass a bill giving the electric railways the right to condemn property for rights-of-way.

Rivalry at Grass Lake reached a climax on the same day when Hawks-Angus also attempted to lay a track through the village. They had assembled a large force of Italian laborers at 4 p.m. and began pushing construction. The Boland people immediately concentrated their forces at the threatened point and by working all night succeeded in getting their rails laid first. The sheriff was summoned, and with deputies spent the night at the scene as it was feared the rival workmen might come to blows. However, all was calm.

Less than a month later, on May 14, 1901, the *Journal* noted the Boland line was being pushed to complete the last gap between Jackson and Grass Lake. The steel for the bridge over the Michigan Central Railroad just east of Michigan Center was being put in place. It was estimated that cars would be running from Jackson to Grass Lake by June 1.

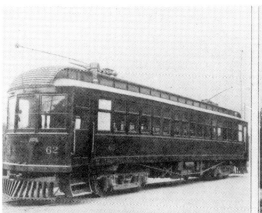

Car 62 was adapted for 5000-volt experimental service on the Grass Lake line.

Henning Collection

In the mid-'20s three cars were acquired from the Interurban Railway & Terminal at Cincinnati. They were numbered 857, 859 and 861 and assigned to the Grass Lake line. Later they were remodeled for one-man operation. Here one of them is in service in Jackson.
Kremkow Collection

A large force of men and teams were grading near Chelsea, while a steam engine and train of dump cars were being used to ballast the roadway from Grass Lake to Michigan Center. According to the *Jackson Daily Citizen* rates of pay were low, $3.50 per day for a team and $1.50 per day for a laborer. Earlier it noted that Boland had 64 teams and 209 men at work on the roadbed.

The *Journal* reported on June 25, 1901, that Worrall Weber, son-in-law of Boland, was elected president of the Detroit and Chicago Traction Company. Also "the company owns private right-of-way and franchises west from Detroit for 285 miles of line and in some 15 villages. Last week the Boland syndicate purchased the Detroit, Plymouth and Northville Railway line which could be used as one of the feeders to the main line. If the road is completed from Chicago to Detroit, it will be one of the longest electrical railroads constructed."

Even though Boland named his company the Detroit & Chicago Traction Co., he used various smaller companies to build the system. Two were incorporated on September 30, 1901; the Jackson & Ann Arbor Railway and the Detroit & Ann Arbor Railway Co.

Grass Lake Line Opens

The formal opening from Jackson to Grass Lake occurred on June 29, 1901. The official party consisted of 150 who rode the new line and then spent the day at *Grey Towers*, Boland's country home two miles from Grass Lake. On August 10, 1901, Boland, according to the *Tribune*, took another group on an inspection trip from Jackson to Grass Lake. They then continued the trip to Chelsea using a steam locomotive to pull the cars, as the electrification was not complete beyond Grass Lake.

As late as October 30, 1901, the *Free Press* reported that construction of the line between Grass Lake and Ann Arbor was at a standstill due to the non-arrival of the new third rail. It also reported the receipt of seven new cars equipped with observation, smoking compartments and lavatories. According to the *Jackson Daily Citizen* the large cars began operating to Grass Lake on December 15, 1901. They noted the ten 56-foot cars built by St. Louis Car Company cost $13,400 each. The cars had steam heat, 4-100 h.p. G.E. motors and were finished in mahogany.

When Boland sold his rail line holdings to the DUR, only the lines east of Grass Lake were transferred. The Grass Lake to Jackson trackage belonged to and was operated by the Jackson city system. During interline DUR-MUR service an agreement allowed each company to use the other's rails (in case of trouble) between Grass Lake and Jackson.

Abandonment of this line occurred in stages, with the tracks from Grass Lake to Wolf Lake Junction being taken out of service in 1924, Michigan Center to Wolf Lake in 1927 and Michigan Center to Jackson the last.

Branching Out

A branch line, the Detroit, Plymouth and Northville Railway, while built independently, was purchased by the Boland syndicate as a link in its plans to reach Detroit. The company was incorporated May 25, 1898, and immediately began obtaining franchises from the townships of Nankin on January 9, 1899, Livonia on May 10, 1898, Plymouth on March 23, 1898, and Northville on August 10, 1898, which was amended on April 22, 1899. The latter town wanted street lighting furnished; three lights of 80 candlepower each to be located between Bradner Road and the Plymouth and Northville gravel road. This provision was amended in 1904 to add lights at Benton's and Wiltsey's crossings.

Villages and towns along the route frequently granted franchises with strings attached. In granting a franchise, on May 3, 1898, for Washington (Wayne Road), the town of Wayne wanted the railway to build a 12-inch sewer from the village's north limits to the north bank of the river, which passed through the village. If a lake was created, the railway was to raise its track and bridge and pay 50% of the cost.

The village of Plymouth wanted a guarantee that the line would not be sold until completed, and for locating the powerhouse there. The railway also was to furnish 80 candlepower lights at each street and railroad crossing which were to be lit from sunset to 1 a.m.

Northville, on March 9, 1899, wanted 80 candle-power lights at each street crossing on the line, and stipulated joint use of tracks by other companies approved by the council.

The *Journal* on July 26, 1898, reported that a first mortgage had been filed by the DP&N securing $150,000 at 5% for 20 years. The mortgage was with the Union Trust Company and was executed by C.W. Casgrain and W.H. Wickham. Construction had already begun on the road, and the powerhouse at Plymouth was started the previous day. International Construction Company won the contract for completion of the road.

The article also noted the territory through which the new line ran was one of the most densely populated in Wayne County. This new connection with Detroit promised to be popular in both Plymouth and Northville, as these villages suffered indifferent railroad service with the city.

The Boland Line had trackage on the main street of Grass Lake. Here car 44 is ready to depart for Jackson.
Henning Collection

October 15 brought news in that work was continuing on the line. The article described the route as "north from Wayne two miles to Cady's Corners, thence west one mile to Tonquish post office, thence north four miles to Newburg, west two and one-half miles to Plymouth and thence north four miles to Northville. In the latter village there will be about two miles of road extending to the U.S. Fish Hatchery (Seven Mile Road). (This extension was never built, and the line ended in downtown Northville, where it shared tracks with the Orchard Lake Division of the DUR.) As of October 15 the section between Wayne and Plymouth was within two weeks of being completed. The grading was completed, and rails and material for the overhead were on the ground.

The first car ran between Wayne and Plymouth on February 14, 1899. Regular passenger service began on this portion four days later. The original equipment used was four small single-truck cars built by Jackson and Sharp Car Company. These cars were painted yellow and green and were obviously not new; local residents nicknamed them "grasshoppers." In fact, these were the original cars purchased by George Hendrie for the Detroit to Pontiac line on Woodward Avenue. Later he had purchased new and larger double-truck cars, built by Kuhlman, for this longer and heavily-traveled line.

Unfortunately, the Plymouth powerhouse was not completed when the line opened, and the tiny cars had difficulty getting up the hills on the Plymouth end of the line. When the powerhouse opened on July 19, 1899, the line began regular hourly service. Initially, power must have been obtained from the DY&AA.

Completion of the line quickly followed, and the first car arrived in Northville on November 10, 1899. Regular passenger service began the following day complete with free rides. Actually, the line was not totally complete due to the unfinished Pere Marquette Railroad underpass at Phoenix (Five Mile Road). The early passengers had to walk across the tracks, changing cars to complete their journey.

Fares throughout the years were 10 cents from Plymouth to Northville; Plymouth to Wayne 15 cents. The minimum was 5 cents, and zone fares prevailed along the line for short rides.

The initial timetable was dated December 9, 1899, and showed cars leaving Northville at 15 minutes past the hour from 6:15 a.m. to 11:15 p.m. with close connections at Wayne for Detroit, Ypsilanti and Ann Arbor.

Westbound cars of the DY&AA line left the Detroit city hall on the even hours to 9 p.m. and connected with the DP&N at Wayne. A special theatre car left Detroit at 11 p.m., connecting with the car leaving Northville at 11:15 p.m. Travel time from Northville to

Possibly taken the same day as the earlier photo, this view shows the front of the car and its number, 4. These four small cars were obtained from the Detroit & Pontiac Railway when it purchased large double-truck Kuhlman-built cars.
Schramm Collection

The first cars later were rebuilt into double-end, double-truck units to avoid reversing in Northville. Renumbered 76 and 77, they were used until the DUR takeover. They were then rebuilt into line cars and renumbered 7762 and 7763.
Schramm Collection

Interurban 29 is standing in front of the depot located in the group of buildings on the right in downtown Plymouth.
Woodard Collection

Plymouth was 20 minutes; from Northville to Wayne 1 hour, and from Wayne to Detroit, 1 hour 15 minutes.

After its debut, the Northville branch seldom made news, but the *Evening News* on May 3, 1901, reported a brief labor dispute. "Due to disagreement over wages, the employees of the DP&N quit work yesterday and resumed work today after satisfactory agreements were made," the road's president, John A. Russell, was quoted as saying.

The original small cars were shortly replaced by cars 76 and 77, which appear to have been built in the company shops. There is a possibility they were rebuilt from the first four originals. The 76 and 77 were double-trucked and double-ended with reversible seats to eliminate a bothersome backup movement in Northville.

Northville's waiting room was on the west side of Center Street. This meant that cars from Farmington, upon entering Northville on Griswold Street, would turn left (east) on Main Street, then have to back up west two blocks to the station. Single-end cars from Plymouth turned right into Griswold Street, backed around and west on Main Street to the waiting room. The Northville freight depot and express office was at the northeast corner of Griswold and Main streets.

Boland In—and Out

Soon there was another flurry of franchise negotiations. On May 14, 1901, the *Tribune* reported that the Springwells Township board had the previous night approved franchises for the DP&N from the Detroit city limits through the township. Additional franchises were obtained from the townships of Livonia on May 23, 1901, Plymouth on April 9, 1901, and Nankin on November 8, 1900. These were for a proposed direct line to run from Plymouth to Detroit, reducing the distance from 28 to 23 miles. The route would follow Ann Arbor Road, Plymouth Road and Warren Avenue into Detroit.

The reason for all this activity was detailed in the *Free Press* on May 26, 1901. "Last week the Boland Syndicate, composed of W.A. Boland, P.H. Flynn, Senator McCarthy, and D.F. Lewis, all of New York, purchased the DP&N line. The Boland-Flynn Syndicate had decided to extend to Detroit via the Ann Arbor Territorial Road from Ann Arbor, via Plymouth and Warren Avenue. It had to purchase the DP&N since it held all the franchise rights through the intervening townships." On July 20, 1901, the *Journal* noted "Boland had completed the deal, paying the balance of the purchase price of $325,000."

As we have seen, the Angus-Hawks syndicate was the first to complete the line between Ann Arbor and Jackson. This seemed to end all actual construction on the Boland line for several years. Through the years there seemed no end of newspaper accounts of pending mergers or one group buying out the other.

The *Free Press* on July 2, 1904, claimed an agreement had been signed between the DYAA&J and the Jackson city lines along with the lines to Wolf Lake and Grass Lake. The pact was signed by Coler & Co., operators of Jackson Consolidated Traction, and

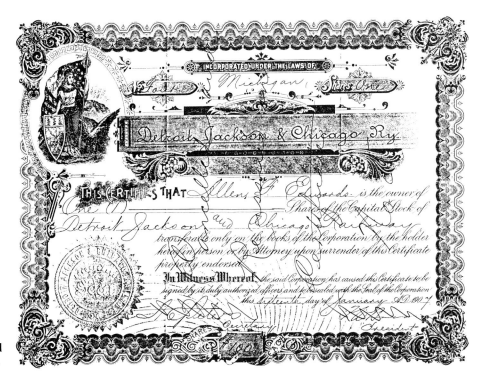

A temporary stock certificate issued prior to the regular printed edition.

The occasion for this photo is unknown, but the men were too dressed up to be "gandy dancers"—maybe it's a group filling pot holes on the early dirt roads.
Schramm Collection

Hawks-Angus, and called for operation as one system; however, neither company would lose its identity. The agreement would enable the companies to more economically operate the two systems.

The closest to a merger we have found was reported by the *Ann Arbor Argus-Democrat* on July 22, 1904. "Wednesday, the DYAA&J Electric Railway ran the first car to Wolf Lake under the new merger arrangements with the Boland lines. In celebration of the opening of switches connecting the two lines . . ." These varying accounts and later denials continued until 1906.

Basically, Hawks-Angus promised to pay off the Boland debts and work toward purchase of the competing system. The general manager of the Jackson system moved his office to Ypsilanti. When the Hawks-Angus group reneged on the agreement, Boland renewed his quest to reach Detroit.

The DUR franchise book stated it thusly:

On November 27, 1906, this company (Boland) conveyed all its assets, franchises, rights-of-way, etc., to the Jackson, Ann Arbor & Detroit Railway.

The Jackson, Ann Arbor & Detroit Railway was incorporated September 5, 1906, under the general railroad law of Michigan, and by purchase of the above referred to, acquired all the property and assets of the Jackson & Ann Arbor Railway, and the Detroit, Plymouth & Northville Railway. This company did some work upon procuring a right-of-way from Wayne to Detroit and some grading was done, but no further work was ever done on this end of the line.

It was too late for Boland to expand toward Detroit because the Hawks-Angus system was sold to the DUR. Effectively this ended any chance of Boland reaching Detroit, so the financial backers sold out to the DUR's DJ&C.

The Detroit, Jackson and Chicago Railway was incorporated by the DUR on January 14, 1907, to purchase and operate the DYAA&J, and on Feburary 1, 1907, received the property, rights and franchises. On July 19, 1907, the Jackson, Ann Arbor & Detroit Railway conveyed all its property, assets, rights-of-way, franchises, etc. likewise to the DJ&C.

The DUR Gains Control

Thus, both companies which had fought each other were now under the control of the DUR. The Hawks-Angus line continued as the main line to Jackson until the end of service. That portion of the Boland line from Jackson to Grass Lake remained in service as part of the Jackson Consolidated Traction but was sold to the Mills group on May 9, 1907, for $1 million.

Angus and Hawks were also losers; Jere C. Hutchins, in his book *A Personal Story*, wrote "Hawks and Angus made for themselves an unfortunate decision;

40

they turned down an offer of $520,000 in cash for their company's 26,000 shares of stock, practically all of which they themselves owned. Two or three years later their property was taken over by assumption of its bonded debt with no profit to them whatever."

In a 1923 valuation report, the Michigan Public Utilities Commission gave more details of this take-over. There were no winners, it seems, in this particular transaction:

The Detroit, Jackson & Chicago Railway Company was originally incorporated with a capital stock of $25,000, and authorized a bond issue of $4,000,000, of which $2,600,000 was used in paying off the outstanding bonded indebtedness of the Detroit, Ypsilanti, Ann Arbor & Jackson Railway, and $805,000 was issued to purchase the stock of that company. The balance, $595,000 was issued to pay for "Additions and Betterments" as made. This bond issue was guaranteed by the Detroit United Railway both as to principal and interest. The Detroit United Railway purchased the capital stock of the Detroit, Jackson & Chicago Railway Company for $25,000, paying for the same by crediting the running account of that company; the advances to this company, shown on the books, exceeded that amount.

In 1916, the capital of the Detroit, Jackson & Chicago Railway Company was increased to $1,000,000, and on August 31, 1916, $589,000 additional stock was issued to the Detroit United Railway to pay for "Additions and Betterments." The total cost to the Detroit United Railway Company for the stock of the Detroit, Jackson & Chicago Railway issued to it was, according to the books, $614,000.

For good or ill, the DUR had now taken over the DJ&C and its important east-west interurban route. It turned out to be its last addition.

This is the Ice House Curve trestle located approximately a half-mile north of Plymouth. Further north was Phoenix Lake.

Faber Collection

Leaving Northville for Plymouth, interurban cars had to cross this trestle over the Mill pond.

Schramm Collection

Main Street, Northville, with an early auto parked at the extreme left. The car in the background is on the Northville-Farmington run.

Woodard Collection

41

The same car as 31.

Formerly 31, this car was now DUR 7773. In 1906 it was
lengthened to a 15-window car. Note the third-rail shoes.
Schramm Collection.

3
THE D.J. & C. UNDER THE D.U.R.

WITH THE FORMATION of the Detroit, Jackson & Chicago Railway on July 19, 1907, the DUR now had seven operating divisions. And finally had control of all the major interurban roads leading into Detroit.

The 76-mile Jackson division was the longest of all DUR interurban lines. It was a busy operation, second only to the Pontiac division in the amount of local traffic carried. On an average day, 34 cars left Detroit for Ann Arbor, with 19 trips terminating there. The DJ&C offered three classes of service: local, express and limited. With the exception of one or two late night cars, local cars ran only between Detroit and Ann Arbor. The two latter classes alternated the through trips to Jackson.

The terrain between Detroit and Ann Arbor is relatively flat; from there to Jackson it's gently rolling with a few low hills. Leaving the downtown Detroit station, cars followed Michigan Avenue through Dearborn, Inkster, and Wayne to Ypsilanti. It was a double-track line to Dearborn, then single-track with frequent passing sidings to Ypsilanti, from there the route featured a couple of lengthy passing tracks along Packard Road before reaching the Ann Arbor station.

From there the line continued along the highway past Lima Center to the edge of Chelsea. Then it cut across the south side of that village and swung in alongside the Michigan Central Railroad tracks, which it paralleled to Grass Lake. It left the railroad and passed through town on private right-of-way and rejoined the railroad west of Grass Lake. Upon reaching Leoni, the line cut across country to reach the north shoulder of Page Avenue and followed that road to the Jackson city

DUR Pass.

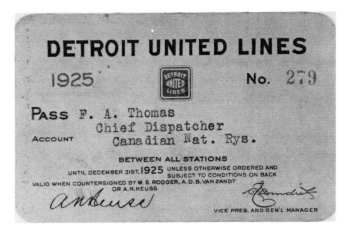

43

limits. Turning, it paralleled Henrietta Street; then on Chapin Street and finally reached the Jackson terminal. Passing tracks were spaced at two- to three-mile intervals.

The two busiest stations on the DJ&C were Wayne and Ypsilanti with 40 daily cars each way. Plymouth-Northville cars met the main line at Wayne, while Saline cars connected at Ypsilanti, accounting for the high total.

An operating oddity on this division was the practice that had some "express" or "limited" cars overtaking and passing a local at some given point. For example, the 7:25 a.m. local from Detroit would reach Ypsilanti at 9:19 a.m., and be in Ann Arbor at 9:55 a.m. The 7:50 a.m. express out of Detroit would stop at Ypsilanti at 9:20 a.m., but arrive in Ann Arbor at 9:50 a.m., five minutes ahead of the local car. Several daily schedules were set up in this manner, with an equal number of Detroit-bound cars running similar patterns.

On the DUR, the DJ&C was the only division which faced competition from another electric line. This was a rarity, as few such situations existed nationwide. Between Grass Lake and Jackson the DJ&C and Michigan Railway were mostly in sight of each other, and in one 4½-mile stretch were running along the opposite shoulders of Page Avenue. They had separate bridges over the Michigan Central Railroad near Michigan Center.

Both routes were just over eleven miles, but the DJ&C was the fastest, usually covering the distance in 30 minutes, while the Michigan Railway consumed nearly 50 minutes per trip. Both lines shared the Jackson terminal, but used separate facilities in Grass Lake. For years the combined schedules of both systems provided Grass Lake with 27 daily trips in each direction. When stops made by Michigan Central trains are also considered, this village of 800 was literally drowning in rail passenger service.

DUR renumbered the cars into its own fleet system, assigning numbers 7765 through 7787 to this division. An unusual feature was the choice of numbers 7750 through 7759 for the Ann Arbor city cars. The 7000-series had always been used strictly for passenger interurbans, though some cars retained their old number after being reassigned to freight or utility uses. Numbers 7760 to 7764 were assigned to work or line cars, including 7762 and 7763 which were the former 76 and 77 from the DP&N.

On July 2, 1907, the first of five new cars, numbered 7790 to 7794, made an initial run. These cars were painted yellow with the interior finished in cherry and the seats upholstered in green plush. They all had push button signals and were built with lower platforms.

Little was changed in operating procedures, with the DJ&C functioning in its normal manner and retaining its own dispatching, as did the Rapid Railway. The cars began using the DUR's downtown Detroit terminal with no change of crews at the city limits. The fares remained on a mileage basis as before.

But improvements were promised. The November 12, 1907, *Ann Arbor News Argus* reported the DUR's plans, which included enlarging the power plant at Ypsilanti, straightening the right-of-way to cut down on accidents, and re-laying the Saline branch with heavier rail. In December 1907, the DJ&C quit making local stops "at your door"; stops were now to be made at least ¼ mile apart.

These were still the so-called "golden years" of interurbans in Michigan, before the building of highways and the onset of automobiles and competing buses. Freight business on this line was good, too. On June 3, 1909, the *Street Railway Journal* reported that the railway had received a contract early that year to carry 160 tons, or between four and five million bricks, from the west end of Detroit to Kalamazoo. Detroit in those days had several large brick kilns on the west side of the city.

In an effort to build profits, an express service was started in 1908 between Detroit, Plymouth and Northville via Dearborn and Wayne. The freight car would leave Dearborn at 6 a.m. heading for Northville.

An attempt to use large cars on the Saline branch was dropped. They were unable to reverse on the Saline 'Y' due to the downhill grade. Since city officials would not allow a change in track location, smaller cars were substituted.

During 1908, a Detroit-Saline through-car service was begun for a six month trial; however, 80% of the passengers alighted at Ypsilanti. It was found that the through service also hampered operation on the Plymouth and Northville line, so on October 13 it was discontinued. From then until abandonment in 1925, the Saline line remained a branch and was never extended to Adrian as planned by the DUR at the time of takeover.

Another betterment came in December 1908 when the "theater car" was upgraded. The original cane-seat cars were replaced with ones having plush-seats. The *Dearborn Independent* reported this, but never noted whether the cars or just the seats were changed.

Through To Kalamazoo

In April 1911, a four-hour, 28-minute "limited" car through service to Kalamazoo was started in conjunction with the Michigan United Railways. Detroit's Mayor William Thompson had opposed the move because the MUR cars were equipped with third-rail shoes. However, the objections were overcome and the operation started.

This 145-mile, every two-hour service included stops at Ypsilanti, Ann Arbor, Jackson, and Battle Creek. At the same time, another service was started in conjunction with the Michigan United Railways on a run from Detroit to Lansing via Jackson. This 114-mile run took three hours and 55 minutes. The first DUR cars in use were furnished with third-rail shoes for use on the MUR system. Cars known to have been so equipped included 7303, 7520-22, 7267, 7772-73, 7790-94. In later years additional cars were added.

A new Jackson barn was reported completed by the *Jackson Press*. The original Jackson barn had been at Pearl Street and North Park; the new one in the same block at Pearl and Milwaukee Street.

Traffic was increasing, and in 1912 the DUR received approval to lay double track in Dearborn. The company has to give concessions, including putting on two additional cars to increase the hours of service, and contributing to the paving of Michigan Avenue. In May 1913, property in Dearborn was purchased on the south side of Michigan at Mason Street. A new station and a 'Y' was built so cars could turn off Michigan Avenue to pick up passengers and freight.

Heavy rains came in the spring of 1916, and the Rouge River inundated Michigan Avenue. Interurban traffic was halted for several days and people commuting through Dearborn had to be ferried through the flooded area. The vehicle used was a large milk truck owned by Walker Dairy. By March 27 the cars returned to normal operation.

Six new cars ordered the previous year arrived in February 1917. The order took a year to fill due to the shortage of motors caused by World War I. All six were to be assigned to the Detroit-Kalamazoo run and were fitted with third-rail shoes. They were numbered according to division as follows: two from the Rapid, 7311 and 7312; two from the DM&T, 7524 and 7525; and two from the DJ&C, 7595 and 7596.

Responding to inflation, the DUR raised the minimum cash one-way fare from ten to fifteen cents during the summer of 1918. The action also included changes to the fare zones limits. One notable change was in the Dearborn area. Originally, St. Joseph's Retreat (Outer Drive) was a zone limit going west; beyond was an additional nickel. Now the zone was moved eastward 1½ miles to Duffield Station near the Henry Ford & Son Tractor Plant (Michigan and Elm). Most workers refused to pay the additional five cents and walked the four extra blocks to the plant.

The unpredictable Henry Ford nearly complicated life for the DUR in 1919. In that year Ford asked for a 30-year franchise to operate an interurban line into Dearborn, via a route that would pass right through present-day Greenfield Village. The proposed route was to go out Fort Street to South Dearborn Road and thence into Dearborn. Also proposed was service into Ecorse Township.

Ford, it seems, planned to use gas-propelled cars, eliminating the cost of building overhead. He did build one such car (a cross between a "doodlebug and a Budd railcar"—see *Detroit's Street Railways*, Book One), which was named *Dearborn*. It became his private railway car and was used on the Ford-owned Detroit, Toledo & Ironton Railroad.

But, after receiving a 20-year franchise from officials of Dearborn and Ecorse Township, Ford suddenly lost interest and line was never built.

Financial Problems Begin

After World War I it was downhill all the way for Michigan interurbans in general, especially for those in the Detroit area. The cost of operation had risen alarmingly during the war years, and now ridership was falling.

In 1918 Michigan's trunk highway and road system was ranked 19th nationwide in mileage. On April 7, 1919, the voters approved a $50 million bond issue to build or improve 3600 miles of road over 10 years. By April 17, 1923, Gov. Groesbeck reported to the state legislature that $32 million had already been spent. During the recession of 1921 much of the money had been spent on make-work projects, an idea which was becoming politically popular.

By 1924, Michigan had 6600 miles of trunk highways and was a national leader. As funds were needed to continue highway building, new taxes were enacted, including license fees and gasoline levies.

All these new highways were an invitation to a new group of promoters. These were the touring car and bus operators, who quickly set up operations in various parts of the state. The largest number were concentrated in the Detroit area.

But there was little coordination, and the state wanted to spread service out and limit duplication of operations. Thus in 1923 the Atwood Act (Public Act 209) was passed which gave the Michigan Public Utilities Commission (MPUC) the authority to issue "Certificates of Convenience and Necessity." These were franchises good for operations over fixed routes.

It was not long before Michigan's interurbans felt the threat. In 1923 the Wolverine Transit Company, operating buses on Gratiot Avenue from Detroit to Mt. Clemens, applied for and received a franchise from the MPUC. The Rapid Railway, already operating interurbans on Gratiot, appealed this decision.

The Michigan Supreme Court upheld the decision of the MPUC and would not allow the Rapid to begin operating a competing bus line. The feeling at the time was that bus service should develop without regard to existing rail service. However, in considering new bus

A FTER THE DUR TAKEOVER, the 23 DJ&C passenger cars were rerostered into the standard DUR 7000 series. In previous acquisitions, Detroit United had renumbered the cars in the same order as the company being taken over. Now, however, the newest cars were assigned the lowest numbers, which started at 7765.

The cars acquired were: **7765-7771**, purchased 1904; total length 51'9". Built by Barney & Smith, they had been numbered 23 through 29. Car 7768, on February 16, 1925, was converted to a trailer, then on February 8, 1930, made into a camp car. Few DJ&C cars carried names, but 7771 was named *Seneca*.

Car 7770 was assigned to the Wayne local service when this photo was taken at Dearborn substation switch. The motorman is Herbert Hinds; the conductor, John Shaw.
Andrews Collection

Cars are Renumbered

7772-7774, probably part of the 1904 purchase; total length 53'3". Built by Barney & Smith, these cars had been numbered 30-32. However, records show they had been spliced with cars 1-3 in 1906.

L. Caplin and Bert Curtis with unit 7774 laying over in Ann Arbor.
Schramm Collection

7775-7780, purchased in 1901 when the line was extended to Jackson. Total length of these six Barney & Smith-built cars was 49'9". Originally numbered 15 through 20. Newspapers reported there had been seven. However, car 14, damaged in a wreck, was rebuilt into a line car and renumbered 7813. There was no number 13. Car 7776 was destroyed in an accident at Chelsea, on July 20, 1918, in a collision with freight motor 1936. 7779 was destroyed in Detroit on Michigan Avenue just east of Military, near Pere Marquette Railroad crossing in 1908.

Four of a kind: car 7777 is on Michigan Avenue, Dearborn, heading for Jackson. At least 48 "7s" were used in numbering this car inside and outside.
Faber Collection

7781-7784; these consisted of two DJ&C groups. First was 11 and 12 which may have been trailers purchased along with the first order of cars. The second cars were listed as 21-22 and were trailers. Cars 7781, 7783 and 7784 originally had 11 windows, which were replaced with 13 narrow windows. Later the first and last windows were blocked in. Their length was listed in 1922 as 42'5". Car 7782 was rebuilt in 1906, and was the only combine on the DJ&C. In 1923 it was rebuilt for either one- or two-man operation; its 1922 length was 44'9".

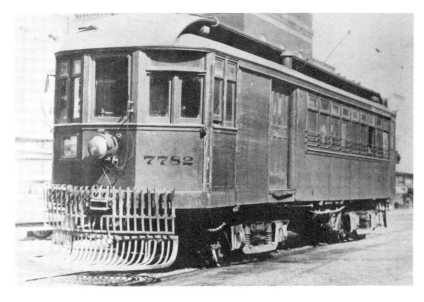

The last car operated on the Ypsilanti to Saline run was unit 7782.

Schramm Collection

Here are 7783 and 7784 at the Ypsilanti barn. These cars started out as trailers 21 and 22. Notice the different front window arrangements.

Schramm Collection

7785-7787; these three cars were all the remaining operating passenger cars from the original order. Originally numbered 4-6, cars 1-3 had been spliced as noted. Cars 7-10 were converted into freight units, and renumbered 407-410. The DUR renumbered them 7800-7803. Cars 5 and 6 were converted by the DUR in 1906 to freight units, retaining their same number. Car 4 had its motors removed September 18, 1926; whether it was used as trailer is not known. It was destroyed at Oakwood February 14, 1930.

There were no cars **7788** or **7789**.

The 7785 sits in front of Ypsilanti carhouse as the division's safety car.

Stoner Collection

In 1907 the DUR purchased **7790-7794** from Kuhlman Car Company. These cars were 52'2" in total length.

This view of the interior of car 7790 shows the type of seats. Most interurban cars included a separate smoking section. Besides a restroom, the car had a water cooler. Usually one common cup served the passengers, but the State of Michigan Health Department abolished the public drinking cup July 20, 1911. At first, passengers had to purchase their own waxed paper cup at the station. Later the cups were provided on the cars.

Schramm Collection

Car 7791 stands on the wye at the Ann Arbor station.

Schramm Collection

7795-7796; the last cars purchased for this division, in 1916. They were quickly assigned to the interline service to Kalamazoo, and when that ended in 1925, were transferred to the DM&T division. When Receiver John F. Collins took over operation in 1928 these two cars were not included. Total length of the cars was 58'3", making them the largest on the line.

We see 7796 at the end of the DJ&C line in Jackson.

Radway Collection

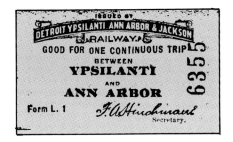

ISSUED BY
DETROIT YPSILANTI ANN ARBOR & JACKSON
RAILWAY
GOOD FOR ONE CONTINUOUS TRIP
BETWEEN
YPSILANTI
AND
ANN ARBOR
Form L. 1
F. A. Hinchman, Secretary

	WYANDOTTE DIV.	**DETROIT UNITED LINES.**	FLINT DIVISION
JAN. FEB. MAR. APR. MAY	RAPID RAILWAY SYS.	**Employee's Ticket Receipt**	PONTIAC DIVISION
	D., J. & C. RAILWAY		ORCHARD LAKE DIV.
JUNE JULY AUG. SEPT. OCT.	D., M., & T. S. L. RY.	**NOT GOOD FOR PASSAGE.**	Form WK-1

Conductor must punch both portions of Ticket in space provided showing date. Passenger will retain this receipt and return it to his foreman.

F. W. BROOKS, President.

Conductor		15	14	13	12	11	10	9	8	7		5	4	3	2	1
Foreman		15	14	13	12	11	10	9	8	7		5	4	3	2	1
Conductor	31	30	29	28	27	26	25	24	23	22	21	20	19	18	17	16
Foreman	31	30	29	28	27	26	25	24	23	22	21	20	19	18	17	16

(NOV. DEC. 1917 1918 1919)

routes, existing bus operations on the route had to be taken into consideration. This regulatory doctrine sealed the eventual doom of every electric interurban in the state of Michigan.

To protect its routes, the DUR formed the Peoples Motor Coach Company on September 14, 1924. The original DUR incorporation papers would not allow operation of buses. Now, with dwindling revenues, the DUR was forced into the bus business.

A 1922 *Bus Transportation* article indicated that bus service between Detroit and Ann Arbor was limited to touring cars. An Ann Arbor newspaper on November 11, 1924, noted "the Highway Motorbus Company organized sometime ago to operate between Detroit and Ann Arbor was purchased by the Peoples Motor Coach and they will begin operation next week." At least the interurban cars going out Michigan Avenue to Ann Arbor would now be competing with their own buses. By 1926 the bus route had been extended to Jackson.

Fares Controlled by State

Another blow to the interurban was the state legislature's passage of the Glaspie Bill (Act 115 of 1921), which went into effect August 18, 1921. It gave the MPUC authority to regulate the fares of interurban companies. An extensive study of the assets and investments of the DUR was immediately made.

During the first year the MPUC relied on the DUR annual report, which showed gross passenger earnings per mile of $15,945. This exceeded the minimum $14,000 per mile of mainline track allowed and permitted a fare of 1½ cents per mile.

The DUR had a complex fare structure, as each division had continued with its original method of fare collection at the time of takeover. Now it was unable to meet the MPUC August 18, 1921, deadline for filing the new rates of fare. This angered the MPUC, which then denied a dividend request a few days later.

DUR was able to put the new fares into effect on September 4. This upset some communities which, notwithstanding the original and unchanged fran-

chises, received a fare increase. They indignantly demanded improved service from the DUR.

Early in 1922 revenue fell below $14,000 per mile, so the rate was increased to 2 cents per mile. On June 21, 1923, the MPUC received its long-sought independent study made by the Froelich & Emery Engineering Company. It could now make a final decision on the basic rate. The DUR agreed to maintain the 2 cents per mile rate and it was further agreed that the accounts for the various divisions would be kept and reported separately in the future.

The study, while treating the DUR as a single company, made an in-depth study of each division.

Highlights of the MPUC study of the DJ&C:

● Mainline consists of 70.2 miles of track. It is single-track road throughout its entire length, with frequent passing sidings, lying either within the confines of highways or on private right-of-way.

● Northville branch is 14.5 miles in length and is single track lying in a highway its entire length.

● Saline branch is 10.1 miles in length and also lies within the limits of a public highway.

● Wayne cut-off is an uncompleted mainline cut-off located north of the main line at Wayne.

● City lines in Ann Arbor consist of 3.5 miles of city track built between 1890 and 1894.

● Total trackage: First main line, 98.488 miles; Second main and passing sidings, 9.118 miles; Other track, 4.468 miles; 112.074 total miles.

On May 15, 1922, .441 miles of track from Addison 'Y' to Detroit city limits was sold to the city of Detroit. The report continued:

The principal buildings are passenger stations, at Wayne, Ann Arbor, Lima Center, Francisco and Michigan Center. Car barns and other terminal facilities are located at Ypsilanti and Jackson. The power-houses at Dearborn and Ypsilanti and substations at Wayne, Ann Arbor, Francisco and Michigan Center are no longer used for these purposes, but have been partially remodeled and are now being used as car barns and passenger stations, respectively. All current is purchased at the direct current bus in the stations of

Family Tree

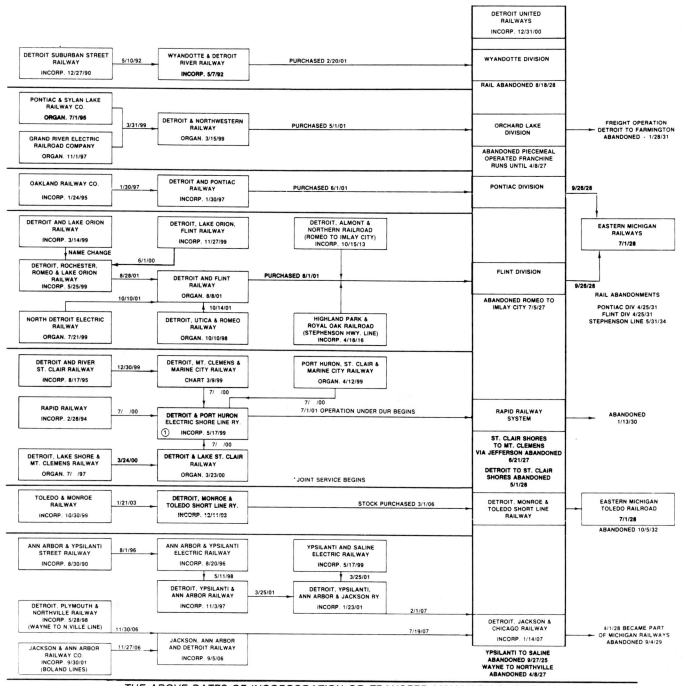

THE ABOVE DATES OF INCORPORATION OR TRANSFER MAY VARY SLIGHTLY,
DEPENDING ON WHETHER THE DATE OF AGREEMENT OR DATE OF FILING IS OBSERVED.

① "ELECTRIC" DELETED 8/30/99 FROM CORPORATE NAME

ABANDONMENT DATES - LAST DAY OF OPERATION

THE SANDWICH, WINDSOR AND AMHERSTBURG DIVISION IN CANADA AND VARIOUS CITY
OPERATIONS WILL BE COVERED IN THEIR RESPECTIVE CHAPTERS.

REVISED 7/1/85

Heading for Detroit, car 7791 passes the Duffield carhouse located near Michigan Avenue and Brady Street in Dearborn. This facility was originally a powerhouse, later it became a substation.
Schramm Collection

DJ&C's main carbarn was on Congress Street, Ypsilanti. On the left were the shops where major repairs were made.
Radway Collection

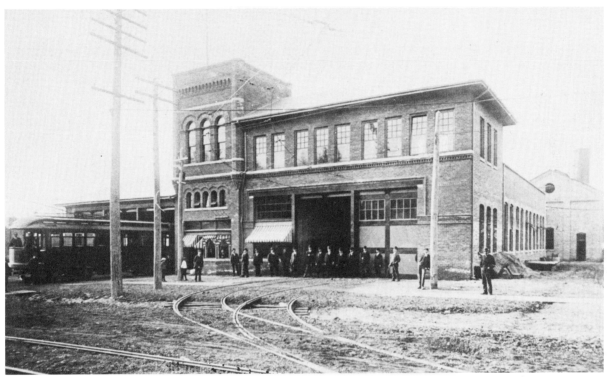

the Detroit Edison Company and Consumers Power Company located at Beecher Street in Detroit and at Dearborn, Wayne, Pusilanti, Ann Arbor, Chelsea, Grass Lake and Jackson."

On November 15, 1923, the DUR requested a rate of 2½ cents per mile for all passengers it carried. The MPUC reviewed the various divisions and for the DJ&C noted the following. "That at 2¼ cents a mile this system would not earn a profit, but that at 2⅜ cents a mile it would be able to earn a fair return, and the rate is therefore fixed at 2⅜ cents per mile."

Finally, on January 10, 1924, the various divisions received approval for new rates per mile, as follows: DJ&C, 2⅜ cents; Rapid Railway, 2½ cents; DM&T, 2⅜ cents; DUR, 2½ cents.

On May 15, 1922, the City of Detroit finally won its 30-year campaign to own its own transit system. The fight had been initiated in the mid-1890s by Mayor Hazen Pingree and was finally completed under the leadership of Mayor James Couzens. Of all misfortunes befalling the interurban company, this probably was the worst blow. Now the interurban cars entering the city would be forced to pay a high rental to use tracks they used to own. The Department of Street Railways (DSR), as the city system was now known, could and did schedule its cars totally without regard to the interurbans and their carefully-crafted timetables.

Earnings continued to fall during 1924, and the *Electric Railway Journal* reported on March 25, 1925, that earnings per mile fell from 8.53 in 1923 to 5.36 in 1924. On March 10, 1924, the DUR went into receivership.

Electricity and Power Plants

Territory control was equally important to electric power and interurban companies. Detroit Edison Company was organized on August 19, 1903, as seven small companies were consolidated, each previously serving a portion of a much smaller Detroit. This was accomplished under the direction of Alex Dow who joined Edison Illuminating Company in 1896.

Prior to the amalgamation, the management of Detroit's electric supply had been confusing, each company having different rate structures for electricity. Some charged by lamp hour, some by fixed contract, others by kilowatt hours. One reason for this lack of uniformity was the lack of a reliable meter. Finally an accurate meter appeared in 1900, manufactured by General Electric. At the time of consolidation there were four different meters in use, and more than one method to produce electricity by steam. It took years to standardize the electric industry in Detroit, under Dow's direction.

Edison had been selling power to streetcar companies prior to the formation of the DUR. As the original interurban companies built their lines, they also built their own power plants. This resulted in a mixture of plants and capacities when taken over by the DUR. The following is a summary of the power supply capabilities of the various DUR related companies:

Wyandotte and Detroit River Railway: original DC power plant in Ford City (Wyandotte) closed prior to DUR purchase with power purchased from Detroit Citizens' Street Railway.

Rapid Railway: First DC plant built at Roseville to power the line from Detroit to Mt. Clemens on Gratiot. The Shore

Line, operating from Detroit to Mt. Clemens along Jefferson, purchased power from the Mt. Clemens system's Lakeside plant. When the line was extended to Port Huron, a new AC plant was built at New Baltimore. Roseville became one of five substations. The Lakeside plant was taken out of service and removed. The New Baltimore plant was closed in 1925.

Orchard Lake: Pontiac and Sylvan Lake Railway had a DC plant in Pontiac, later used for stand-by; abandoned by 1915. Grand River Electric Railway purchased power from Edison Illuminating Company. When taken over by the Detroit & Northwestern Railway, a new plant was built at Farmington Junction using DC power; it operated until 1925.

Pontiac Division: A DC plant was built at Birmingham which was out of service by 1915.

Flint Division: A DC plant was built at Rochester which also provided power to that city. When the line was extended to Flint an AC plant was installed. Detroit Edison Company won the lighting franchise in Rochester May 14, 1909. On December 16, 1914, the sub at Flint closed and power purchased from Commonwealth. The power plant at Rochester closed in 1925.

DM&T Division: produced AC power at a plant located in Monroe; also a small plant at Monroe Piers provided power for the resort. The Piers plant closed by 1915; the Monroe plant in 1925.

DJ&C Division: original operation. Ypsi-Ann purchased power from the Ann Arbor Electric Company. When the line was built to Ann Arbor, two DC plants were built—one in Ypsilanti,

the second in Dearborn. When the line was extended to Jackson, the system was converted to AC and the Ypsilanti plant enlarged; Dearborn became a substation. The plant was closed by 1915. The Detroit, Plymouth and Northville line had a DC plant at Plymouth; it closed by 1915.

As soon as electric service in the city of Detroit was consolidated by Edison, the next step was expansion into the suburban area. As happened with the electric railways, the existing companies had to be purchased. One such early purchase was in Grosse Pointe Farms, where a small power plant and water system had been built by local residents. The company was unable to show a profit due to antiquated equipment. Dow purchased the plant, selling the water plant to the city of Grosse Pointe Farms. This allowed him to eliminate an undesirable operation, and at the same time obtain a steady customer for his power.

In Port Huron the purchase was not made until 1919, and then only because Consumers Power Co. was thinking of bringing in competing power. This small plant had supplied the early streetcar lines.

In Pontiac the first takeover attempt was in 1904, which ended in failure, even though the DUR wanted power there. Dow felt he could not afford the line. Then in 1909, Dow did sign a contract to furnish the DUR with power. This was in response to W.A. Foote of Consumers Power, who in 1908 threatened to bring in his power.

Foote was planning, along with E.W. Clark & Company, which controlled the Bay City & Saginaw Power Company, and Walbridge & Hodenpyl, which controlled gas and power sales in Pontiac, to bring in power from the Au Sable River. Their banking associate, N.W. Harris and Company, arranged the financing.

With the rapidly expanding demand for power due to the growing auto industry in Pontiac, Dow agreed to provide the DUR with power. Edison supplied the area around the old central city while Consumers Power, who gained control of

Pontiac Light and Power Company, provided power within the old 1910 boundary. On October 2, 1987, Consumers Power transferred control of the electric power in this special district to Edison, while retaining the gas rights.

In 1905, Edison made an attempt to purchase the city-owned plant in Monroe. The residents of Monroe voted against the sale, and with the railway in receivership, the necessary right-of-way was tied up in court. It was not until 1917 that Edison was finally able to purchase the plant.

The largest Edison purchase in 1904 was the Washtenaw Light and Power Company. Scattered along the Huron River were small dams built to generate power for WL&P. This acquisition also gave Edison an opening towards Jackson, the home of Consumers Power Company. Thus, when the DJ&C offered Dow a contract for power to Lima Center, it was eagerly accepted. This brought Edison half-way to Jackson and established a boundary 50 miles from downtown Detroit. For this reason Dow agreed to purchase the property for far more then its true worth.

Unfortunately, the hydro-electric power never developed, even during World War I with its coal shortage. During this period, only a maximum of 1.7% of the total demand was met by water power. Dow, in a letter dated May 7, 1907, noted that this purchase in effect established an economic boundary for Detroit Edison.

Through the years Dow had worked with the DUR, providing power and establishing new boundaries. On August 1, 1904, the Delray power plant's first furnace was fired up and started providing the DUR with power. Dow had always felt the DUR was overcapitalized, fighting to maintain solvency, and quite unable to afford additional capital investments. Therefore, he decided Edison would continue to sell power to the DUR, equal to or less in cost than they could produce their own. By courting the interurbans, he reasoned, Edison could expand its territory into areas which otherwise would have been uneconomical. This was especially true in the early days when the only large users were electric railways and city street lighting.

Downtown Detroit

Above: Michigan Avenue and Griswold Street, once one of Detroit's busiest corners. It's June 9, 1920, and the DJ&C car in the center will turn right (south) on Griswold and head for the Bates Street station.
Manning Brothers Historical Collection

Griswold Street, just north of Jefferson, showing a DJ&C car loading at Detroit's first unified interurban depot. In 1915 the Detroit station moved to Bates and Jefferson, which DJ&C used until abandonment on September 4, 1929.
Henning Collection

Car 7765 sits on Farmer Street between Bates and Monroe in 1917. The large building to the right was the Crowley-Milners Department Store, torn down years ago. Straight ahead is the famed J. L. Hudson store which, at that time, was not built to its ultimate height; today it stands nearly empty.
Manning Brothers Historical Collection

Rapid Railway car 7299 heads west on Michigan Avenue and has just crossed Livernois Avenue on its way to Jackson. Since it is equipped with third-rail shoes it might be going all the way to Kalamazoo or Lansing over the Michigan Railway.
Hildebrandt Collection

Leaving Detroit

An outbound interurban car has stopped at Addison wye on a cold winter day. This was the end of the city track until May 15, 1922, when the City of Detroit purchased the city lines and the portion to Wyoming Avenue. It was also here that the city and interurban crews exchanged cars prior to the DUR takeover of DJ&C.

Woodard Collection

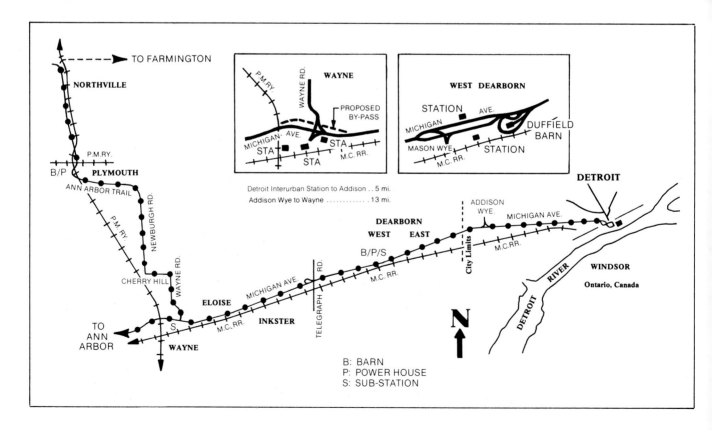

Through Dearborn

Looking west on Michigan Avenue, Dearborn, in 1905. The building with the turret was built in 1896 as the Wagner Hotel. Located at Monroe, it still stands today. Across the street at the right was the Commandant's House, dating back to the 1830's when the arsenal was moved from Detroit to what was then called "Dearbornville." In later years the line was double-tracked in this area.

Dearborn Historical Commission

7805 heads a work train along a flood-swollen Michigan Avenue in the vicinity of the Rouge River, March 14, 1918.

Kremkow Collection

Westbound car 7794 at Westwood switch, a half-mile west of Telegraph Road.
Motiligan Collection

Michigan Avenue at Wayne County General Hospital. The car is westbound, heading for Wayne.

DUR

Wayne County General Hospital was also known as *Eloise* through the years. The small shelter was later replaced by this larger depot.

Aigeltinger Collection

Wayne

Passengers can transfer to the DP&N Line

Detroit-bound car 16 pauses at the Wayne depot. The rear of a Plymouth-Northville line car is just visible at the right.

Moore Collection

The baggage carts in front of the Wayne depot are evidence this was a busy transfer point between the two lines. There were 40 cars each way every day during the golden years of interurban travel.

Andrews Collection

This is the Wayne substation and depot after it had been enlarged. It was needed to supply additional power to the branch line from Wayne to Northville after the Plymouth powerhouse was closed.

Hildebrandt Collection

59

We look west on Michigan from Wayne Road. The next major stop was Canton, four miles further on. Notice how the track swings from the center to the side of the road.
Andrews Collection

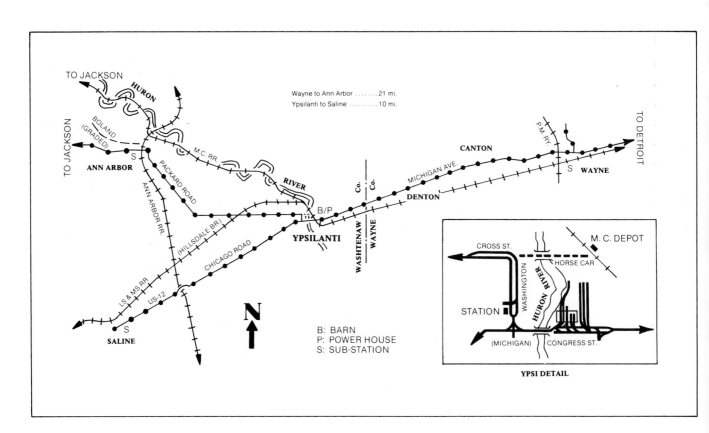

This was Denton stop in Canton Township between Wayne and Ypsilanti. The dirt road is now U.S. Highway 12.
Helen Maloney

Car 7785 is standing on the barn lead. The bridge in the background is the Congress Street span over the Huron River. In later years the line was double-tracked in the barn area.
Schramm Collection

This photo of the Ypsilanti depot shows the track into the freight room which came off the westbound track.

Faber Collection

The only known photo of the obscure Ypsilanti horsecar line. Here the car sits at Cross and Washington streets, its connection with the interurban. Little is known of this operation, other than it ran a scant half-mile along Cross Street to the Michigan Central depot. It is thought this track may have been part of the Ypsi-Ann prior to electrification. The operator was allowed to keep all receipts collected, and when he died, the line quit.

Hildebrandt Collection

A westbound car about to turn off Congress Street. In later years a straight track was installed at this corner.

Andrews Collection

Then to Ann Arbor

Line car 7263, usually found on the Rapid Railway, was running along Packard Road, Ann Arbor, in this February 11, 1923, view. DUR line cars, not confined to any one division, roamed the entire system.
Lloyd Morris

Passengers and crew await their car at Ann Arbor.
Schramm Collection

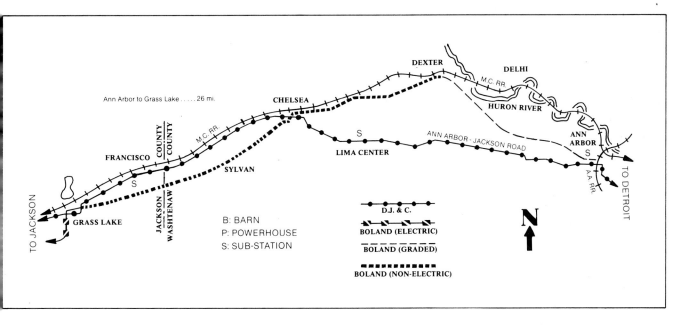

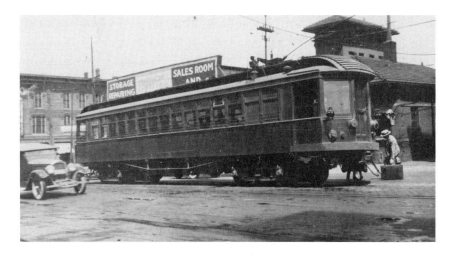

Lloyd Morris caught #7773 the 5:30 pm westbound Jackson express in front of the Ann Arbor station, on June 13, 1925. Suppose the man with a suitcase is a "drummer"?

7794 is at milepost 37, near Berry switch west of Ann Arbor, en route to Chelsea.
DUR Files

Right and Opposite, top: Unlike the Boland line, the DJ&C entered Grass Lake on the outskirts. These two photos show the private-right-of-way.
Manning Brothers Historical Collection

The DJ&C Grass Lake depot.
Stoner Collection

The Michigan Center substation and depot was typical of DJ&C construction. The tower on these buildings contained the switching gear and transformers. As originally built, 2000 volts AC were supplied to each substation and then reduced to 390 volts AC for the rotary converters. The converters in turn supplied 600 volts DC to the trolley line for a distance of about five miles. Power was supplied at Dearborn, Wayne, Ypsilanti, Ann Arbor, Lima Center, Francisco, Michigan Center and Saline. By December 1907 the last three named substations were closed, and power was purchased from Commonwealth.
Henning Collection

End of the Line

Interurban Station, Jackson, Mich.

MICHIGAN UNITED TRACTION CO.
INTERURBAN STATION
DETROIT, JACKSON & CHICAGO RY.

Street loading in Jackson, always a problem, was solved by the construction of an off-street terminal on Francis Street in late fall 1910. Both MUT (owner) and DUR shared the terminal when it opened in January 1911.
Hague Collection

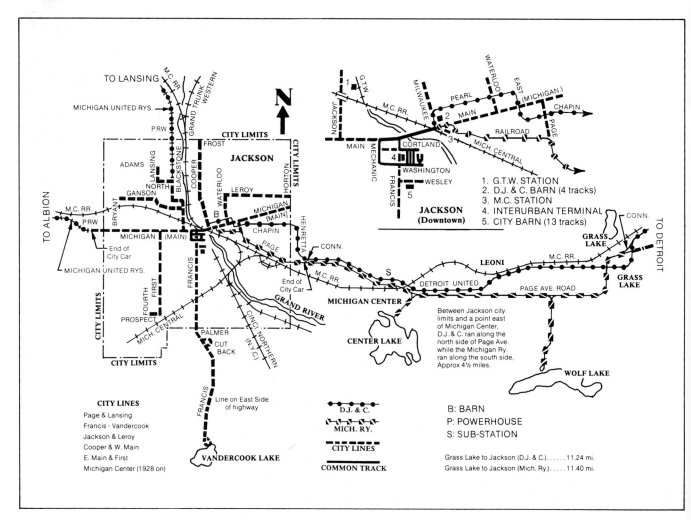

TO LANSING
MICHIGAN UNITED RYS.
M.C. RR.
GRAND TRUNK WESTERN
PRW

N

CITY LIMITS
JACKSON
CITY LIMITS

FROST
ADAMS
LANSING
BLACKSTONE
COOPER
WATERLOO
LEROY
NORTON
NORTH
GANSON
BRYANT

TO ALBION
M.C. RR.
PRW
MICHIGAN (MAIN)
B
MICHIGAN (MAIN)
CHAPIN
HENRETTA
CONN.

End of
City Car
MICHIGAN UNITED RYS.
PAGE

FRANCIS
FIRST
FOURTH
CITY LIMITS
MICH. CENTRAL
PROSPECT
PALMER
CUT BACK
CINCI. NORTHERN (N.Y.C.)
GRAND RIVER

End of
City Car
M.C. RR.
MICHIGAN CENTER
CENTER LAKE

CITY LIMITS
FRANCIS
Line on East Side
of highway

CITY LINES
Page & Lansing
Francis - Vandercook
Jackson & Leroy
Cooper & W. Main
E. Main & First
Michigan Center (1928 on)

VANDERCOOK LAKE

• • • • D.J. & C.
^^^^ MICH. RY.
---- CITY LINES
─── COMMON TRACK

G.T.W.
JACKSON
MILWAUKEE
WATERLOO
PEARL
EAST (MICHIGAN)
MAIN
CHAPIN
RAILROAD
PAGE
MICH. CENTRAL
CORTLAND
MECHANIC
WASHINGTON
FRANCIS
WESLEY

1
2
3
4
5

JACKSON
(Downtown)

1. G.T.W. STATION
2. D.J. & C. BARN (4 tracks)
3. M.C. STATION
4. INTERURBAN TERMINAL
5. CITY BARN (13 tracks)

CONN.
GRASS LAKE
TO DETROIT
M.C. RR.
LEONI
DETROIT UNITED
PAGE AVE. ROAD
GRASS LAKE
S

Between Jackson city limits and a point east of Michigan Center, D.J. & C. ran along the north side of Page Ave. while the Michigan Ry. ran along the south side, Approx 4½ miles.

WOLF LAKE

B: BARN
P: POWERHOUSE
S: SUB-STATION

Grass Lake to Jackson (D.J. & C.)......11.24 mi.
Grass Lake to Jackson (Mich. Ry.).....11.40 mi.

The Branch Lines

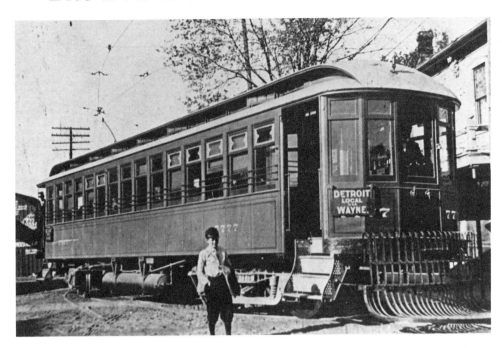

Wayne to Northville

Unit 7777 turns off Wayne Road onto Michigan Avenue at Wayne. In later years DUR introduced through cars into Detroit from Northville, eliminating the need to transfer at Wayne.

Wayne Historical Society

JAN. FEB. MAR. APR. MAY JUNE JULY AUG. SEPT. OCT. NOV. DEC.

Keep this transfer until taken up by Conductor. It will be accepted for fare only on date and from and to stations punched. Transfer will be accepted only on first train due to leave Wayne or Ypsilanti after time punched.

J. F. KEYS, G. P. A.

DETROIT, JACKSON & CHICAGO RY. 89374

DJ&C Transfer.

A very early view looking north on Wayne Road, just north of Michigan.

Aigeltinger Collection

Wayne Road, looking north, in March 1919. Today this is a five-lane street. Note the double overhead, a standard DUR practice on single track.
Manning Brothers Historical Collection

Bound for Wayne, 7785 meets 7780 at Newburg Station. This DP&N station was located at Newburg Road and Ann Arbor Trail. The building has been preserved by the Livonia Historical Society at its Greenmead facility.
Livonia Historical Society

First, Plymouth

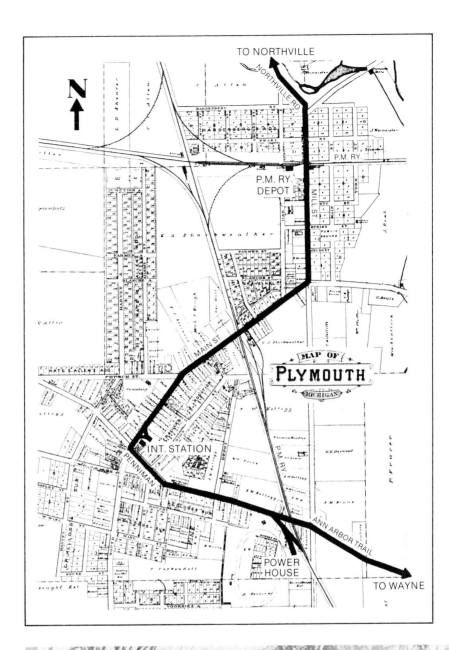

Map of Plymouth.

The interurban brought mobility to small towns such as Plymouth. Enroute to Northville, the car is turning the corner from Sutton onto Main Street. The station is just out of sight to the right.
Schramm Collection

From Plymouth to Northville

The *Yolande* is passing Kellogg Park in downtown Plymouth. Today the well-kept park is still there, but the rails are gone, replaced by parking spaces for automobiles.
Schramm Collection

Here the *Yolande,* on its way to Northville, leaves the shoulder and heads cross-country. This is near the present Cass Benton Park between Plymouth and Northville.
Moore Collection

Car 7781 has just passed under the Pere Marquette Railroad tracks through the Phoenix Tunnel. It was located near the point where the Northville Road crosses the C&O tracks by Phoenix Lake. Today nearly all traces of the tunnel are gone (the authors found a short piece of track buried in the roadway on the far side of the tunnel). Both train and interurban are heading toward Northville.
Faber Collection

Northville

Badge used on DJ&C.

DJ&C button.

To enter Northville, the car had to cross the Mill Pond. Waterpower was still an important item of the early days in this area, as its availability led to early settlements.

Schramm Collection

A car laying over on Main Street in Northville. It has already been turned on the wye, ready to head for either Wayne or Farmington.

Robertson Collection

An early Northville funeral in progress. The car in the foreground marked *Special* was rebuilt from a single-truck passenger car into a funeral car. The interurban car in the rear will leave for Wayne or Farmington.

Northville Historical Society

The Northville freight depot was on the northeast corner of Main Street and Griswold. Later a Ford factory was built on the site.

Northville Historical Society

As soon as the photographer has finished, the crew will re-board, and 7775 will leave for Wayne.

Northville Historical Society

Scenes along the Saline Branch

After wying at Hall Street, car 7782 backed up the hill to town center. Now it's loading for the return trip to Ypsilanti. The curving track in the foreground is the depot spur. The depot was located in the block southeast of the Michigan and Ann Arbor road intersection.
Michigan Historical Collections, Bentley Historical Library, University of Michigan

Heading for Saline, 7794 is passing the Ypsilanti-Pittsfield township line. The dirt highway is the Chicago Road, later paved and now U.S. 12.
Schramm Collection

DETROIT, JACKSON & CHICAGO RAILWAY
DETROIT, BATTLE CREEK, KALAMAZOO AND LANSING

West Bound—Read Down   East Bound—Read Up

Express Cars							Limited Cars									MII	STATIONS	Limited Cars								Express Cars.					
6 00	4 00	2 00	12 00	10 00	8 00		7 00	5 00	3 00	1 00	11 00	9 00	7 00			0	Lv....xDetroit (E.T.)Ar	10 55	12 55	2 55	4 55	6 55	8 55	10 55	9 15	9 55	11 55	1 55	3 55	5 55	7 55
6 47	4 47	2 47	12 47	10 47	8 47		7 47	5 47	3 47	1 47	11 47	9 47	7 47			10	...Dearborn...	10 07	12 07	2 07	4 07	6 07	8 07	10 07	8 31	9 07	11 07	1 07	3 07	5 07	7 07
7 02	5 02	3 02	1 02	11 02	9 02		8 02	6 02	4 02	2 02	12 02	10 02	8 02			18	...Wayne...	9 56	11 56	1 56	3 56	5 56	7 56	9 56	8 21	8 56	10 56	12 56	2 56	4 56	6 56
7 26	5 26	3 26	1 26	11 26	9 26		8 26	6 26	4 26	2 26	12 26	10 26	8 26			30	...Ypsilanti...	9 33	11 33	1 33	3 33	5 33	7 33	9 33	7 58	8 33	10 33	12 33	2 33	4 33	6 33
7 48	5 48	3 48	1 48	11 48	9 48		8 48	6 48	4 48	2 48	12 48	10 48	8 48			39	...Ann Arbor...	9 10	11 10	1 10	3 10	5 10	7 10	9 10	7 35	8 10	10 10	12 10	2 10	4 10	6 10
8 10	6 10	4 10	2 10	12 10	10 10											50	...Lima Center...								7 43	9 43	11 43	1 43	3 43	5 43	
8 20	6 20	4 20	2 20	12 20	10 20		9 11	7 11	5 11	3 11	1 11	11 11	9 11			54	...Chelsea...	8 45	10 45	12 45	2 45	4 45	6 45	8 45	7 34	9 34	11 34	1 34	3 34	5 34	
8 33	6 33	4 33	2 33	12 33	10 33		9 20	7 20	5 20	3 20	1 20	11 20	9 20			60	...†Francisco...	8 33	10 33	12 33	2 33	4 33	6 33	8 33	7 20	9 20	11 20	1 20	3 20	5 20	
8 42	6 42	4 42	2 42	12 42	10 42		9 27	7 27	5 27	3 27	1 27	11 27	9 27			65	...Grass Lake...	8 26	10 26	12 26	2 26	4 26	6 26	8 26	7 10	9 10	11 10	1 10	3 10	5 10	
8 48	6 48	4 48	2 48	12 48	10 48											68	...Leoni...								7 04	9 04	11 04	1 04	3 04	5 04	
9 20	7 20	5 20	3 20	1 20	11 20		10 00	8 00	6 00	4 00	2 00	12 00	10 00			76	Ar...Jackson(E.T.)Lv	8 00	10 00	12 00	2 00	4 00	6 00	8 00	6 40	8 40	10 40	12 40	2 40	4 40	
							9 20	7 00	5 00	3 00	1 00	11 00	9 00			0	Lv...Jackson (C.T.)Ar	6 58	9 00	11 00	1 00	3 00	5 00	7 00							
								8 28	6 28	4 28	2 28	12 28	10 28			44	...Battle Creek...	7 36	9 30	11 30	1 30	3 30	5 30								
								9 28	7 28	5 28	3 28	1 28	11 28			69	...Kalamazoo...	6 35	8 25	10 25	12 25	2 25	4 25								
							10 45									37	Ar...Lansing (C.T.)Lv	5 40													

DETROIT TO JACKSON—West Bound

Local Trains

MII	STATIONS																											
0	Lv xDetroit(E.T.)Mich	415	430	530		600				6 30		7 30	8 30		9 30	1030		1130	1230		1 30	2 30		3 30	4 30		5 30	6 30		7 30	8 00	8 30		9 00	1000	1100		1200
10	Lv Dearborn....Mich	454	520	620		649			7 20		8 20	9 20		1020	1120		1220	1 20		2 20	3 20		4 20	5 20		6 20	7 20		8 20	8 50	9 20		9 50	1050	1150		1242
18	Lv Wayne........Mich	543	643				7 43	7 43	8 43	8 43	9 43	1043	1043	1143	1243	1 43	1 43	2 43	2 43	3 43	3 43	4 43	4 43	5 43	6 43	7 43	8 43	179	43	1017	1017	1113	1209	1209	1259
27	Lv Plymouth....Mich	608	708				3 08		9 08		1008	1108		1208	1 08		2 08	3 08		4 08	5 08		6 08	7 08		9 08		1041			1235
33	Lv Northville..Mich	625	725				8 25		9 25		1025	1125		1225	1 25		2 25	3 25		4 25	5 25		6 25	7 25		9 25		1100			1254
30	Ar Ypsilanti....Mich				540		718	8 20	9 20		1120		1 20		3 20		5 20		7 20	8 20	9 20		9 50	1020		1050	1150	1240		1 25
0	Lv Ypsilanti....Mich					652	8 45	1045		1245		2 45		4 45		6 45		8 30		1050		1150		1250
10	Ar Saline........Mich					720	9 15	1115		1 15		3 15		5 15		7 15		9 00		1115		1215		1 15
39	Lv Ann Arbor...Mich		605	748	8 50	9 48		1148		1 48		3 48		5 48		7 48	8 50		1020		1120	1220	110
50	Lv Lima Center .Mich		622	810															1040		1240
54	Lv Chelsea ....Mich		630	820															1051		1251
60	Lv †Francisco ..Mich		642	833															1103		1 03
65	Lv Grass Lake...Mich		653	842															1110		1 10
68	Lv Leoni ......Mich		704	848															1116		1 16
76	Ar Jackson(E.T.)Mich		725	910															1140		1 40

JACKSON TO DETROIT—East Bound

Local Trains

MII	STATIONS																					
0	Lv Jackson......Mich												5 30		7 30		9 20			1206
8	Lv Leoni........Mich												5 59		7 59		9 44			1223
11	Lv Grass Lake...Mich												6 05		8 05		9 50			1230
16	Lv †Francisco...Mich												6 14		8 14		1000			1238
23	Lv Chelsea......Mich												6 30		8 30		1013			1251
26	Lv Lima Center .Mich												6 39		8 39		1023			1 00
37	Lv Ann Arbor...Mich		535	640	705			9 05		1105		1 05		3 05		5 05		7 05	8 05	9 05		1050		1145	1 10	1 20
0	Lv Saline.......Mich	*	*		7 20		9 45		1145		1 45		3 45		5 45		7 45	9 00		1115		1215	1 15
10	Ar Ypsilanti....Mich				7 50		1015		1215		2 15		4 15		6 15		8 15	9 30		1140		1240	1 40
46	Lv Ypsilanti....Mich	438	503		600	710	735		9 35			1135		1 35		3 35		5 35		7 35	8 35	9 33		1120		1213	1 38	1 48
43	Lv Northville....Mich	520	630			730	8 30		9 30		1030	1130		1230	1 30		2 30	3 30		4 30	5 30		6 30	7 30		9 30		1115
49	Lv Plymouth....Mich	§ 538	648			748	8 48		9 48		1048	1148		1248	1 48		2 48	3 48		4 48	5 48		6 48	7 48		9 43		1131
58	Lv Wayne........Mich	506	536	606	636	713	743	813	9 13		1013	1013	1113	1213	1213	1 13	2 13	2 13	3 13	4 13	4 13	135	136	136	137	138	13 9	13 1013	1010	1155	1155
66	Lv Dearborn....Mich	500	527	557	627	657	733	805	833		9 30			1030	1130		1230	1 30		2 30	3 30		4 30	5 30		6 30	7 30		8 30	9 30	1030		1215
76	Lv xDetroit (E.T.)Mich	555	625	655	725	755	825	855	925		1025			1125	1225		1 25	2 25		3 25	4 25		5 25	6 25		7 25	8 25		9 25	1025	1125		1 00

*To and from Ypsilanti Car House only.   §Daily except Sunday.   †All Cars stop at Pere Marquette Crossing West of Wayne.
Limited Cars westbound stop at Francisco to let off Detroit passengers and eastbound to take on Detroit passengers.

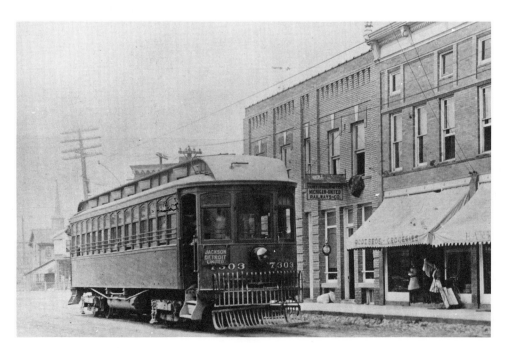

DJ&C Timetable

Rapid Railway car 7303 at Galesburg in front of the Michigan United Railways depot. Through cars to Kalamazoo and Lansing began April 1, 1911. MUR cars in the Detroit service had to be lowered 6½ inches to fit DJ&C trackage.

Krentel Collection

Interline Service

With an extensive interurban network west of Jackson, it is easy to understand the DUR's desire for interline service. Likewise, by using DUR tracks, the Michigan Railway would have access to Detroit, Michigan's largest city.

The original agreement for interline service was dated January 30, 1911. In it the DJ&C was to pay 55 cents for each car entering Jackson, but less than $9 per day. The terminal in Jackson was to be used jointly, with all expenses divided equally. Passenger accounts were to be based on the number of cars in and out, except for through cars. The freight account was to be based on tonnage, but not to include through express cars.

A clause was inserted permitting operation over each other's tracks between Jackson and Grass Lake in case of blockade. For through service, each party was to furnish cars in proportion to total miles on the route. In addition, each railroad was to charge two cents per mile for the use of its car while on the tracks of the other, except for switching purposes.

Rates increased on June 30, 1915, and again February 6, 1917, as amendments were made. The last figure recorded was 3.0375 cents per car mile for passenger cars and 2 cents for trailers.

Much of the Michigan Railway was equipped with a third rail instead of overhead wires to deliver power to the trains. The cars furnished by the DJ&C for interline operation can be identified only by checking the roster for cars equipped with third-rail shoes. Included were cars 7303, 7311-12, 7520-22, 7524-5, 7767,

7772-3 and 7790-6. No records exist that show what cars were furnished by Michigan Railway.

Through service was discontinued about March 1, 1924, according to the DUR notes from which most of this data was obtained. Apparently the service was halted at the behest of the Michigan Electric Railway.

In 1927 the question of through car service was revived, but apparently nothing came of the idea. A study indicated that it would cost about $100 per car to be re-equipped with third-rail shoes. This was necessary since all the third-rail shoes had been removed and scrapped by the DUR. Also, in 1925, cars 7311-7312, 7524-7525 and 7795-7796 had been transferred to the DM&T Division.

One reason that through car service was apparently never reinstated is that DUR Receiver A.L. Drum increased parallel bus operation from Detroit to Jackson from a two-hour to a one-hour headway. Interurban rail service between Jackson and Kalamazoo was abandoned on November 30, 1928. Operation between Jackson and Lansing lasted until May 18, 1929. After John F. Collins was appointed receiver, some Michigan Railway cars were assigned to the DJ&C. One of the cars used the last day of operation was Michigan Railway car 825. There was a shortage of DJ&C cars, with many not in shape to operate; others had been scrapped earlier by Drum.

A Kalamazoo-Detroit Limited eastbound on Packard Road, near the Ann Arbor city limits, on February 11, 1923. *Lloyd Morris Photo*

Freight and Work Cars

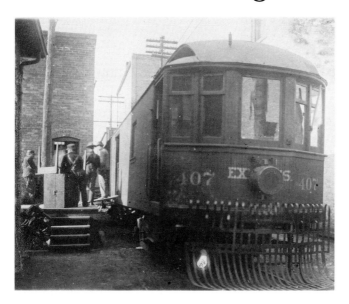

Originally passenger car 7, this vehicle was rebuilt into express car 407. DUR renumbered it 7800 when it took over operations. *Schramm Collection*

Little is known of the DJ&C freight operations, and newspapers often reported conflicting stories. Package freight was handled between stations. The *Detroit Free Press* reported on May 19, 1905, the first carload lot service. A 300 h.p. freight motor and four flat cars equipped with air brakes, were hauling bricks from the west side of Detroit to Kalamazoo.

Apparently the interurbans had no plans then to operate freight trains over the city streets in Detroit. A February 2, 1906, *Ann Arbor Argus-Democrat* article described contemporary freight operations as being limited to a flat car equipped with a tower for the motorman and a trolley. This unit could pull two flat cars.

It was probably shortly after that time that the first passenger cars, 7 through 10, were converted for freight operations. These were renumbered 407 through 410 and were the only cars listed at the time of the DUR takeover at which time they were renumbered 7800-7803. Later, two additional cars, 7786 and 7787, were converted, but they retained their passenger car numbers.

The first purchase of freight cars for this division was in 1921 when car 2006 was obtained for use as a freight trailer. (In 1923 it was motorized.) Freight trailers 2142 to 2147 were also purchased in 1921.

We see 7800 as the Gabel's Creamery milk car. It was designed and painted by the creamery as a rolling advertising billboard.

Schramm Collection

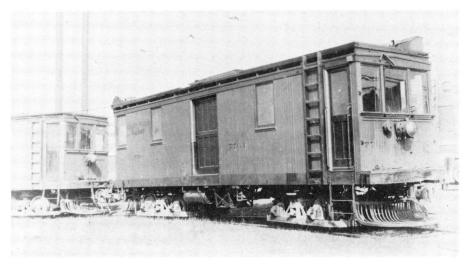

About 1915 DUR replaced the bodies on many of the old line cars with new bodies from the Niles Car Company. Here is the appearance of 7763 with its new body and painted in Eastern Michigan colors and logo. When DJ&C split from DUR this car was retained by Eastern Michigan. Today it still exists at the Ohio Railway Museum at Worthington, Ohio.
Nichols Collection

In August 1912, car 7773 derailed seven miles east of Ypsilanti. Here, a line car, acting as a wrecker, is attempting to correct the problem. The motorman this day was Pat Briggs, and the conductor was Everett Hicks.
Dearborn Historical Commission

The 7755 is a former city car converted to a line car.
Schramm Collection

Car 7804 fights heavy snow-drifts to free 7774 on the Saline Division in February 1912.
Schramm Collection

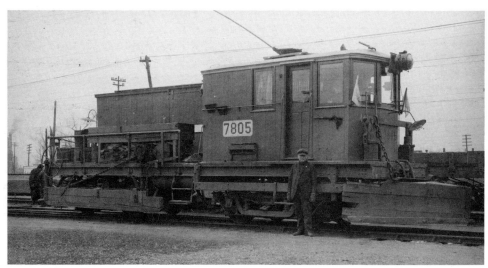

One of the large work cars used by the DUR was the 7805. It was assigned to the DJ&C Division.
Schramm Collection

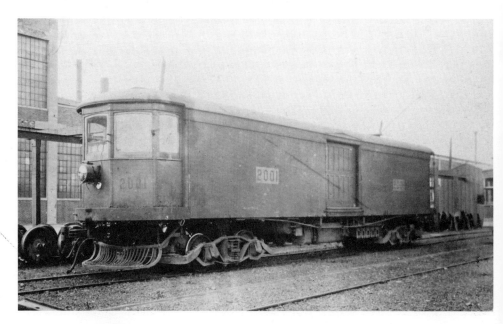

Motor 2001, purchased in 1916, was equipped with two Standard arch bar trucks and four Westinghouse 562A5 motors. Here it is standing at the Highland Park main shops.
Schramm Collection

This washout at Phoenix curve was caused when the Ford Dam near Northville on a branch of Rouge River collapsed and water carried away the DUR bridge; it happened on December 3, 1920.
Wayne County Road Commission

Phoenix Curve on March 23, 1920. At this time the county was replacing the older bridge and straightening the highway. Our photo is south of the Rouge River looking north-*DUR*

One of the many lakes and ponds created by damming the Rouge River. This provided water power for generating electricity in various parts of the river's flood plain, thus attracting small industries to the area. Here, the interurban tracks follow along the water's edge en route to Northville.
Wayne Historical Society

Throwing the switch for perhaps the last time, the motorman of 7782, *Old Maud*, makes ready to depart Ypsilanti
for Saline on the final day of operation, September 27,
1925.   *Schramm Collection*

4

BANKRUPTCY AND FINAL YEARS

BANKRUPTCY FOR THE DUR came on March 10, 1925. Times were changing, the public deserted the interurban for the bus; it was unable to make payments to the Yellow Coach Company for coaches it had purchased. The first co-receivers appointed were Joseph M. Simard and Security Trust Company. There was an attempt to refinance the company on July 29, 1925, but the plan was voted down. A few weeks later, on August 24, 1925, Simard resigned and was replaced by W.C. Dunbar as co-receiver.

Then, on January 22, 1927, A.L. Drum was appointed as sole receiver. He had been hired on May 8, 1925, as a consultant to help reduce the cost of operation. He remained as receiver until replaced by Federal Judge Charles Simons in response to petitions filed by the bond underwriters. They were concerned that with the formation of a new company, there might be a conflict of interest.

Drum was replaced by the Security Trust Company, which continued as receivers, but they retained Drum in an executive capacity to organize a new company to take control of both the rail and bus lines.

Of course, DUR had been retrenching for some time. The Windsor property was sold in 1920, and the Detroit operations were taken over by the city in 1922.

One of the first DUR track abandonments took place on the DJ&C when the line from Ypsilanti to Saline was discontinued. The state highway department wanted to widen and pave the Chicago Road to create a second major road connecting Detroit and Chicago. The cost of moving the track would, of course, have to be borne by the railway.

Newspapers noted that while residents along the line were against the abandonment, businessmen in Saline

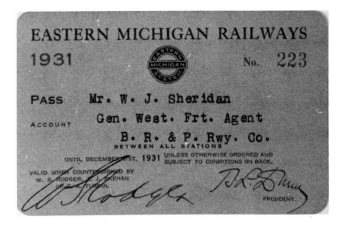

EASTERN MICHIGAN RAILWAYS
1931   No. 223

PASS   Mr. W. J. Sheridan
ACCOUNT   Gen. West. Frt. Agent
           B. R. & P. Rwy. Co.
           BETWEEN ALL STATIONS
UNTIL DECEMBER 31ST, 1931 UNLESS OTHERWISE ORDERED AND
                          SUBJECT TO CONDITIONS ON BACK.
VALID WHEN COUNTERSIGNED BY
W. S. RODGER, C. J. SKEHAN
OR C. T. TURPIN.
                                            PRESIDENT.

were all for it. They felt it would improve business to have an all-weather highway. What they didn't realize was that shoppers would continue on to larger cities such as Ypsilanti and Adrian for their needs.

So, on September 27, 1925, the rail service was abandoned. In its place, on October 15, 1925, the Peoples Motor Coach Company began operating buses with a fare up to 35 cents. This was the second bus replacement of streetcars in the area. On February 1, 1925, buses had replaced city streetcar service in Ann Arbor, supposedly for a one-year trial. The streetcars never returned.

Another early abandonment was the Wayne-Northville line. In the mid-1920's service was reduced to two-hour headways. However, some of the cars continued on into Detroit, saving a transfer at Wayne. Service was further reduced on December 5, 1926, when a single daily round trip was made to protect the franchise and retain ownership of the right-of-way.

A similar reduction occurred on the line from Northville to Farmington Junction to Redford on December 30, 1926. From that date until April 8, 1927, a single through car was run from Redford, to Farmington, to Northville, to Plymouth and to Wayne.

This expedient allowed the DUR to continue freight operations on this trackage. But there was insufficient

traffic, and on February 1, 1927, the bankruptcy court authorized abandonment, which occurred April 8, 1927. Reversion of the right-of-way property to former owners began October 10, 1927. During 1928 most of the trackage was removed except in city streets.

Replacement bus service was provided by the Outer Belt Transit Line, taken over by the DUR in 1927. The road from Plymouth to Northville was paved in 1922, making it part of a network of concrete roads reaching Ann Arbor. Then on May 23, 1925, the Outer Belt Transit was organized to provide bus service.

The route of the Outer Belt line duplicated part of both rail lines serving Northville. Buses operated from Ann Arbor, through Plymouth, Northville, Farmington, Orchard Lake to Pontiac.

Beginning in 1925 the Detroit Motorbus Company was also operating buses to both Plymouth and Northville directly from Detroit via Plymouth Road and via Seven Mile Road. These direct routes were not only faster, but eliminated the transfer at Wayne. After this service started, DUR's rail branch was doomed.

The DUR Fights Back

All this competition left the interurban starved for cash, and DUR receivers were granted a fare increase, effective July 1, 1925, which allowed a rate of 3 cents

---

Eastern Standard Time   **DETROIT, JACKSON AND CHICAGO RY.**   JOHN F. COLLINS, Receiver   **Eastern Standard Time**

Detroit-Ypsilanti-Ann Arbor-Jackson-Lansing-Battle Creek-Kalamazoo-Grand Rapids and Intermediate Points

WEST BOUND   READ DOWN   SUBJECT TO CHANGE WITHOUT NOTICE

(railway timetable — westbound)

STATIONS	Miles
Lv. DETROIT Lv.	0.00
DEARBORN	10.87
INKSTER	13.60
ELOISE	16.10
WAYNE	18.12
YPSILANTI	30.55
ANN ARBOR	39.18
LIMA CENTERS	49.33
CHELSEA	53.85
FRANCISCO §	60.82
GRASS LAKE	64.94
LEONI §	68.08
Ar. JACKSON Ar	76.18
Lv. JACKSON Lv.	76.18
Ar. LANSING Ar	114.52
Lv. JACKSON Lv.	76.18
BATTLE CREEK	120.00
Ar. KALAMAZOO Ar.	145.14
Ar. GRAND RAPIDS Ar.	194.86

Grand Rapids - Kalamazoo - Battle Creek - Lansing - Jackson - Ann Arbor - Ypsilanti - Detroit

EAST BOUND   READ DOWN

(railway timetable — eastbound)

Miles	STATIONS
0.00	Lv. GRAND RAPIDS Lv.
50.00	Lv. KALAMAZOO Lv.
74.00	BATTLE CREEK
119.00	Ar. JACKSON Ar.
0.00	Lv. LANSING Lv.
37.00	Ar. JACKSON Ar.
0.00	Lv. JACKSON Lv.
8.10	LEONI §
11.24	GRASS LAKE
15.36	FRANCISCO §
22.33	CHELSEA
24.60	LIMA CENTERS
37.00	ANN ARBOR
45.63	YPSILANTI
58.06	WAYNE
60.08	ELOISE
61.33	INKSTER
65.31	DEARBORN
76.10	Ar. DETROIT Ar.

† Does Not Run between Ann Arbor and Jackson on Sundays and Holidays.   * Daily Except Sunday and Holidays.   o Does Local Work between Wayne and Detroit.

§ Trains stop on signal

per mile. This time the MPUC approved the same rate for all divisions except the Wyandotte Division which had received a new franchise subsequent to the effective date of the act.

Hoping to slow the loss of riders, the DUR raised the rate to just 2¾ cents per mile. To attract new business, on August 12, 1925, the railway introduced commuter tickets. These were booklets of 20 tickets which sold at two cents per mile. There was also a 30-ticket family book and a smaller packet of 12 tickets. These books were good for only 30 or 90 days.

Under Drum, the DUR attempted to improve its image. In 1925 a new color scheme was adopted and some of the cars were repainted. The new livery was desert sand or light gray body, red band under the windows, and a vermillion red roof. This replaced the tuscan red body and gray roof then in use. As with other divisions, not all the cars were repainted, which meant an interesting mixture of colors on the line.

Another bold 1925 venture was the introduction of a deluxe parlor service on several lines. One schedule showed a single such car on the Detroit to Ann Arbor run. What car was assigned is not known, but cars in this service had their interiors extensively rebuilt. On the Pontiac Division, trailers were rebuilt and motorized. Almost all these cars were renumbered in the 8000 series.

The DJ&C Separates

The financial news kept getting worse, and on April 1, 1928, DJ&C's bondholders voted to remove Drum from management of their company. When DUR originally took over operation of the DJ&C, only the stock was purchased; the bonds remained outstanding. Now the bondholders, upset over the lack of earnings being received from their property, got news that Drum was not going to include the DJ&C in the reorganized Eastern Michigan Railways (EMR). Upset, they confronted Drum on his scheduling of buses along the route to Jackson. He responded that the buses were merely being co-ordinated with the electric cars (the cars and buses alternated on a two-hour headway).

But Drum's credibility with the bondholders was badly damaged, and at this point they placed DJ&C in the hands of a new receiver, John F. Collins, of the Michigan Electric Railway. Collins was in the process of closing down the interurban system in mid-Michigan. Of course Drum was still running the DUR, and he was now free to schedule buses when he pleased, so he began operating DUR subsidiary company buses once an hour from Detroit to Jackson in direct competition with the electric cars.

Under Drum's receivership of the DUR, only a single used interurban car, No. 20 from the Grand Rapids, Grand Haven & Muskegon Railway was purchased. It became 7556 on the Flint Division. Most other changes were cosmetic, such as repainting old cars, although there was some rebuilding of trailers into motor cars for deluxe service. However, Drum did manage to find money for buses as the company listed 155 such vehicles in the *Bus Transportation* directory of November 1927. The cost to buy out competing bus companies became a considerable drain on the treasury. But the plan was that as the rail operations on all divisions were being phased out, bus operations continued in their place.

As Collins took over the DJ&C, he received the following cars from Drum: Passenger Cars: 7771, 7777, 7780, 7791, 7792, 301 (formerly 7793), 302 (formerly 7773). Trailer Car: 7768. Freight Motor: 77803. Work Motors: 7804, 7805. Flat Cars: 7617, 7814, 7818, 7822, 7824.

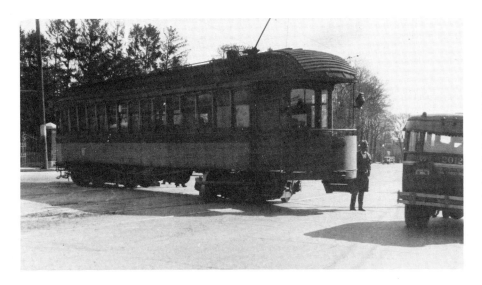

Abandonment was only a few months away when eastbound car 7792 split the switch at Nowlin Street, Dearborn, May 6, 1929. The car is still in DUR colors, which could mean it was on lease or loan to the Collins-controlled DJ&C. Detroit Motorbus Company 2012, at the right, was purchased from Studebaker to combat the jitney threat. When forced off of Detroit streets, these buses were then assigned suburban runs.

Hildebrandt Collection

The foregoing cars, still in serviceable condition, were returned to the EMR during September 1929, after the DJ&C was abandoned.

The following cars, not in serviceable condition, were returned to EMR or were already there and had not been used at all on the DJ&C under Collins: Freight Motor Car: 7806. Line Cars: 7761, 7762, 7763, 7813. Passenger Cars: 7766, 7770, 7772, 7774, 7781, 7782, 7783, 7784, 7785, 7790. Flat Cars: 7809, 7810, 7815, 7816, 7817, 7819, 7820, 7823. Gravel Car: 7811. Boarding Car: 7825. Sand Car: 7821.

Flat Car 7807 was not in serviceable condition and was located at Ypsilanti being used as a freight dock.

DUR inventory cards revealed that in 1929 Collins took two cars to the Albion shops of the Michigan Electric Railway to be rebuilt. The cars were repainted maroon below the windows, light cream above. 7773 became 302 and 7793 became 301. The letter boards were marked "Detroit, Jackson and Chicago Railway."

In 1930, after the line was abandoned, the cars were returned to Detroit's Highland Park shops. The DSR held 302 along with cars 7546, 7548 and 7555 in lieu of trackage payments from the DUR. The DSR placed 302 inside the Detroit barn at Military and Michigan while the rest of the cars went to the Wyoming car house and sat in the yard. Finally, in 1937 the DSR had Art Gustler of the EMR strip 7546, 7548, 7555, then sell the bodies. Car 302 was returned to EMR since it was the property of DJ&C and not DUR. To this day no one has come up with a photo of 302 in service or at the barn.

Car 301 ended up with Eastern Michigan, where according to records and photos we have located, it was repainted in EMR colors and logo and assigned to the Pontiac Division. In July 1931, the body was sold in Pontiac.

Eastern Michigan System Debuts

Detroit United Railway began to bow out on September 12, 1928, when approval to sell portions of the remaining DUR properties was given. On September 26, the sale was confirmed at a price of $2,575,000 for those portions, with the balance remaining in receivership. The Eastern Michigan System (EMS) that was formed included the following:

Ann Arbor's Biggest Bank Deposit

IT WAS PROBABLY the DUR's most spectacular accident; it happened on August 4, 1927, there was no loss of life, but it was expensive! In later years, Sid Ferriss, then an office boy for Eastern Michigan Railways (successor to the DUR) made a copy of the official report:

August 5, 1927

Subject: Derailment of cars at Ann Arbor, Mich.
Mr. G. H. Zapp, Gen Mgr.

Dear Sir:

On D.J.&C. Division, westbound freight consisting of motor car #2004 and 8 trailers leaving Ann Arbor, 11:30 p.m. August 4, 1927, four trailers were damaged due to the necessity of cutting the train in two while making the hill on Huron Street, Ann Arbor, Mich. A field lead wire on #4 motor, in motor car #2004 was burning off, and for that reason unable to pull the entire train up this grade. In coupling up this train at the top of grade, due to improper blocking of one section, four cars rolled down the grade from Glendale siding to Huron and Main Streets in Ann Arbor, and were derailed on curve, wrecking Farmer & Mechanics Building on the corner. The distance from Glendale siding to where the wreck occurred is 1.4 miles.

The M.E.R. car #1629 is a total loss with exception of trucks and air brake equipment. This car should be settled for, along the A.R.A. plan which exists between the M.E.R. and our company,.

DUR car #2103 is damaged about half of body, trucks and air equipment slightly damaged. At this time I cannot say whether body can be rebuilt on account of underframe condition.

Above freight motor car #2004 is equipped with Westinghouse type 562 motors, designed for freight hauling and was not overloaded when pulling an eight car train.

A.J. Challeen
Supt. of Shops

Shortly afterward, there was printed in *Ann's Amazing Harbor* this colorful eye-witness account of the accident by a staff writer whose name seems lost to history:

The cars (trailers) screeched under the railroad (bridge) and up the three block hill at a speed slightly less than its maximum. Naturally it didn't make the sharp turn of the tracks at Main Street, going south—but jumped the rails, scattered the curbstones, and plowed into the old Farmers and Merchants (Mechanics) Bank by way of the front door. Bricks and mortar, stone and glass, banknotes and paraphernalia splashed and flew in all directions. But it was much worse beyond the opposite wall where the air pressure built up and burst the partition. It was like the explosion of a dozen sticks of dynamite—as I heard the tales the next morning.

Elmer Stofflet has his lunch counter and bean hashery in there, and it was well-stocked with hot soup, spaghetti, American fries, beans, hash, soft boiled eggs, hot and cold dogs, mustard, hamburgers and customers. Then the roof caved in. A neighbor was fondling his sweetheart in a dark-corner-booth, and they say she'd slapped his hands away, when all hell broke loose. The poor boy thought her slap was the hand of Satan. Everything mentionable flew all over the place. Women screamed, men cursed, waitresses prayed for forgiveness, and the proprietor yelled: "save the nickels and dimes—leave the due bills."

There were no casualties, but they had to dig the people out from the mounds of dust and dirt. The rats and mice down in the cellar, the kitchen cat, and every cockroach that had been enjoying heaven for all the generations since time began, left the place, never to return. These statistics and many more are from reporters on the spot, and not from me. It was a jarring thunderclap that shook all the downtown area—even the firemen two blocks away were rudely tumbled from their beds and lit running toward the pyrotechnics—some without their breeches. Our city didn't quiet down for a month.

Two views of the August 5, 1928, wreck of the Farmers & Mechanics Bank in Ann Arbor. The top photo shows the wrecked cars, the bottom depicts the bank building after the area was cleared.

Stoner Collection

Flint Division, Pontiac Division and a subsidiary, the Eastern Michigan-Toledo Division, along with the Peoples Motor Coach Company and the trucking operation.

The Rapid Railway, Orchard Lake, and Wyandotte divisions remained in receivership. This would allow the EMS to abandon these lines as soon as they were proven unprofitable to the court, regardless of franchises. As previously mentioned, bus companies under EMS control would continue to service the same routes. More detailed data on this will be covered in the chapter on buses later in this volume.

But what of the Detroit-Jackson interurban? It was a lost cause and did not figure into the Eastern Michigan scheme at all. On September 4, 1929, newspapers reported that the end of passenger service on the DJ&C would occur as of that date. Receiver John F. Collins was quoted as saying that he had received the approval from Federal Judge Charles Simons in Detroit to discontinue operation of passenger service. The shops in Ypsilanti would be closed, laying off 25 men. Repairs to freight cars would be done at the Jackson car barns. The *Free Press* added that about 175 men would be thrown out of work from this action.

On September 12, the papers mentioned that the end of freight service would occur "within a few days."

On the last day of operation to Jackson, September 4, 1929, Michigan Railway 825 has just left the Bates Street terminal and is crossing Jefferson. Note the *Interurban Cars* sign above the car. Within two years only the Toledo line was left, and the station for it was moved to Woodbridge Street.   *Schramm Collection*

The sale was also noted in *Ann's Amazing Arbor*, which interviewed a very anti-interurban old-timer from the area named William Morrison. Morrison was born in 1880 and grew up on a farm on the Dexter-Ann Arbor Road. He had worked for the Michigan Central from 1899 to 1904. He noted that Sylvan Township and Chelsea Village were ruled by Frank Glazier, a banker, industrialist and Republican.

"Glazier told the original interurban builders that their railroad would have to turn off the Jackson Road and enter Chelsea, and they agreed to his command," Morrison said. The article noted that Morrison considered this an arbitrary thing and bad for the community. His town of Dexter was left high and dry by the electric road.

Morrison alleged the electric line used cheaper cedar ties while the railroad used oak ties. (The authors talked to an old Rapid Railway trackman who stated without hesitation that for interurbans the cedar tie was by far the best choice since they did not have to carry as heavy a weight as railroad ties did and were more durable.)

Clearly, old-timer Morrison was not unhappy at the demise of the interurban. The cars were operated in a reckless manner, he said, adding that "anyone could have predicted the death of the interurban with all their accidents . . . [they] killed every living human and beast, at the point where the rails crossed the wagon trails. The cars' own destruction was bound to come."

Morrison wrote "On October 31, (1929) the 'funeral services' were held at the depot on West Huron in Ann Arbor. At 12 noon, a car drove on to the depot's platform. Two men stepped out of this automobile and lifted a crippled man from the back seat of the car. His name was Mr. Sayers, Master of Chancery for the court. The chauffeur and attorney McDonald were the other men. Attorney McDonald bid seventy-two thousand dollars. Twenty-seven years before, this railroad had cost three million dollars. The few persons at this funeral were a local attorney, a farmer from Scio on the Jackson Road, and myself."

The *Dearborn Press* reported on November 7 that the electric railway equipment had been sold to the Woodmere Scrap and Iron Metal Company. Thus ended the Detroit-Jackson interurban.

Surviving Operations

As with other major rail corridors radiating out from Detroit, Michigan Avenue's original DUR rails were used in later years by Department of Street Railway. This arrangement was initiated near the end of the DJ&C service, and unlike other suburban operations, there was no financial agreement with the DUR.

Thanks to Henry Ford, there was a major expansion of streetcar service in the Michigan Avenue corridor just as the DJ&C was dying. Ford decided to build a new and larger Dearborn facility to be known as the Ford Rouge plant. This giant auto factory was designed to replace Ford's earlier complex in Highland Park and produced a change in Detroit traffic patterns from north-south to east-west.

On June 13, 1925, DSR's Northwest Belt (Oakman) line was extended from Grand River in Detroit to Michigan Avenue in Dearborn. The section below Tireman was entirely within Dearborn. Two weeks later, on June 28, the line was further extended to the new Ford Rouge plant along Michigan Avenue to Coolidge (Schaefer) and south to the new facility. There was a gala parade of streetcar equipment that day to the Fordson (Dearborn) city hall.

The DSR's Michigan rail line was extended on September 25, 1928, to Coolidge and down to the Ford plant. Then on October 17, 1929, six weeks after the DJ&C quit, the line was further extended out Michigan to the 'Y' at Mason Street, using idle DJ&C rails. An extra 10 cent fare was charged for riding west of Schaefer.

Finally, on September 7, 1930, the Michigan line was again extended to a new loop at Telegraph Road, 12 miles from downtown Detroit. DSR Bulletin #3069 detailed operations on the single-track section that existed from Coolidge to west of Southfield Road. The three-mile section was governed by automatic block signals.

Alas, DSR's expansion was short-lived. The depression hit, and service was cut back early. The 16 cent fare was reduced to 12 cents on September 1, 1931. Then on December 17, 1931, streetcars were not permitted west of Mason due to track repairs which continued until January 1, 1932. On February 6, 1932, service on the extension was drastically cut to just three cars in the morning and three in the evening rush hours. By February 29, 1932, all service to Telegraph Road was discontinued, and no cars operated beyond Schaefer.

Fourteen years later, on August 4, 1946, the DSR discontinued rail service west of Wyoming Avenue (Detroit's city limits), except for peak hours to the Ford plant. Even this part-time rail service ended on May 1, 1947.

Another streetcar line which served a section of Dearborn was the Crosstown line on West Warren. In earlier days this street had been proposed as part of an interurban route into Detroit. With Detroit expanding westward, it was deemed necessary to extend the Crosstown line across a portion of Dearborn to reach this new territory.

The initial section, from McDonald Street to Manor Avenue, was built to connect with the new Northwest Belt trackage and was opened on October 5, 1925. The final extension, 3½ miles to Rouge Park, was finished on August 5, 1929. This was Detroit's last rail extension; soon DSR management would turn to bus substitution.

DSR 3286 was the first car to run over former DJ&C rails on October 17, 1929, just six weeks after the interurban quit. The Peter Witt, with its colorful bunting, is heading for Mason 'Y'. Note a forerunner of the Edsel running alongside the streetcar.
Dearborn Historical Commission

Interurban Days

The following appeared long ago in a Ypsilanti newspaper called *The Press*. It was written, according to the credits, by Milton Barnes, a blind linotype operator.

ELECTRIC INTERURBAN CARS whizzed through Ypsilanti's main streets from 1898 to about the middle of 1929.

The man at the front, the motorman, was the idol of every subteen boy. You'd wonder why he'd ever, ever, want to change jobs with the man at the back end, the conductor.

But, take it from Alfred Augustus who worked both ends back then, there are reasons.

In the early morning one of these giant orange-yellow cars would set sail from Jackson, first trip out for the day, after the boys at the powerhouse had tunked all the wheels with sledge hammers to make sure they weren't cracked, then tested the compressed air tanks underneath for leaks, then filled them to about 250 pounds of air pressure, for the brakes.

One bell to stop, two to go ahead, three to reverse.

DING! DING! We're on our way, Alfred Augustus at the helm. The car's about half full, the Ohmer Fare Register registering 10 full fares all the way to Detroit, and 20 for stops here and there between.

But it's happened again; someone's auto wheels are stuck in the car tracks ahead.

Maybe a minute, maybe four or five and the auto is extricated. A boy on his bike abruptly crosses the tracks and the motorman taps his foot to sound the large brass gong under the dash.

The railroad crossing; the law calls for a full stop, the conductor climbing out with a little red flag, running ahead to signal the crossing is clear (if some switch engine doesn't pull 60 cars slowly by).

All's well 'til the E. Ganson corners, letting off a passenger. Then over the M.C. tracks at Michigan Center. Two passengers leave; three climb aboard. Then on to Grass Lake village, where the conductor signs with the local agent a bill of lading for a package to be delivered in Detroit.

Next into Chelsea village, a loop into the town and out, a wasted four miles.

There's the odd little brick waiting room at Lima Center where one of the passengers insists on climbing out to buy her son Willie a package of Cracker Jacks for the tedious hours ahead.

The proud motorman, like a Roman Charioteer, sounds his air horn for cross roads at Dexter and Delhi. There are the Jackson Avenue fairgrounds, and after a dip under the Ann Arbor Railroad tracks we've come to the interurban station at Ann Arbor where, at the lunch counter, some of our potential passengers are chewing away at pumpkin pies.

Into the station door the conductor calls, "All Aboard for Ypsilanti, Denton, Sheldon, Wayne, Eliose, Dearborn, Springwells—and Deeetroit."

First half of the 3-hour trek has gone well. At Ypsilanti there were some students with heavy luggage, waiting on Zwergel's steps. Two toots of the air horn and they rush to get aboard.

Down Cross St. hill and we turn into Washington Street, passing the fire house. It's a chilly morning and the passenger agent in the Ypsi depot is stoking the big jumbo stove with floor sweepings, candy wrappers and box wood.

Around the corner, onto Michigan Avenue down the hill to the bridge and the powerhouse on the east side where we take on more air for our brakes. The next 30 miles are rough, though the first half of the ride into Detroit isn't bad, past Denton, Sheldon, Wayne, Eliose and Dearborn, where we meet double tracks.

The rest of the way in, there's our headache.

The foot gong clanging; autos that prefer car tracks, wagons ahead, stalled car, a hay wagon at Western Market; stop-go lights at every corner.

No longer is the motorman King of the Highways.

From the Boulevard, the last three miles, you fight your way in, clanging that big brass gong, sounding the air horn.

By now the conductor is up front, too, for he has to climb down to the street to turn onto Shelby Street. Then down toward the docks and along Woodbridge, the street that parallels the river, past several trucks pulled by horses.

A momentary respite. You sound the horn, three smart toots, and the girl from Vernor's Ginger Ale party store runs out with a tray on which are two cream-soda ginger ales with straws.

We inch along Woodbridge to Bates Street hill to Jefferson, where upon the conductor calls "Deeetroit! Deeetroit waiting room." All the passengers with their packages and umbrellas leave, and a host of new ones climb aboard.

We cross Jefferson Avenue, make a left turn at Larned, cross Woodward and again are on Michigan Avenue, fighting our way past the ball park, Western Market, the Boulevard, to Schaefer's Switch.

At our private phone booth we get orders and now can sigh with relief because we are on private right-of-way, clear sailing past Dearborn, Eliose, Wayne, and over the MC bridge and down the hill—and the conductor yells "Ypsilanti! All aboard for Ann Arbor, Delhi, Dexter, Chelsea, Grass Lake, Michigan Center; making connection at Jackson to Parma, Albion, Marshall, Battle Creek and Kalamazoo!"

Seems there ought to be some easier way to earn a living. All the man at the other end has to do is take tickets, stoke the little hard coal furnace, pull the bell cord when someone wants to get off, count the day's receipts, find lost umbrellas, open and close windows for neurotic passengers, break up a fight, eat candy bars, call stations so folks won't go past their stops, fill the ice water tap rack with more drinking cups, turn the ceiling lights off and on and console a confused farmer late for getting home at milking time.

Three years up front, 1,100 long days, and you've had enough. Al Augustus told me. Then, be content to ride the back end clear 'til pension time.

College Days in Ann Arbor

Morris Lloyd, a railfan from Buffalo, New York, wrote the authors in 1980 about his student days in Ann Arbor. Here is some of what he remembered of the years 1922-25:

As I recall the schedules in effect in those days there were six through runs in each direction between Detroit and Kalamazoo. These were limited runs and the first trip westward started from Detroit about 6 a.m. with following runs every second hour on the even hours up to 6 p.m. A like schedule operated eastbound. Leaving Detroit every two hours on the odd hours was a Jackson Express, with similar service eastbound from Jackson. Limited cars made the run between Detroit and Ann Arbor in about 1 hour 45 minutes; express runs took about 2 hours. In between the limited and express runs were Ann Arbor-Detroit Locals, which required about 2 hours and 20 minutes for the trip.

My first room in Ann Arbor was on East University Avenue a few doors from Packard Road, the street used by the cars entering Ann Arbor from Detroit. The following year I roomed in a house on South Division Street at Packard, where my room faced Packard. This gave me an excellent view of the interurban cars on Packard and I well remember the nights when I studied late after the interurban traffic was over, how the interurban freight runs used to roll through westbound.

The usual freight train consisted of a box motor on the head end, followed by an assortment of interurban freight cars from various lines in Michigan, Ohio, Indiana, etc., with another box motor on the rear end. This pusher helped to get the train up the West Huron Street hill leaving Ann Arbor westbound. Eastbound freight runs usually rolled through Ann Arbor in the small hours of the night.

Cars used in Detroit-Ann Arbor local runs were usually the older type with open rear platforms, such as 7794. These were sometimes used on Jackson Express runs, but generally a heavier car with enclosed rear platform was used, or a heavier Niles car. The Niles cars were also pooled with the steel cars of the Michigan Railway cars to hold down the Detroit-Kalamazoo Limited runs.

The only other MU runs in those days were steel cars, of the 8000 series, I believe used in football specials to Ann Arbor. These were made up into four car trains consisting of motor-trailer-motor-trailer. The trailers were of the same design as the motor cars, but had the passenger door at the front end instead of the rear.

These football specials would stop to discharge their passengers on Packard Road, near the Ferry Field stadium, then run into downtown where they would be turned (as they were all single end cars) and then were parked until time for the return trip, when they would pick up their passengers on Packard Road, near where passengers could walk from the game.

Car 7793 on Woodward Avenue after it was returned to Eastern Michigan from DJ&C. The Eastern Michigan colors and logo were painted on and the car assigned to the Pontiac Division. *Kremkow Photo*

An early Ann Arbor city car stands next to the MCRR depot. To reach this point, the car had to descend a steep grade. After a car lost its brakes and slammed into the building, the line was cut back to the top of the hill. Today the depot is known as the Gandy Dancer Restaurant. In mid-1986 the owner sponsored an event to mark the building's 100th anniversary. Amtrak trains use a smaller facility located about where the roof is visible beyond the tree.

Sturgis collection

5

ANN ARBOR CITY LINES

As long ago as October 13, 1865, the Ann Arbor *Michigan Argus* had an editorial urging the construction of a streetcar system for Ann Arbor. With the hills in Ann Arbor, a horsecar line may have presented a problem. A cable car line would have made an interesting alternative.

On September 30, 1866, the Ann Arbor Street Railway Company was incorporated, and attempts were made to obtain a franchise. The Ann Arbor council met on October 4, and began discussing the route to give the company. No decisions were arrived at, so the company never did receive a franchise.

Two decades went by, and a second Ann Arbor Street Railway Company was formed and received a franchise on August 13, 1888. The proposed route was changed several times before final approval on September 15, 1890. "Commencing at the south end of the Michigan Central bridge (southwest) on Detroit Street," read the ordinance, "to Catherine Street, (west) to Main Street, (south) to William Street, (east) to State Street, to North University, (east) to Washtenaw, (southeast) to city limits at Hill Street. Also from Hill and Washtenaw about 500 feet (west) to Lincoln Avenue. South across Wells Street to the main entrance of county Fair Grounds (Burns park).

"Also commencing at the intersection of Main and William (south) to Packard, (southeast) to city limits (at Brooklyn Street). The latter to be constructed as soon as necessary to make connections with proposed Ann Arbor & Ypsilanti Street Railway *(Ypsi-Ann)* and on or before October 1, 1891."

The *Ann Arbor Argus* reported on January 3, 1890, that a $200 deposit had been made by J.C. McLaughlin and J.B. Corliss to build an electric railway in Ann

Arbor. There was a small snag—the *Ann Arbor Register* on September 4, 1890, reported a dispute taking place at the council meeting the previous Monday. Corliss, "secretary of the Ann Arbor road said he and Mr. McLaughlin had $80,000 invested in the line now building." On the other hand, if the Ypsi-Ann steam dummy was allowed to operate on the streets of Ann Arbor, Corliss and McLaughlin would sell all their electrical appliances, buy steam motors and save $35,000 of their investment in addition to $1,000-$2,000 yearly in reduced operating costs. These threats were persuasive and the council resolved that the Ann Arbor city cars would meet the Ypsi-Ann at the city limits.

City streetcars began operating on September 30, 1890. By January 9, 1891, the Ypsi-Ann began operating regular service but without a connection into Ann Arbor. On January 26, 1891, the owners of the Ann Arbor & Ypsilanti Railway purchased the Ann Arbor Street Railway Company for $84,000 taking possession on January 31. However, the two companies continued to operate separately, with Ann Arbor city lines an electric line and the Ypsi-Ann still a steam dummy operation.

On February 18, 1892, the Ann Arbor & Ypsilanti Street Railway received approval to extend the line on Packard "over and across the territory annexed to the city of Ann Arbor." Then on November 9, 1893, the last grant was given for trackage on North Main Street to Depot Street to Broadway to the city limits. Also on State Street from William Street to Monroe Street, to East University, to Hill Street. The latter route was from the north entrance of the Fair Grounds at Wells, west on Wells to Forest Avenue and southwest along Wells to connect with the track on Packard.

Then calamity hit. On January 24, 1894, the Detroit Street car barn located between Kingsley and Division was destroyed by fire. Also lost were five motor cars and one trailer. A single motor car was spared because the watchman released the brakes and it rolled out of the barn. That fall six new cars were ready and operation began again on September 24. A new barn was built at Wells and Lincoln streets, opposite the present Burns Park, four blocks east of Packard Road.

Upon formation of the DJ&C, the Ann Arbor city lines were included in the new company. The city system reached its greatest extent by 1900, about 6½ miles. Mileage receded slightly at a very early date,

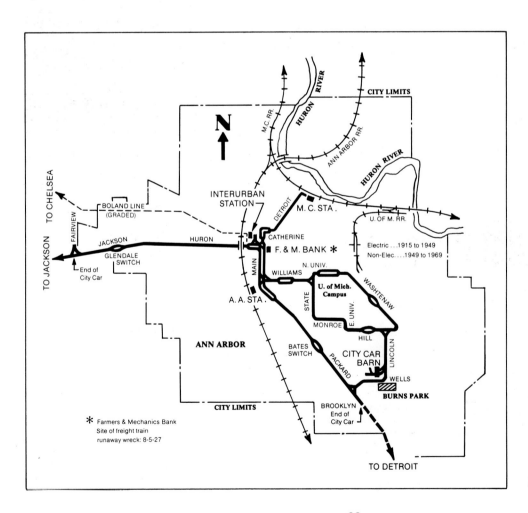

Ann Arbor city rail map

This damaged glass plate is the only photo we have found of the first Ann Arbor cars which burned in 1894.

Hildebrandt Collection

The bodies of the Jackson and Sharp cars are shown loaded on the flatcars for shipment to Ann Arbor.

Lee Collection

An early photo of the cars in service.

Hildebrandt Collection

then held steady until total abandonment in 1925. Except for a half-mile of double track on Main Street, the line was single track with occasional passing sidings.

There were two routes: "Michigan Central Depot-University" about 3½ miles long, and "Packard-Huron," just under 3 miles in length. The University route was split into two sections. At the State and William streets switch, cars would alternate between "North" and "South"; each following a different route around the University of Michigan campus. The Packard-Huron cars served the west and south portions of the city over trackage shared with the interurbans.

Although the Ann Arbor system was complete by the early 1900's, plans for extensions appeared from time to time. The last proposal occurred in 1921, to build to the newly-constructed U. of M. Hospital. But nothing was done to serve this area until the coming of the motor bus in 1925.

Operating the System

Accidents were always a threat. On January 8, 1902, a city car lost its brakes coming down the Detroit Street hill, went off the end of the track, and slammed into the Michigan Central Depot at the foot of the hill. After that, the cars terminated on the brow of the hill, and the last 500 feet to the station was done on foot.

Not many new cars were sent to Ann Arbor. On December 24, 1902, the *Ann Arbor Argus Democrat* reported on a new yellow car in the barn having a stove installed. Whether more followed was not reported. Then on March 10, 1913, hand-me-down Pay-Enter cars began operation, with the first starting on the Depot-University line. These one-man cars required front door loading and alighting, and were equipped with hand brakes. They likely were ex-Detroit city cars rebuilt for this service.

As is well known, Ann Arbor is the home of the University of Michigan. This probably led to many unusual situations for the motormen operating the city cars. At least one car was recorded to have been destroyed by the students in a fire. Other occurrences were recorded from notes in *Ann's Amazing Harbor*.

Ann Arbor did allow one-man cars and Alfred Augustus recorded some experiences: The small single-truck cars were double-ended. The seats on the closed cars ran along the side lengthwise. During the summer open bench cars were used.

Augustus related how the small cars could be made to jump the tracks. This was a favorite pastime of students, standing on the rear platform and jumping in unison, causing a derailment. Then to return the car to the tracks and continue the trip, the youths usually assisted the motorman, having had their fun.

Leo Nowicki, Department of Street Railways General Manager, remembered that in his student days at U. of M. he had been in one (or more) of these escapades. A fellow student lost a leg during one such prank, but continued his studies to become an outstanding doctor. Near the end of streetcar days, motormen finally developed an answer to the students' threat on cars equipped with air brakes. If the car was empty of other passengers, he could slam on the air brakes. The momentum would send the students sprawling.

Interurbans and express cars had the right-of-way over the city cars. Augustus also noted that the large cars had a clearance problem under the West Huron Street railroad bridge. The trolley pole would be bent almost flat and if going faster then a snail's pace it would jump the wire.

Augustus remembered more. A brilliant football star of the old days jumped on Augustus' car one evening with the bald statement "I'm riding free. Want to make anything of it?" "No, my boy, you and I see eye to eye." And he never did pay a five cent fare after that understanding.

High-spirited youths celebrating football victories caused plenty of amusement to Augustus. The boys habitually gathered along Washtenaw Avenue and met Alfred's car on the corner of Hill Street. They'd pile on and take over. One boy with ability would handle the control wrench and motor the vehicle through the crowd clear downtown, out to the MCRR depot and back, while the boys sang "The Victors" and raised the

City car 7752, formerly 102, remained in service until April 9, 1913.

Hildebrandt Collection

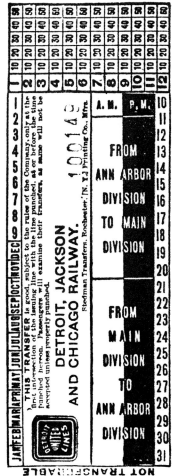

Two postcard views of open
bench cars in service. Since
the DUR did not provide any
open bench cars for Ann Arbor,
these were some of the early
Ann Arbor city cars.
Schramm Collection

dickens. Alfred sat on the side and enjoyed the whole business. If it was near suppertime, they'd take him a plate full of victuals and he'd relish them as they rocked along.

A new conductor-motorman came along one fall, who figured the only way to keep students in their place was to be stern and commanding with them. He had the "celebration" run, and when the gang hopped aboard demanding a free trip, the man said "No. Every last fare who boards pays his nickel or gets off, quick!"

Alfred said the boys refused, not that they were poverty-stricken; some of the students actually had coins jingling in their pants pockets, but it was the principle of the thing. Not one stayed on; the boy with

the plate full of supper placed it on the steps of his frat house and joined the gang that followed the slow-moving dinky on its troubled journey, on Washtenaw, along North University and on to State Street—interrupted by the trolley-rope getting "accidentally" tangled up in the feet of the boys, and consequently having the wheel yanked off the wire. The lone attendant had to get off and go back among them to fix it. Of course he may've been jostled a few times . . .

When the car was about to turn south at State, the boys reckoned their gang had been augmented by enough other celebrants, so they took the trolley off the wire, lifted the rear end of the lightweight car around, and nosed it north, the wrong way. Then they pushed the dinky on up State Street where there were no

City car and crew at the end of the Packard line, on tracks shared with the interurbans.

Stoner Collection

An ex-Detroit car southbound on Main. *Stoner Collection*

tracks, for three blocks, to let it come to rest in the middle of Huron Street. There it badly disrupted the carriage traffic of professors on their way to banquets, of out-of-town visitors sightseeing around the campus area, and downtown merchants trotting their smart horses home to a badly-needed supper. Everyone stopped to behold the misplaced streetcar where it stood, well off its beaten path.

The wrecking car had to be summoned from the Wells Street carbarns and anchored at the corner of State and North U. Several lengths of wire cable weren't enough to reach the beached trolley. All the log chains the wreckers could assemble were put together, end-to-end, to reach the stranded car. In a couple of hours the new motorman resumed his run, a beaten but wiser man. The students gathered from far and near to cheer the workmen and to celebrate their victory in song and dance.

The kindly Augustus kept a black account book full of entries recording students who had ridden when they had no carfare. The lost revenue came out of his pocket, and was seldom redeemed, but he and the students remained good friends.

Alfred was always a sharp-eyed observer of DUR special equipment movements, especially the parking

Here's a view taken January 30, 1925, in the 100 block of North Main Street. The lone streetcar led a parade of 12 new Yellow Coaches.
Michigan Historical Collections, Bentley Historical Library, University of Michigan

of a maximum of 21 interurban cars along Wells Street to handle the crowds returning to Detroit after the big U. of M. games. He said it was not unusual to leave a mob of 500 stranded football fans yelling on the corner of State and Packard, when the last coach took off for the city with its aisles and seats packed to the gunwhales.

How did the conductor collect his fares? He didn't. It was almost impossible to squeeze himself through the packed humanity—and he'd often find his side pockets lightened by slick-fingered gentry. That was where he carried his change; nickels and dimes in the left, quarters and four-bit pieces in the right. All the passenger had to do was reach in and help himself, while the frustrated conductor inched his way along, leaving the flapping ends of his double-breasted uniform coat to bring up the rear, or having the brass buttons yanked off it they were in the buttonholes where they belonged.

Ann Arbor Bows to the Bus

As early as May 9, 1924, Wellington F. Evans, president of Detroit Motorbus Company, held a meeting in Ann Arbor Mayor Lewis's office and presented a bus system plan for Ann Arbor. Few details were released, except that the routes would duplicate the rail lines and serve some new areas. Evan's plan called for 13 single-deck buses; about two-thirds would seat 16 to 20 and one-third seat 20 to 29. However, the fare proposed was not the 5 cent streetcar fare but much more—from 8 to 10 cents.

The DUR-owned Peoples Motor Coach Company presented a competing all-bus plan to the Ann Arbor city council on November 4, 1924. This was to be a one-year experiment; if the buses proved unsatisfactory, the streetcars would be returned. The council approved, and abandonment of the streetcars was set for early the next year.

And so on January 30, 1925, there was an unusual parade with 12 new coaches following the old, tired dinky. The streetcar had signs on each side; one reading "Goodbye Folks! Scrap for Mine," the other "I leave you without reproach, I humbly bow before the Coach." The new buses carried signs reading "Our up-to-date service for this up-to-date city begins Feb. 1." Aboard the first coach were musicians playing funeral dirges.

Thus ended streetcar service in Ann Arbor after 34 years of operation. However, not all was to be as grand and glorious as planned in the DUR's first all-bus city.

Local newspapers carried stories of the last day of streetcar service, noting that the last six dinkys had made their final run. They were destined for the scrap heap. Now in their place were 12 shiny new buses built by Yellow Coach Company, painted brown and trimmed in yellow. Of course, there was a price: instead of the old 5 cent streetcar fare, the buses started out with a 10 cent cash fare; tickets were three for 25 cents or six for 50 cents.

Bus routes were changed constantly, and after eight months of operation, the company was losing money. The reported revenue was $75,338.08 and expenses $93,424.24, for a net loss of $18,086.16. With taxes and depreciation added, the loss was $40,402.31, from February 1 to September 30.

Alarmed, T.P. Pinckard, president of Peoples Motor Coach, vowed to find ways to at least break even. By November 24, the city council approved dropping one route; there were now three instead of the four original routes. In 1928, while retaining the 10 cent cash fare, ticket prices went to 12 for $1 and weekly passes up from $1.24 to $1.75.

Whether the bus service ever made money is doubtful, although it continued to operate after the end of the first year. Newspapers reported route changes and complaints on the service, especially during the summer months when U. of M. students were on vacation. On May 29, 1930, the *Ann Arbor Daily News* reported that Eastern Michigan Motorbuses (EMM) was moving into the old DJ&C building on West Huron near Main.

EMM took over from Peoples Motor Coach in 1928, and finally in 1933 announced it was going to stop operating buses in Ann Arbor. The beginning of the end occurred on March 5, when it proposed to drop Sunday service and issue a new ticket giving two rides for 15 cents. The new ticket was approved and Sunday service was limited but not dropped. Headways were lengthened—all to no avail.

The end came on Friday, June 17, 1933, when the company ended all bus service at 11:20 p.m. In reviewing the operation, the *Ann Arbor Daily News* noted the bus company had started with eighteen 29-passenger coaches (actually the first 29-passenger Yellow coaches had been replaced with 21-passenger Reo coaches on a three-for-two ratio early in 1925). Later in 1925, this number was reduced to twelve 21-passenger coaches. This fleet continued until 1931, when 12 new buses were put in service with some routes shortened or eliminated. On January 13, 1933, service was curtailed further, employing just five buses until the end of operations. The peak year was 1928 when the system was carrying 5,000 daily passengers, but by 1933 this figure had dropped to 1,350 per day.

Try, Try, Again

Ann Arbor was not to be without buses for long. Soon formed was the Ann Arbor Transportation Company. Sewell H. Platt, manager of the local Ford agency, was the owner and A.H. Cady was bus superintendent. Cady started as a conductor for the DJ&C, and in 1907 was a train dispatcher in Ypsilanti. (He saved the scrapbooks from the DUR that became a major source for this series on the DUR.)

On July 24, 1933, new buses arrived and service began; the bodies were painted blue to the center line, maize from there to the top, with black wheels and top. The name "Ann Arbor Transportation Co." was lettered on the blue portion of the bodies. The fare was 10 cents or three tickets for 25 cents, with free transfers. Service began on three routes, two having 20-minute headways and the third a 30-minute headway. All lines started at Main and Washington streets.

By the spring of 1936 Platt dropped the Ann Arbor bus operation. Having lost the franchise renewal, he refused to operate through the summer to the end of his franchise period, eliminating bus service for the summer. Cady, however, offered to operate through the

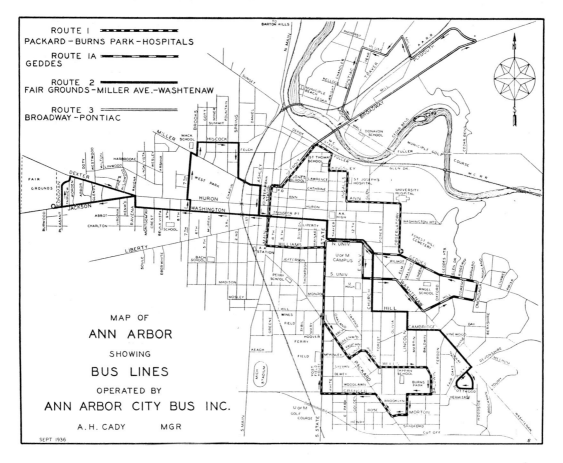

MAP OF
ANN ARBOR
SHOWING
BUS LINES
OPERATED BY
ANN ARBOR CITY BUS INC.

A. H. CADY   MGR

Coaches 20 through 24 of the Ann Arbor Transportation Company fleet were lined up on July 15, 1933, for this advertising photo for the Velvet Power Brake Co. These small 10-passenger buses were built on Ford chassis.
Manning Brothers Historical Collection

summer on a temporary franchise and attempted to purshase or lease the buses.

Failing to reach an agreement with Platt, Cady was able to obtain temporary use of two 20-passenger buses, two eight-passenger station wagons and a five-passenger sedan to be used on the Pontiac-Broadway run. On another route Cady planned to use one large and one small bus. The new company was named Ann Arbor City Bus Company, with William A. Scholey as president and Cady vice-president. On September 1, 1936, when the new franchise took effect, the *Ann Arbor Daily News* reported that six 17-passenger buses were to start operating Thursday.

The population of Ann Arbor had now increased 10% between 1930 and 1940 to 29,721. On November 8, 1940, the *Ann Arbor News* reported the bus company would launch a three-month experiment starting December 1, to provide Sunday service. Churchmen had petitioned for the service, which consisted of two buses operating on a loop. The article pointed out the previous Sunday service (in June 1933) had attracted an average of only 22 passengers.

In 1941 the *Ann Arbor News* noted that the bus line had obtained two 27-passenger Ford coaches similar to those used in Detroit, bringing the fleet up to ten. On June 2, 1942, the franchise was extended for an additional three years beyond the August 31, 1944, expiration date. World War II was on, and bus service was a needed commodity, as citizens were now using public transit instead of their own cars whenever possible. To conserve fuel, some routes, such as the Broadway line, were discontinued, and some stops were eliminated by order of the Office of Defense Transportation (ODT).

With passenger traffic up 25%, two more new 27-passenger Ford buses arrived on October 22, 1942; the ODT would allow these new buses to operate a maximum of 3,000 miles per month.

The Hound Moves In

A major development came on May 4, 1943, when the *Ann Arbor News* reported that the Ann Arbor City Bus Company had been sold to Great Lakes Greyhound Lines Inc., with Cady remaining as superintendent of the local lines. The new company was named Ann Arbor City Bus, Inc.

Ann Arbor was to become the base for 40 intercity buses and four giant Ann Arbor-Willow Run buses. The takeover had been effective as of May 1, with the fleet now consisting of eight 17-passenger and four 27-passenger buses. The garage, located at 117 N. First Street, was to be remodeled to handle both the city and intercity buses.

With a war on, small companies had little clout. One reason given by Cady for the sale was that when he ordered a new 27-passenger bus in January, the ODT turned him down. Operators with 13 or fewer city buses (he had 12) could not qualify for new equipment.

Time passed, the war ended, and the old problems returned.

In October 1947, the *Ann Arbor News* reported the arrival of twelve 29-passenger buses, and that routes were again being changed. On January 6, 1948, Greyhound received a new seven-year franchise. The downtown terminal was to be moved to Main and Huron streets instead of Main and Washington streets. Regular fare climbed to 12 cents in 1951.

Business got worse, and on February 29, 1956, the *Ann Arbor News* mentioned that Greyhound was planning to drop city service in Ann Arbor within six months. By August 28, the city had agreed to subsidize Greyhound $1,900 monthly and, in turn, service would continue at least until February 28, 1957. By this time there was talk of a city-run system.

Greyhound threw in the towel on Saturday, April 6, 1957. The company reported it had been losing money since 1948. The 11 buses were sold to a Chicago firm.

By April 12 a new company, Ann Arbor Transit, Inc., was ready to start with 12 used Checker and Transit buses from Detroit. There would be four new routes totaling 39 miles, the fare was 25 cents or five tickets for $1. School fare (except U. of M. students) was 15 cents. There were to be free transfers with no service on Sundays and holidays. The green and cream buses began operating on April 15, 1957. To assist the new company, a five-year formal agreement was approved to obtain tax benefits; however, this agreement was not considered as a franchise.

AAT was no more successful than its predecessors. By June 12, 1959, the company had dropped all service, and the city was considering an election to approve a tax for city bus service.

Then, amazingly, another new company offered to provide service. On September 1, 1959, City Bus Company of Ann Arbor, headed by Arvin Marshall, put six 21-passenger Divco-Wayne "Bantam" jitneys into service on regular routes. Painted black with white trim, the jitneys were leased from Wayne with a purchase option. The fare was 25 cents with free transfers. The six routes were combined into three.

Six 66- to 72-passenger school buses, painted yellow and black, also were placed in service. Sometime later a green and cream 20-passenger coach was acquired for downtown shuttle service.

By May 1, 1963, the City Bus Company was pulling out. One of the drivers, Leonard B. Jones from Dexter, took over the city lines on May 8, and operated with the seven buses. Marshall continued to operate the school buses and make payments on the other seven, leasing them to the city. The new operator, Public Bus Co., was to receive fuel without paying taxes on it, and its license fee was set at 50 cents per bus. But Jones was also unsuccessful and discontinued operations on January 4, 1964.

Still, hope endured. On January 13, 1964, Marshall returned and bus service was to be restored and buses repaired. In September 1965, the City Bus Company of Ann Arbor (II) put seven new 24-passenger buses into service. These vehicles featured a rear door and were painted white with a red band beneath the windows. On May 18, 1966, the bus fares increased from 25 to 30 cents, with free transfers.

On May 22, 1968, hundreds of bus patrons were stranded when drivers called in sick. The drivers wanted a raise from $2.09 to $2.72 per hour and a cut in daily hours to eight. Marshall talked of raising fares to 35 cents. But on May 24, Marshall informed the drivers he was through with bus operations in Ann Arbor, giving as one reason that the city was negotiating with Short Way Lines for operating the system. However, he did continue operating the school charter business and suburban runs.

On July 15, service resumed after a 54-day lapse under the name Ann Arbor City Transit Inc. The ten buses needed came from Saginaw and were operated by the St. John Transportation Company of Dayton, Ohio. The city agreed to cover any losses incurred by the firm and would pay a management fee of 5% of gross revenues. Base fare was 30 cents, and the office and garage was at 415 W. Washington Street. There was no Sunday or holiday service.

Great Lakes Greyhound was providing local service when this photo was taken April 1957, at Observatory and Geddes.

Hildebrandt photo

Ann Arbor Buses

After Greyhound quit, Ann Arbor Transit, Inc. took over, using these used DSR Transits. Here is 7754-3 still painted in DSR cream and green colors, on Huron St. in May 1957. The renumbering seemed to be limited to adding a dash and a single number while retaining the old DSR number. This bus had been retired on DSR order number 7825 along with 7613, 7638, 7647, 7650, 7657, 7718, 7720, 7738, 7740, 7745, and 7758.

Hildebrandt Photo

Main and Huron in June 1962. The bus at the right was numbered 005. The new color scheme used by City Bus Company of Ann Arbor was black with white trim.

Hildebrandt Photo

This white-painted Divco bus was at the corner of Ingalls and Lawrence in March 1962. It was being operated by City Bus Co. of Ann Arbor (II).

Hildebrandt Photo

The corner of Hill Street and Church in March 1968. Now the color scheme used by City Bus Co. was white with red striping.

Hildebrandt Photo

A Ford Van bus painted green with a cream top was operated by Ann Arbor City Transit, Inc., in January 1969, at Ashley and Ann Street.

Hildebrandt Photo

This GMC model TGH-3101 painted blue with a white top was in service at Main and Huron when taken January 1969. The operator was Ann Arbor City Transit, Inc.

Hildebrandt Photo

This photo was exposed in March 1970, at the Ann Arbor Transit Authority's 4th Avenue transfer station. The TA's colors were orange bottom, cream top with a dark green belt rail.

Hildebrandt Photo

A speeding GMC TDH 5105 AATA bus was photographed in May 1970, going through the intersection of Liberty and Third.

Hildebrandt Photo

Painted in purple with yellow and green striping, this AATA-owned GMC TDH 3301A coach is shown in September 1970, on Main Street between Liberty and William.

Hildebrandt Photo

City Operation Begins

Now, Ann Arbor's buses were to become public property. On July 15, 1968, the council approved creation of a Mass Transportation Authority, under which St. John would operate. This authority was incorporated "for the purpose of acquiring, owning, operating or causing to be operated a mass transportation system within the City of Ann Arbor, and beyond the said corporate limits."

But it was a false start, and by January 28, 1969, the city was again without bus service. Faced with excessively high monthly charges, the council cancelled the contract with St. John effective January 31.

On May 7, 1969, service was begun by the reorganized Ann Arbor Transportation Authority (AATA). The AATA began with three routes: Miller-Hospitals, Stadium-Seventh-Washtenaw, and Huron-Packard-Plymouth Road. The first garage was at 315 W. Huron Street. In June, 11 used GMC model 4512 buses were purchased and full service restored on September 2. Former Saginaw Transit, Inc. manager John C. Zielinski was named manager in November.

In 1971 Ann Arbor was one of 13 U.S. cities selected for a test of the feasibility of a coordinated Dial-A-Ride/fixed route service. At that time AATA was operating 18 buses over radial routes covering most of the city. All lines met at a central downtown transfer point once every half hour during high demand periods and hourly at other times. The adult fare was now 35 cents, senior citizens and children 20 cents, with free transfers.

From September 22, 1971, to September 1972, a pilot project was in force, with 60 cent fares or $10 for a monthly pass, permitting members of the same family unlimited use. Free transfers to all AATA fixed routes buses were given to cash fare patrons. A transfer from fixed route service to Dial-A-Ride required a 25 cent payment.

It was decided that ridership of fewer than 200 riders per day would be considered unsuccessful, 200 to 300 per day moderately successful, and 300 to 400 per day successful. Ridership did reach 200 per day by the close of the project and stayed well over that level during the winter months in 1972.

Pleased with the results, Ann Arbor went to the voters for additional funding which was approved by a 61% vote in April 1973. This gave AATA a dedicated property tax of 2½ mills, or about $1,500,000 annually. The new Dial-A-Ride along with the linehaul service was named "Teltran" from TEL-ephone TRAN-sportation.

On February 18, 1974, Ann Arbor and Ypsilanti were connected with a bus route, and some local service was instituted within Ypsilanti. By June 1976, Dial-A-Ride service was extended to the entire city of Ann Arbor during the daytime hours. The Dial-A-Ride buses were so coordinated with the loop buses that two or more met at each transfer point.

As ridership increased in areas being served by Dial-A-Ride, fixed routes were established. This policy continued until October 1, 1979, when the system was reorganized into a fixed route system and Dial-A-Ride used only to transport the elderly and handicapped.

By 1985 there were 18 fixed routes serving Ann Arbor, Ypsilanti and the surrounding portion of Washtenaw County. Dial-A-Ride was still used on a limited basis, and provided Sunday service in Ann Arbor. Base fare was 60 cents, or 20 tokens for $9. Service to Dexter and Chelsea in western Washtenaw County began the spring of 1987.

Finally, it seemed, bus service was a success in Ann Arbor.

Pictured on September 6, 1977, on Carpenter Road just south of Packard, coach 242 is in front of the garage located in Pittsfield Township. *Motor Bus Society*

Dodge Maxivan number 73 at William and Fifth, September 10, 1977.

Motor Bus Society

Ann Arbor Buses, July 18, 1985

GMC coach 313, a model RTS-4, on 4th between Liberty and William. It wears an AATA color scheme of white with a dark red band. *Drouillard Photo*

AATA's GMC new-look coach 244 in the new paint scheme. *Drouillard Photo*

Coach 603, an Orion II built by Ontario Bus Industry, was used for handicapped service. *Drouillard Photo*

A Flexible "Metro" numbered 330. *Drouillard Photo*

East end of the power plant railway, over the ash drop in May 1941. The length of this line was about 4000 feet.
Hildebrandt Photo

Below: Not many railroads used coal hoppers as line cars. Here was one used by the U of M's in a photo taken November 1948 by Henry Elsner.

Ann Arbor's Freight Only Service

AFTER THE END of the DJ&C, Ann Arbor still could boast of an electric rail line. This ¾-mile spur operated between the Michigan Central Railroad (now Conrail) tracks and the University of Michigan powerhouse on Huron Street. When the powerhouse was built in 1915, it was decided to bring in coal and ship out the ashes using an electric locomotive.

This operation employed a two-wire power system similar to trolley coach operation. However, where the clamshell bucket would swing, bringing in coal from the storage piles to the boilers hoppers, the wire was in the way. To get around this problem, the power pickup was mounted on the side of the building, and an arm on the locomotive made contact, allowing the locomotive to operate through this portion of the line.

In 1949 electric operation was discontinued and the locomotive sold to Warwick, R.I., where it has been preserved. It was replaced by two 35-ton internal combustion Plymouth locomotives. One was needed to provide motive power and other was cannibalized for parts. In 1960 a used 70-ton General Electric locomotive was obtained from Navy surplus to replace the Plymouths. Finally, in 1968 the powerhouse was converted from coal to natural gas, and in 1969 the GE locomotive was sold and the following year the tracks were removed.

Looking north with the Fuller Avenue bridge in the background, in April 1948.

Mark Hildebrandt

NYC engine 2005 is shown in May 1941, interchanging coal cars. This line was all uphill from the NYC tracks to the power plant.

Hildebrandt Photo

During its last days of service, the Plymouth locomotive was photographed on North Hospital Drive in fall 1960.

Hildebrandt Photo

Kuhlman-built car 45 of the Jackson & Battle Creek Traction Company was used to provide local service. Note the fancy striping. The local cars alternated with the larger and faster express cars, making local stops and carrying freight, including newspapers and other light express items.
Michigan Historical Collections,
Bentley Historical Library, University of Michigan

6

MICHIGAN RAILWAY COMPANY

MUR and MR passes.

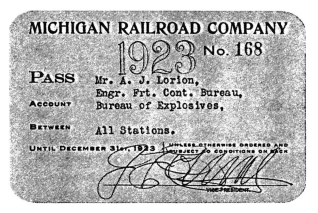

S ITUATED IN THE CENTER of the state of Michigan was an electric rail system that, in size, rivaled the Detroit United Railway. This huge operation, unlike the DUR, was controlled by officials of a powerful electric syndicate associated with the present Consumers Power Company in Jackson. The Michigan Railway (MRY), organized during March of 1914, brought together some 22 railway operations that spread as far north as Bay City, west to Lake Michigan, and east to Grass Lake.

Officially, the *McGraw Electric Railway List, 1918* sorted out the maze of inter-connecting companies. Commonwealth Power, Railway and Light Company, a holding company, controlled through stock ownership, among other companies: Grand Rapids, Holland & Chicago Railway; Grand Rapids Railway Company; Saginaw-Bay City Railway Company; Consumers Power Company (Maine); Michigan Railway Company; and Michigan United Railways (MUR).

The Michigan United Railways (operated by Michigan United Traction Company from April 1, 1912 to 1916) owned the city systems in Lansing, Kalamazoo, Battle Creek, Jackson and interuban roads between Lansing and St. Johns, Jackson and Battle Creek, Kalamazoo and Battle Creek, Jackson and Lansing and Lansing and Owosso. This company was leased to Michigan Railway Company.

In turn, the Michigan Railway Company both leased the MUR and Grand Rapids, Holland & Chicago Railway, and operated Saginaw & Flint Railway and the Grand Rapids to Kalamazoo and the Battle Creek to Allegan lines.

When, in 1916, the Michigan United Traction Company turned over operations of these holdings to the Michigan Railway, the large network of rail lines was organized into five electric and one steam divisions. Because of the complexity of this corporation, we will briefly trace the growth and demise of the independent companies within their separate divisional units.

We already have covered the MRY's Northeastern division in *When Eastern Michigan Rode the Rails, Book One.* Part one of this chapter will focus on the routes controlled by the Michigan United Railways that made up the Southern division (Kalamazoo to Jackson), and Northern division (Jackson to Lansing, St. Johns and Owosso). Part two will cover the remaining divisions; Western (Kalamazoo to Grand Rapids and Allegan to Battle Creek), Northwestern (Grand Rapids to Holland, Macatawa and Saugatuck) and Steam (Kalamazoo to South Haven). Included will be some of the work and freight equipment used on all the divisions.

SOUTHERN DIVISION
Battle Creek to Kalamazoo

City operations of both the Citizens' Street Railway of Battle Creek and Kalamazoo came under the control of the Michigan Traction Company on October 1,

1898. By early June of 1899, the company had under construction a 28-mile link between the two towns. On June 26, 1900, the first trial run to Galesburg from Battle Creek was made in the interurban car the *Comstock.* The motorman was Major Loren N. Downs, its promoter. The following day, service between Galesburg and Battle Creek was started with a fare of 20 cents. Two cars began service, *Queen City* and *Comstock,* while three cars, *Augusta, Galesburg,* and *Kalamazoo,* were held in storage for completion of the line. The 45-foot cars were variously built by St. Louis Car Company and J.G. Brill. Three open-bench cars also were purchased for the Gull Lake branch.

Newspapers on July 22, 1900, were reporting that the original promoter and builder, Major Downs, had retired and pulled out of the project. A new financial group, the Railways Company General of Philadelphia, would complete the line.

On August 2, 1900, the line opened for service from Galesburg to the tracks of the Grand Rapids and Indiana Railroad at Washington Avenue in Kalamazoo. The crossing was delayed until a grade-separation agreement was reached with three steam railroads in March of 1901. The settlement forced the interurban to build an awkward 22-foot bridge over both the Chicago, Kalamazoo & Saginaw Railroad and the Belt Line

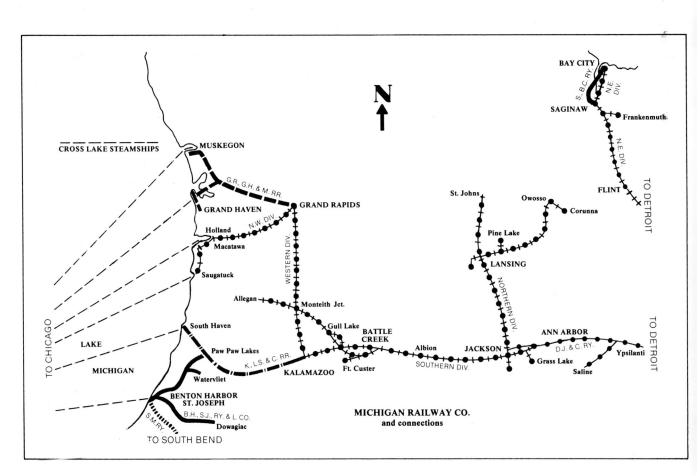

MICHIGAN RAILWAY CO.
and connections

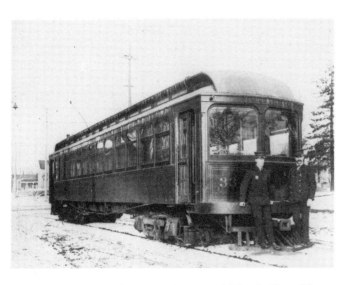

A 1910 view of car 33, originally named *Marshall*, in Albion on a cold winter's day, if the icicles are any indication.
Michigan Historical Collections,
Bentley Historical Library, University of Michigan.

Railroad, then drop 44 feet to pass under the Grand Rapids & Indiana Railroad. This "roller coaster ride" opened for service to downtown Kalamazoo October 21, 1901.

Many of the early promoters of traction lines failed to take into account the need for expensive grade separations, because according to state rules, their project could not cross a steam railroad at grade. This rule also applied to the Galesburg crossing of the Michigan Central Railroad.

Wishing to take advantage of the summer traffic to the resort at Gull Lake, the company constructed a three-mile branch leaving the main line at Augusta. These efforts were temporarily blocked by a hotel property owner located on the proposed right-of-way, who wanted to hold out for a higher sale price. Undaunted, the company built around his property to another point on the lake. Though the line was not completed by July 4th, cars were soon operating from the junction to the lake—almost. Unfortunately, the promised short walk from the cars to the lake proved to be half a mile.

Equipment operated by the Michigan Traction Company on both the city and interurban lines totaled 36 motor cars and 20 trailers by 1901. MTC operated a total of 49 miles of track. Power was purchased from the Kalamazoo Valley Electric Company owned by W.A. Foote. Trowbridge hydro dam (25 miles northwest of Kalamazoo) fed power to converter stations along the route.

Within both Kalamazoo and Battle Creek, city tracks were used. Kalamazoo controlled the streets the cars were to use, and the stops to be made within the city. Included in the franchise was a clause that the offices of the company would be in Kalamazoo. In later years this clause would force subsequent owners to continue to keep a token representation of officials in town.

Railways Company General received a buyout offer from William Boland during August of 1901, when the company was in poor financial shape. Boland, with dreams of building to Chicago, had created the Detroit and Chicago Traction Company. He was then building from Jackson to Detroit with plans to expand west, and the Michigan Traction would have been an added bonus. But the deal did not take place. Instead, Railways Company General backed another Boland plan for building from Battle Creek to Jackson.

Michigan United Expands

Michigan Traction Company directors met on November 11, 1905, to discuss an offer to sell their company. A month later the *Detroit Journal* reported that the Michigan Traction Company was in the hands of Myron W. Mills of Port Huron. As of December 19, the company became part of the new MUR controlled by Mills, George G. Moore (both from the Port Huron area), and James R. Elliott of Lansing.

Officially, the MUR filed for status as a Michigan company on March 31, 1906. Its purpose was to consolidate all holdings which included Lansing City Electric Railway, Lansing, St. Johns & St. Louis Railway; Lansing & Suburban Traction Company (Haslett Park and Waverly Park), Michigan Traction Company and the Michigan Traction Extension Company (city lines in Kalamazoo and Battle Creek—interurban lines Kalamazoo to Battle Creek and Gull Lake) and Battle Creek to Jackson.

After stockholder approval on April 11, the consolidation was put into action on May 1, 1906. Then on May 9, 1907, control of the Jackson Consolidated Traction Company was secured. Now, one firm was operating 185 miles of trackage and building a line from Lansing to Jackson to connect its properties. To complete this project, $5 million in stock was issued—$4 million in common and $1 million in preferred.

Battle Creek to Jackson

William Boland's dream of building an interurban network in Michigan began with the purchase of the Jackson city lines. Next, he set his sights on a route eastward toward Detroit and came up against the Hawks-Angus group (see Chapter One). While battling the group east of Jackson, Boland and W.A. Foote, with the help of eastern financial interests, including P.H. Flynn, D.F. Leeds, John McCarty, F. Cochell and Worrall Wilson (grandson of the owner of the Detroit Citizens' Street Railway), started work

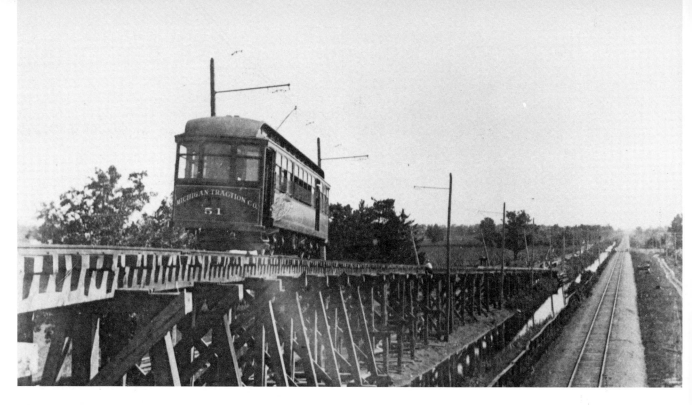

Michigan Traction car 51 starting up the trestle at Galesburg to cross the Michigan Central Railroad tracks. *Lenderink collection*

west of Jackson. The *Detroit Free Press* on May 26, 1901, reported that work would start the following year on the line to Battle Creek. Foote promised that Railways General would back the project.

By August 3, 1901, newspapers reported that the line to Battle Creek was ready to be placed under contract. The Detroit and Chicago Traction Company organized the Calhoun County Railway Company to build the first section from Albion to Marshall and on October 26, 1901, set up the Battle Creek & Marshall Traction Company to continue the line into Battle Creek.

Officially, this route connecting Jackson to Battle Creek was owned and operated by the Jackson and Battle Creek Traction Company formed May 17, 1902.

Service from Battle Creek to Albion began May 17, 1903. Just west of Albion the company built its Taylorville shops. These buildings were to serve as the major repair center for all lines under the control of the syndicate.

Financial problems with Railways General continued to plague the project. A frustrated Boland approached the backers during late October 1901 to try to clear the air. Foote complained later that Railways General really wanted to take the project away from him and his associates. The squabbling eventually resulted in a new financial backer being found in Toledo.

This new angel, C.N. Spitzer, was apparently behind the project prior to the completion of the Jackson-

Battle Creek line on June 24, 1903.

When placed in service, the 45½-mile line had 37½ miles of private right-of-way and eight miles of street running in cities. Running time was 1 hour and 35 minutes for the limiteds, which made an average of six stops.

Two styles of cars were purchased for service. Express cars, 58'-4" long, were built by the St. Louis Car Company. They were elaborately outfitted, having smoking and toilet compartments and high-backed red upholstered seats. Next to the motorman's cab were three viewing seats facing the large front end picture windows, which gave the passenger an exciting view of the road ahead. The General Electric #66 motors were geared to 60 mph. Air compressors were on each car for the brakes. (At this time, DUR cars still used storage air.)

Four trailers, also 58'-4", were designed for use behind the limiteds on busy days. For local service, the railway had five 50-ft. combination baggage and passenger cars, built by the G.C. Kuhlman Company. Each of these cars was equipped with four General Electric #57, 50 h.p. motors and geared to 40 mph. The company alternated express and local cars all day.

The fare was 1¼ cents per mile, with a minimum of five cents. A 400-mile booklet sold for $5. To attract publicity, the company began to name each car after some on-line community, but it confused the passengers. Some thought the car name meant the car would only go to that town and would wait for the next car. After the Michigan United Railways took control of the company on May 9, 1907, the names were removed from the cars.

Again, W.A. Foote's hydro plants produced the electric power for the interurbans at his dams on the Kalamazoo River. High voltage lines of 40,000 volts supplied substations at Battle Creek, Marshall, Albion, Parma and Jackson. The stations, averaging 11 miles apart, converted the three-phase, 60 cycle, a.c. transmission to direct current.

Unlike the average midwest interurban, the company built a third-rail electric propulsion system for rural running but used overhead trolley wire in the cities. Unfortunately, every winter the third rail was subject to ice interrupting the flow of electricity to the pickup shoes on the car. Newspapers were full of reports of trouble during winter and spring ice storms, when the cars would stall, stranding the passengers miles out in the country.

The year 1905 began with great excitement for the men involved in building segments of the interurban lines in mid-Michigan. On January 14, the *Detroit Tribune* reported the formation of the Commonwealth Power Company of Maine. All of Foote's power plants and electric lines were to be placed in this new corporation. Foote's interurban lines would not be in the new company. Then the *Detroit Free Press* on April 29 reported the sale of the Foote-Spitzer Jackson & Battle Creek Traction Company to the Mills-Elliott-Moore group—the MUR.

In between those dates the *Detroit News* on March 28 quoted J.D. Hawks that Coler and Company would finance a line from Jackson to Lansing. Mills and Boland also were involved in arranging for financing a line between these two locations.

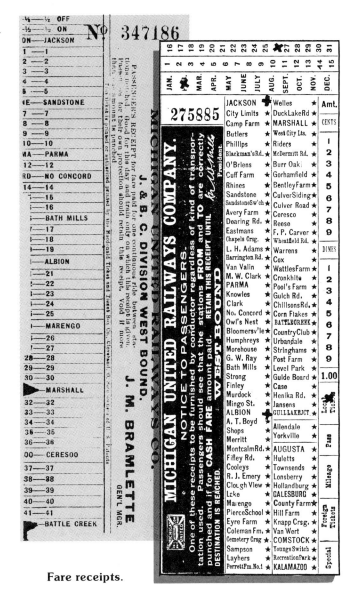

Fare receipts.

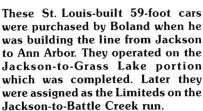

These St. Louis-built 59-foot cars were purchased by Boland when he was building the line from Jackson to Ann Arbor. They operated on the Jackson-to-Grass Lake portion which was completed. Later they were assigned as the Limiteds on the Jackson-to-Battle Creek run.
Dearborn Historical Commission

A view of Main Street in downtown Jackson. This early postcard shot pre-dated the auto-filled streets.
Schramm Collection

From Jackson to Parma

Main Street in downtown Parma.
Stoner Collection

The interurban depot, far right, was twice the size of the Michigan Central depot at Parma. Actually, the Michigan Railway depot also housed the sub-station and freight house. Presently it is the home of the Parma Library.

Stoner Collection

Over the Trestle into Albion

Albion trestle looking west. The bridge spanned both the MCRR and LS&MS railroads, which crossed each other underneath. The car is heading for Jackson.

Schramm Collection

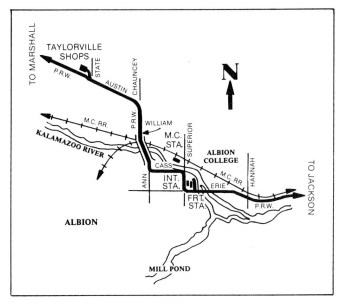

Above, right: DUR car 7791 on the long Michigan Railway trestle in Albion.

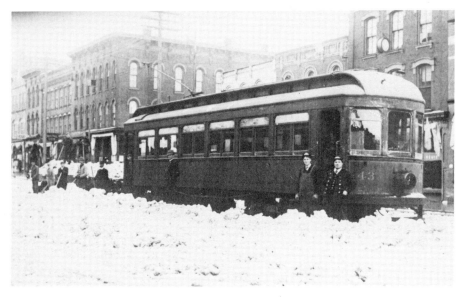

Niles-built car 43 on Superior Street near the station in Albion. It is being used in work service hauling a flatcar onto which snow is being shoveled.

Andrews Collection

Through Marshall

Battle Creek-bound car 47 clatters through the freight house switch and eases to a stop at the Marshall station in this 1910 view. Among the waiting passengers is the arch-typical salesman with his sample cases.
Schramm Collection

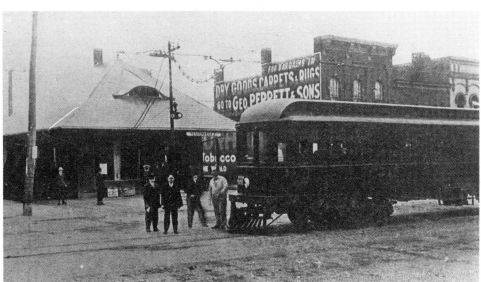

The depot in downtown Marshall with passengers loading a westbound Limited.
Schramm Collection

to Battle Creek

Main Street and Jefferson in Battle Creek looking northwest. The approaching car is a Michigan Traction car arriving from Kalamazoo, passing a local city car.
Woodard Collection

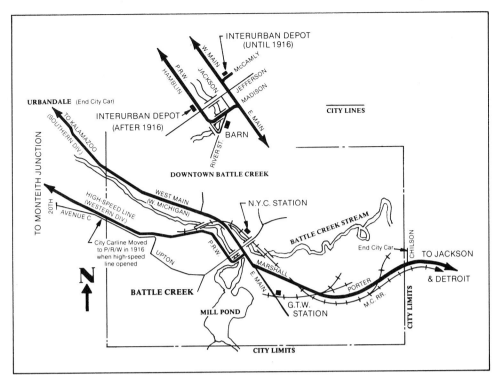

Map of Battle Creek.

A Michigan Traction car eastbound at Finley siding, just east of Level Park. This photo shows the reason for the early popularity of interurbans in rural areas.

Andrews Collection

A view of Gull Lake with a car approaching the curve.

Lenderink Collection

We see two two-car trains standing at a wye in a rural setting, perhaps on the Gull Lake line. Lead car 27 was reported to be one of the country's first all-steel interurbans to go into service. It began operating on the Jackson-Lansing line on May 30, 1914. The trailer behind 27 was one of the 50 series.

Andrews Collection

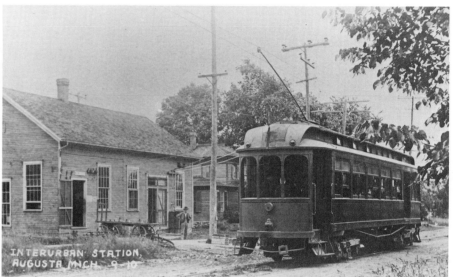

Car 44 in front of the interurban station at Augusta.

Moore Collection

FAST FREIGHT SERVICE
TIME TABLE
In Effect Feb. 1, 1910

JACKSON, LANSING and ST. JOHNS

SOUTH			NORTH		
A. M.	A. M.		A. M.	P. M.	P. M.
10.00		Lv. St. Johns Ar.	9.00		
11.00		DeWitt	8.00		
11.30		Ar. Lansing Lv.	7.30		
12.00	7.30	Lv. Lansing Ar.		1.20	7.00
12.30	8.10	Holt		12.50	6.20
12.50	8.25	Mason		12.35	6.05
1.00	8.45	Eden		12.20	5.50
1.15	9.30	Leslie		12.10	5.40
1.25	9.40	Rives Junction		12.00	5.30
2.00	10.15	Ar. Jackson Lv.		11.30	5.00
P. M.	A. M.		A. M.	A. M.	P. M.

JACKSON, BATTLE CREEK and KALAMAZOO

WEST			EAST		
A. M.	A. M.		P. M.	P. M.	P. M.
10.30	5.30	Lv. Jackson Ar.	9.00	5.15	
11.00	6.00	Parma	8.15	4.45	
11.30	6.30	Albion	7.45	4.15	
12.15	7.15	Marshall	6.45	3.20	
1.00	8.00	Ar Battle Creek Lv	6.00	2.30	
1.30	8.30	Lv Battle Creek Ar		1.30	7.30
2.15	9.15	Augusta		12.48	6.48
2.45	9.45	Galesburg		12.33	6.33
3.05	10.05	Comstock		12.18	6.18
3.20	10.20	Car Barns		12.07	6.07
3.30	10.30	Ar. Kalamazoo Lv.		12.00	6.00
A. M.	A. M.		A. M.	Noon	P. M.

Through connections at Jackson with D. J. & C. Ry. for Detroit and intermediate points. Your patronage is solicited. Rates quoted on application to local agents or G. E. & P. Agt.

J. L. MILLSPAUGH, Gen. Supt., Jackson, Mich.   F. W. BROWN, Gen. E. & P. Agt., Jackson, Mich.

The new Kalamazoo Terminal was located at Rose and Water streets. The large terminal building was still standing in 1987.

Courtesy Consumers Power

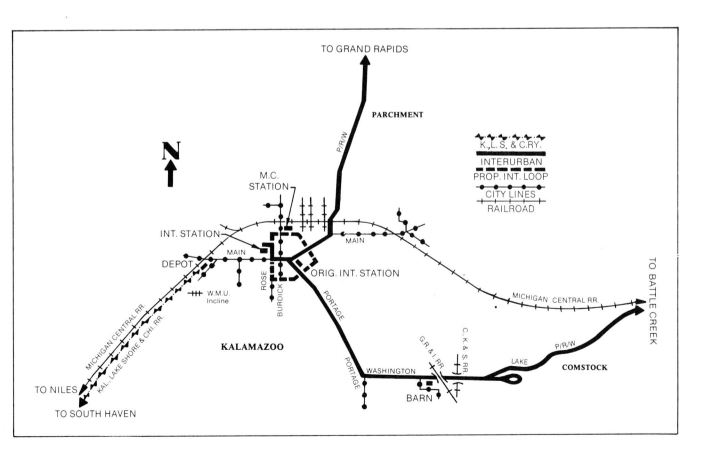

NORTHERN DIVISION
Lansing to St. Johns

North of Lansing in the small community of Maple Rapids lived Issac Hewitt, businessman and promoter. Hewitt hoped a rail line would pass through his out-of-the-way town, a dream he held for over 20 years. But, no steam road or interurban ever made it to Maple Rapids.

Nevertheless, Hewitt's last promotion almost fulfilled his dream, the Lansing, St. Johns and St. Louis Railway (LStJ&StL). That idea began in St. Louis, Michigan, on March 17, 1900. At a gathering of local citizens were John E. Mills of Port Huron/Marysville and well-known traction promoter Bion J. Arnold of Chicago.

Mills told the audience that a rail line would cost $1,500,000, and he was ready to place $200,000 along with Arnold's $100,000 if the communities along the route would put in another $100,000. If funding was in place within two months, cars would run by September.

Little time was lost. Lansing businessmen and Issac Hewitt combined on April 10, 1900, to form the Lansing, St. Johns and St. Louis electric Railway. The company was capitalized at $500,000, making Mills and Arnold the largest stockholders in a company run by local businessmen. Even though the communities did not reach the requested $100,000 on time, the project officially began June 2, 1900.

Right-of-way acquisition problems quickly developed, so on September 4, 1900, the Lansing & Northern Railway was created to be able to use a steam road charter to condemn property for the line. With interurban fever at a peak, the Crystal Lake Railroad, in the planning stage of a line to Maple Rapids, merged with the LStJ&StL.

Surveyors began establishing the route of the electric railway on May 21, 1900. Men and materials started to collect at the community of DeWitt by June 25. Throughout that summer, fall and following spring, rights-of-way were acquired and the ground prepared for the tracks. A bridge over the Looking Glass River took a long time to complete. About a year later, May 11, 1901, the company received its first order of rail and ties.

But the new interurban could not transfer the cars bearing these necessary supplies to its own line as the Pere Marquette Railway refused to connect to the electric company tracks. After transhipping the materials, laying of the rails began. Poles arrived by the end of July for distribution along the line.

On the morning of September 17, 1901, the traction company began digging the foundations for its overhead crossing of the Pere Marquette in Lansing against the wishes of the steam line. On orders from above, a Pere Marquette roadmaster began filling up the excavations.

By October 9, some of the air was cleared and a direct connection between the two lines was agreed. But the bridge dispute took longer to resolve.

This locomotive was used in constructing the line from Lansing to St. Johns. Typed on the photo were the following notes: Taken in North Lansing. Standing on the running board was engineer Dan Baxter, standing next to the locomotive fireman Frances Korff, next to him Harry Allee. Others in photo (conductor) Gran Britten, A. D. Bush and Bert Lee.

Lansing-North Lansing Electric Railroad Museum

Still, progress was swift, and on Monday morning, November 25, 1901, a party of St. Johns businessmen and capitalists boarded a train of the 20-mile electric line for a tour. This train was powered by steam, using construction equipment that included two flatcars covered with canvas with seats provided in the middle and along the sides.

Meanwhile, three new passenger cars were on order from Jewett Car Company. They were 56½ feet long with three compartments—50 seats for general passengers, a smoking and baggage area. Car No. 1 was to be named "Lansing," Car 2 "DeWitt" and Car 3 "St. Johns." They cost $8,000 to $10,000 each.

Because of delays getting the electrical equipment newly designed by Arnold, the company purchased two non-powered passenger cars and inaugurated steam-powered service beginning February 1, 1902. As of January 12, 1902, the company was operating under the name Michigan Suburban Railroad, with a steam railroad charter, so as to be able to make connections with the various steam railroads. On February 3, regular scheduled service for the public began at 7:00 a.m. from the sheds of the company shops in North Lansing, because the company was not able to complete the bridge across the Pere Marquette Railroad. During the first two weeks a daily average of 150 passengers rode the cars pulled by steam locomotives.

Trolley wire began being placed on the poles by December 4, 1902. On Christmas Day, 1902, it was reported that the trains were using the new overhead trestle into North Lansing to within one block of the city's streetcar track. The three electric passenger cars were on the way from the factory and the Arnold motors were to be installed at the North Lansing shops.

Bion J. Arnold was a builder, consultant, promoter, investor and inventor all rolled up into one. As contractor, he was planning a new approach to electric propulsion for the St. Johns line. He felt that using alternating current would reduce the cost of construction and eliminate the need for expensive substations. Accordingly, he invented a new a.c. motor system using 2400 volts, 25 cycle alternating current.

After various delays, testing began June 15, 1903. But car motors were too small and the results were disappointing. Larger motors had been ordered, but delays in shipment caused the management of the interurban company to overrule Arnold and convert to the usual 600-volt d.c. system

Another blow to the company was the death of its president and financial backer, John Mills, at the age of 38 on August 3, 1903. His father, Nelson Mills, took command of the company. First on the agenda was the purchase of the Lansing City Railway from the Angus-Hawks group for $175,000 on August 27, 1903. Prior to this purchase, Mills had difficulty obtaining trackage rights to get his cars to downtown.

After installation of a d.c. substation, the line opened for electric service November 14, 1903. Still hoping to convince the owners to revert to a.c. operation, Arnold continued to wait for the new, more powerful motors. During early December the three big new cars ordered by Arnold were replaced by three suburban cars purchased in Buffalo. Management felt Arnold's cars were too heavy for the track. Still undaunted, Arnold continued to perfect his new a.c. system for the big cars, now in disrepute.

Then a fire on the night of December 18 consumed the North Lansing barns, detroying the building, two of the big new cars and Arnold's new motors being installed in the cars. The barn and contents were partially covered by insurance, but Arnold's $30,000 motors were not insured. This was the last straw. A new fireproof 40 x 180-foot building was constructed on the site of the old barn, but nothing further was heard of big cars and a.c. motors.

President Nelson Mills died March 15, 1904, and another son, Myron Mills, became president. Again, the interurban line changed names as the Lansing and Suburban Traction Railway purchased the Lansing, St. Johns & St. Louis Railway on March 26, 1904. The Mills group also owned the new company.

Myron continued to expand by creating the Michigan United Railways Company on March 31, 1906. All the holdings were merged into the new system, including the Lansing-St.Johns line and the Lansing City Railway.

Lansing to Jackson

Big, bold lines were drawn on maps connecting almost every major city in mid-Michigan by interurban promoters. But financing such a project was a task beyond the ability of most. Even if the project had funding, unexpected factors often stepped in to stymie the completion of the line. Angus and Hawks, after reaching Jackson, began promoting a line connecting Lansing and Grand Rapids with their Grand Rapids, Grand Haven & Muskegon Railway. The *Detroit News* on March 28, 1905, reported the men had found funds to build their line to connect Jackson to Lansing. But it was the last time any mention of this project ever appeared in our scrapbooks.

A clue to the mystery may lay in a *News* story dated November 26, 1907, which said: "S.F. Angus was in a very bad plight. He fell off a streetcar three years ago and his leg never healed. Presently, a stroke and blindness have confined him." At the age of 52, Samuel Floyd Angus, one time book agent, builder of the Toledo, Fremont & Norwalk Railway, life insurance salesman and Detroit Base Ball Club owner died on February 7, 1908.

The Jackson terminal plays host to a 20 series MUT on the left and DUR cars which are loading. In later years buses were also to be found using these facilities.
Schramm Collection

The prize route connecting Jackson to Lansing fell into the hands of the aggressive Mills syndicate. The *Free Press* on April 2, 1905, recorded the March 30, 1905, formation of the Lansing & Jackson Interurban Electric Railway Company by Mills-Moore-Elliott-Boland.

We may never know exactly what happened, but William Boland, the promoter, now did some strange maneuvering. The *Lansing State Journal* on April 24 stated that Boland planned to re-use the rail from his ill-fated line from Grass Lake to Chelsea for the Lansing-Jackson interurban, but by September 19, 1905, the *Michigan Investor* reported that Boland was reorganizing the Jackson & Ann Arbor company. A rueful Boland explained that the deal he had with Angus and Hawks had gone bad and now he would head to Detroit. Therefore, he did not remove the track for use on the Jackson-Lansing line.

In the meantime, the town of Mason would not give the company a franchise unless the line would go through the center of the community. To do this, the company would have to build bridges it could not afford, including an expensive span at Rives Junction over the Grand Rapids branch of the Michigan Central Railroad.

As rail lines and interurbans became commonplace, farmers and other property holders along a proposed new route were increasingly reluctant to give a right-of-way free; they often asked a very stiff price. And money markets would sometimes go dry and promotions would have to await the influx of new money. Whatever the reason, it was not until July 28, 1907, that the contract for construction was awarded to W.E. Tench and Company. Six carloads of equipment were on the way from Roscommon to Holt. On Septembr 22, 1907, the *Jackson Patriot* reported route changes out of the city

of Lansing. Today, portions of old U.S. Hwy. 127 follow the alignment and became part of the former interurban line north of Mason.

On June 29, 1908, the *Free Press* reported that the Michigan United Railway raised its stock from $5 million to $7 million to complete the line from Lansing to Jackson. Finally, on November 24, 1908, a test car with company officials and politicians rolled over the line from Lansing to Mason. The next day, Thanksgiving, service began on a 90-minute headway.

At this time the operating portions of the line were turned over to the MUR by the construction company. Usually a construction company would operate a new line for six months to warrant its construction. But in this case only the MUR had cars ready to operate over the line. No new cars were then on order, so older MUR interurban cars were converted for use on the third-rail line by the addition of power pickup shoes.

The *Jackson Patriot* on January 27, 1909, reported construction of the $15,000 viaduct over the Michigan Central at Rives Junction was under way. A most interesting note in the newspaper was mention of a new company policy of training men for use on various divisions so they could be moved to any location and used where needed.

Progress seemed to be slow; as of April 14, 1909, the line was still three miles from Jackson. On May 26, 1909, it was reported that to get through Mason on a route bypassing the center of the balky community, the company created a two-mile steam railroad, Lansing Southern Railroad.

Finally, on September 21, the last spike was driven on the Lansing-Jackson line, and now it was a matter of awaiting the completion of the bridge at Rives Junction. Then on the 23rd, the line opened from Lansing to Leslie. At last, on November 5, 1909, the *Jackson Patriot*

The interurban car is facing north on Washington at Michigan, with the state capitol building in view. It will turn east (toward the camera) on Michigan Avenue and head for Owosso or St. Johns. In later years St. Johns cars continued out Washington.

Schramm Collection

Effective May 23, 1915

JACKSON - LANSING - OWOSSO - ST. JOHNS

THROUGH CARS JACKSON-OWOSSO   **THROUGH CARS JACKSON-ST. JOHNS**   **THROUGH CAR LANSING-DETROIT**

NORTH BOUND   **CENTRAL STANDARD TIME**   **NORTH BOUND**

Loc AM	Loc AM	Loc AM	Lim AM	Loc AM	Lim AM	Loc AM	Lim AM	Loc NOON	Lim AM	STATIONS	Loc PM	Lim NOON	Loc PM	Lim PM	Loc PM	Lim PM	Loc PM	Loc PM	Loc PM	Loc PM
				6 00		8 00		10 00		Lv. DETROIT Lv		12 00		2 00		4 00		6 00		
+5 05	6 00	7 05		8 00	9 05	10 00	11 05	12 00	1 05	Lv JACKSON Lv		3 05	4 00	5 05	6 00	7 05		8 00	9 20	11 00
+5 27	6 25	7 29	8 28	9 29	10 28	11 29	12 28	1 29	RIVES JUNCT'N	2 28	3 29	4 28	5 29	6 28	7 29	8 28	9 48	11 29
+5 35	6 37	7 38	8 41	9 38	10 41	11 38	12 41	1 38	LESLIE	2 41	3 38	4 41	5 38	6 41	7 38	8 39	9 57	11 38
+5 42	6 48	7 44	8 52	9 44	10 52	11 44	12 52	1 44	EDEN	3 44	3 52	4 52	5 44	6 52	7 44	8 49	10 05	11 46
+5 49	6 59	7 52	9 01	9 52	11 01	11 52	1 01	1 52	MASON	3 01	4 05	5 01	5 52	7 01	7 52	8 58	10 14	11 53
+6 00	7 14	8 03	9 15	10 03	11 15	12 03	1 15	2 03	HOLT	3 15	4 05	5 15	6 03	7 12	8 03	9 08	10 24	12 02
+6 19	7 40	8 21	9 38	10 21	11 38	12 21	1 38	2 21	Ar LANSING Ar	3 38	4 21	5 38	6 21	7 34	8 21	9 28	10 45	12 20

										STATIONS										
6 20	8 22	10 22	12 22	2 22	Lv LANSING Lv	4 22	6 22	7 35	9 30	11 00
6 38	8 38	10 38	12 38	2 38	EAST LANSING	4 38	6 38	7 52	9 45	11 17
6 50	8 50	10 50	12 50	2 50	HASLETT	4 50	6 50	8 03	9 57	11 27
7 06	9 06	11 06	1 06	3 06	SHAFTSBURG	5 06	7 06	8 18	10 11	11 39
7 14	9 14	11 14	1 14	3 14	PERRY	5 14	7 14	8 26	10 19	11 45
7 18	9 18	11 18	1 18	3 18	MORRICE	5 18	7 18	8 30	10 23	11 51
7 45	9 45	11 45	1 45	3 45	Ar *OWOSSO* Ar	5 45	7 45	8 54	10 45	12 11
7 50	9 50	11 50	1 50	3 50	Ar WEST TOWN Ar	5 50	7 50	8 58	10 49	12 15

					STATIONS					
6 00	8 00	9 40	11 40	1 40	Lv LANSING Lv	3 40	6 00	8 23	10 50	
6 26	8 26	10 06	12 06	2 06	DE WITT	4 09	6 28	8 48	11 15	
6 50	8 50	10 30	12 30	2 30	Ar ST. JOHNS Ar	4 35	6 55	9 10	11 38	

SOUTH BOUND

Loc AM	Loc AM	Lim AM	Loc AM	Lim AM	Loc AM	Lim AM	Loc AM	Lim AM	Loc PM	STATIONS	Lim PM	Loc PM	Lim PM	Loc PM	Lim PM	Loc PM	Loc PM	Loc PM	Loc PM	Loc PM
		7 00		9 10		11 10		1 10	Lv ST. JOHNS Lv		3 10		5 10		7 10		9 15		11 45
		7 27		9 35		11 35		1 35	DE WITT		3 35		5 35		7 35		9 40		12 07
		7 56		10 02		12 02		2 02	Ar LANSING Ar		4 02		6 02		8 02		10 07		12 30

										STATIONS										
7 55	9 55	11 55	Lv WEST TOWN Lv	1 55	3 55	5 55	7 55	9 06	10 50
6 05	8 05	10 05	12 05	Lv *OWOSSO* Lv	2 05	4 05	6 05	8 05	9 15	11 00
6 33	8 33	10 33	12 33	MORRICE	2 33	4 33	6 33	8 30	9 39	11 26
6 39	8 39	10 39	12 39	PERRY	2 39	4 39	6 39	8 35	9 45	11 31
6 47	8 47	10 47	12 47	SHAFTSBURG	2 47	4 47	6 47	8 43	9 53	11 39
7 01	9 01	11 01	1 01	HASLETT	3 01	5 01	7 01	8 58	10 06	11 52
7 14	9 14	11 14	1 14	EAST LANSING	3 14	5 14	7 14	9 11	10 16	12 02
7 30	9 30	11 30	1 30	Ar LANSING Ar	3 30	5 30	7 30	9 28	10 30	12 15

Loc AM	Loc AM	Lim AM	Loc AM	Lim AM	Loc AM	Lim AM	Loc AM	Lim AM	Loc PM	STATIONS	Lim PM	Loc PM	Lim PM	Loc PM	Lim PM	Loc PM	Loc PM	Loc PM	Loc PM	Loc PM
5 40	+6 10	7 32	8 05	9 32	10 05	11 32	12 05	1 32	2 05	Lv LANSING Lv	3 32	4 05	5 32	6 05	7 32	8 05	9 30	11 00		
6 00	+6 34	7 54	8 30	9 54	10 30	11 54	12 30	1 54	2 30	HOLT	3 54	4 30	5 54	6 30	7 54	8 29	9 54	11 23		
6 11	+6 47	8 05	8 42	10 05	10 42	12 05	12 42	2 05	2 42	MASON	4 05	4 42	6 05	6 42	8 05	8 41	10 09	11 38		
6 19	+6 53	8 09	8 47	10 09	10 47	12 09	12 47	2 09	2 47	EDEN	4 09	4 47	6 09	6 47	8 09	8 45	10 09	11 38		
6 24	7 07	8 18	9 01	10 18	11 01	12 18	1 01	2 18	3 01	LESLIE	4 18	5 01	6 18	7 01	8 18	8 57	10 19	11 45		
6 35	7 19	8 28	9 13	10 28	11 13	12 28	1 13	2 28	3 13	RIVES JUNCTION	4 28	5 13	6 28	7 13	8 28	9 07	10 27	11 57		
‡6 58	+7 53	‡8 50	9 47	‡10 50	11 47	‡12 50	1 47	‡2 50	3 47	Ar JACKSON Ar	‡4 50	5 47	‡6 50	7 47	8 50	9 37	10 50	12 25		
9 55		11 55		1 55		3 55		5 55		Ar DETROIT Ar	7 55		9 55							

†Except Sunday. ‡Connection for Points West. ||Cars stop on flag. *Connection at Owosso with cars for Corunna. ⌂Station stop for Pine Lake passengers. ¶Connection for Albion. Light figures A. M. Dark figures P. M. NOTE--Limited cars make local stops between Lansing and Owosso.

From Jackson to Lansing

The Rives Junction trestle with car 16 crossing over Michigan Central's Jackson-Grand Rapids subdivision tracks.
Schramm Collection

On November 6, 1909, the trestle at Rives Junction was complete and the first interurban, number 39, arrived at Leslie.

Moore Collection

This Lansing-Mason Niles-built shuttle car is operating to the temporary Mason depot. Judging from the construction material, the line must be new. The passengers or officials are dutifully waiting for the cameraman to finish.
Schramm Collection

The Mason depot, showing the freight awaiting transport by car.
Schramm Collection

The postcard reads: A Bird's Eye View of Mason. It shows the closeness of the railroad and interurban tracks.
Schramm Collection

Car 42 loading at Holt.
Woodard Collection

Two views of De Witt, the main stop on the line from Lansing to St. Johns. Below: A north-bound car loading at the station. Left: The depot with a large amount of freight waiting to be moved.
Lansing-North Lansing Electric Railroad Museum

Lansing to St. Johns

This 1906 photo of car 100 at the Pine Lake loop was captioned "the first electric freight that ran out of Lansing, left to right Wesley Barnes, Frances Korff, and A. T. Mann, general freight and passenger agent for the Lansing and Suburban Railway."
Lansing-North Lansing Electric Railroad Museum

Substation No. 2, County Farm, on the St. Johns line.
Lansing-North Lansing Electric Railroad Museum

Car 3 at the St. Johns depot of Michigan United Railways.
Schramm Collection

A view of the business section of St. Johns. The postcard was dated 1912 and the future depot on the right was still a law office. The 49-52 series car is northbound on Clinton Street en route to the Wye at Railroad Street.

Schramm Collection

127

Merle Beach substation, which replaced early ones at De Witt and County Farm Crossing.
Lansing-North Lansing Electric Railroad Museum

Left: A worker in the power plant. Above: A temporary substation set up in boxcar 900 by Michigan United Traction.
Lansing-North Lansing Electric Railroad Museum

reported that the next day, Saturday, the line would open for through service, but the cars would go slow until the sub-station at Mason was completed and the third-rail tested.

Jackson was becoming an interurban hub, and early in 1909 the MUR began construction of a new terminal east of Francis Street between Cortland and Washington. The new terminal opened for service Monday, January 2, 1911. Cars into the terminal would use Washington Street and leave by Cortland to Main Street. The public entered by Francis Street. It was anticipated 58 cars would leave the terminal daily, besides the local freights.

Lansing to Owosso

With the line from Lansing to Jackson completed and operating, George Moore, the Mills family attorney, incorporated the Lansing & Northeastern Railway on January 10, 1910, which would construct a line from Lansing to Owosso. This company had $500,000

in capital stock. Most of the officers were from the Michigan United Railway. The remaining officers were K. Lathrop, S.W. Lad and T.W. Atwood. The company issued, in addition to the stock, $800,000 in bonds by March 13, 1910, to cover the cost of the grading which was well under way. This was to be another third-rail line, with the power to come from the Commonwealth Power group dams.

Moore had big ideas. On May 4, 1910, he promised that his new line would be extended to Saginaw. And he told of plans being developed for a Jackson-Detroit line to compete with the Detroit United Railway system.

On the northern end of the new route, the *Detroit News* on June 15, 1910, reported that the four-mile Owosso & Corunna Street Railway, cars and power-house had been sold to William Eaton, a stockholder in Commonwealth Power, to satisfy the $80,000 mortgage. This segment was considered a city line under the Michigan Railway (MRY) operating setup, with

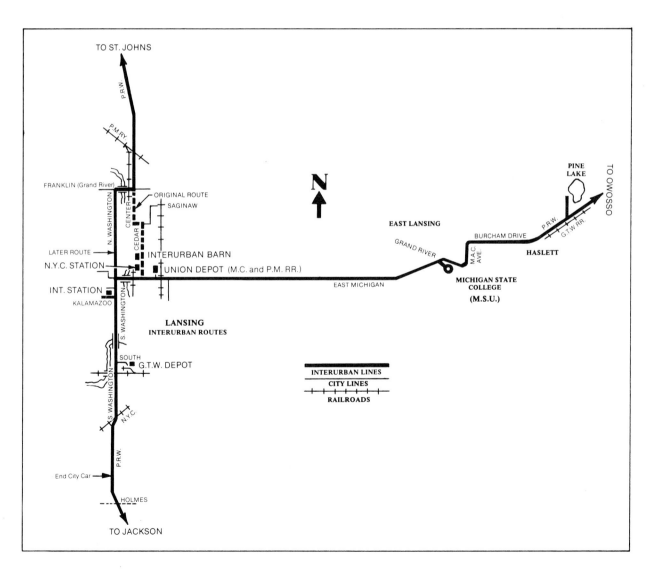

Bakers switch between Lansing and East Lansing along Michigan Avenue, looking west.
Michigan State Archives

Morrice station, with a car about to curve north away from the paralleling Grand Trunk Railroad, toward Owosso.
Michigan State Archives

An early photo at the Owosso car barn of the Healy-type steam motors used on the 4-mile Owosso-Corunna line prior to electrification.
Michigan State Archives

Two photos taken at the Pine Lake loop of the early cars used by Lansing and Suburban Traction. Above is car 115 and below, 117. The destination sign reads COLLEGE-PINE LAKE indicating the cars were assigned to Pine Lake, a short turn on the Owosso line.

Lansing-North Lansing Electric Railroad Museum

McGuire-Cummings-built car 68, coming off private right-of-way onto Washington Street, Owosso, from Lansing.

Sumner Collection

its own superintendent. In later years, Corunna city officials, upon hearing that the MRY group would build to Flint via Corunna, tried to extract funds to support their local park; the company refused to pay.

All went well on the main project, and a month later, on July 16, the *Michigan Investor* reported the grading of the electric line to Owosso from Lansing was practically complete. The Commonwealth Power Company would share the right-of-way for its power lines and supply power to operate the interurban cars. A year later, on July 2, 1911, the Lansing-Owosso division prepared to open for service on a 90-minute schedule. First day of scheduled service was July 8, 1911.

Later, under the management of the Michigan Railway (and unique to the Northern Division) cars were operated hourly from Jackson to Lansing. At that point the cars would alternate final destinations, St. Johns or Owosso, effectively giving each terminal two-hour service. Running time from Jackson to Owosso was 2 hours and 45 minutes. One round trip a day was given by a through car between Detroit and Lansing via Jackson.

After Michigan United Traction took over the Moore-Mills MUR on December 27, 1911, plans were drawn to expand east to Flint. But it was realized that the numerous delays in securing a right-of-way and then shortages of materials would prevent completion of the line until after World World I. By that time traffic was on the decline and management decided to abandon the expansion plan.

Anyway, as early as 1910, a bus company was connecting Owosso with the Flint interurban station. First named the Motor Bus Line, then in 1916 the Owosso-Flint Bus Line, today it is still operating under the Indian Trails banner.

Commonwealth PR&L Formed

The men who met to form the Commonwealth Power Railway and Light Company as a holding company on March 8, 1910, were W.A. Foote and E.W. Clark, representing the Commonwealth Power Company; plus A.G. Hodenpyl and H.D. Walbridge, representing the Michigan Light Company. Even though both companies had an interest in street railways and interurbans in Michigan, only Foote was involved in the building of interurban lines. Walbridge was concerned in gas lighting, and Hodenpyl and Clark controlled financial investments.

Foote remarked that if a power company wished to sell bonds, it would need a contract to sell power to a major user, such as an interurban system. Beginning in 1895, Foote devoted his energy to developing a string of hydro-electric power plants and high voltage distribution systems starting with the Trowbridge power dam, which went on-line September 20, 1899. His hydro

plants supplied power to many local traction systems. To concentrate on expanding his hydro-electric holdings, Foote sold his interurban investments in 1905 to the Mills-Elliot-Moore syndicate (MUR). By 1911 this group controlled interurban and city car lines from Kalamazoo to Battle Creek, Jackson to Battle Creek, Jackson to Lansing, Lansing to St. Johns and Lansing to Owosso.

Roster data for any of these companies is fragmentary, but in the Bentley Library at U. of M. Ann Arbor we found the following 1910 data:

Type	Builder	No. of Cars	Fleet Numbers	Seats	Length
Limited	Jewett	1	30	58	56'-6"
"	St Louis	10 (a)	31-40	62	58'-4"
Local	Niles	2	42-43	46	44'-10"
"	Kuhlman	5 (b)	44-48	62	50'-0"
"	Kuhlman	4 (b)	49-52	62	54'-6"
"	Niles	2	205-206	46	44'-10"

Michigan Traction Cars

Type	Builder	No. of Cars	Fleet Numbers	Seats	Length
Local	St Louis	6	52-57	46	44'-8"

(a) Original Boland cars purchased for Jackson-Grass Lake service.

(b) Purchased by Jackson and Battle Creek Traction Co.

Assignments	Limiteds	Locals
Jackson-Kalamazoo	4	4
Jackson-Lansing	2	2
Lansing extra	1	1
Jackson extra	1	1
Albion shop extra	3	3
Kalamazoo	—	1
Battle Creek	—	1
	11	13

Michigan Traction Cars

Gull Lake (double ended)	2
Wolf Lake & Grass Lake	3
To be rebuilt	1

Foote Re-enters the Picture

It is possible that a chance remark by George Moore in a Jackson newspaper on February 7, 1911, caused Foote's return to interurban management. Moore spoke of plans to build a line into Detroit to compete with the DJ&C. This included construction of a huge power generating plant in Jackson which would compete with Commonwealth Power. It all triggered a chain of events that eventually led the power syndicate to purchase stock in the Michigan United Railways owned by the Mills-Moore group.

That summer, Moore sent his representative, George Blakelock, to England for the purpose of securing financial backing for his expansion plans which, if possible, would include the purchase of the DJ&C and the DUR. The grand design would bisect the territory of the two electric power combines. If Moore's plans came to reality, both Edison and Consumers Power would face bonding and territorial problems.

The Detroit Edison Company, under the leadership fo Alex Dow, worked closely with the North American Company. Dow was securing for the Edison the service area of St. Clair, Macomb, Oakland, Wayne and Washtenaw counties. The Commonwealth Power group served the area beyond Edison. But their gas plants remained within a portion of this area.

So the power companies now drew their territorial lines, which remain unchanged to this day. The Detroit Edison Company supplied power to the DUR as far as Lima Center on the DJ&C while Consumers Power served the rest of the line. The Moore plan of building to Detroit was shelved.

Companies Formed and Reformed

The Mills and company network of interurban lines extended from St. Johns to Kalamazoo. Mills' first line to St. Johns was not a financial success, but the other lines proved profitable. This taste of good luck spurred expansion plans under the direction of the family attorney, George Moore, which included a line into Detroit.

Defensively, the electric power groups feeding power to Mills' interurban began to buy into the Michigan United Railway to the extent they could force a 999 year lease of the property. The company formed on December 27, 1911, to run the operation was the Michigan United Traction. According to the *Journal* of October 24, 1911, the power syndicate signed preliminary agreements in London, but the official takeover seemed to be, as reported, February 24, 1912.

At that point Moore was replaced as spokesperson for the Michigan United Railway. He continued to serve on that board for many years beyond the takeover, even though Commonwealth officials served various positions on the board. These officials determined the future course the company would take in the

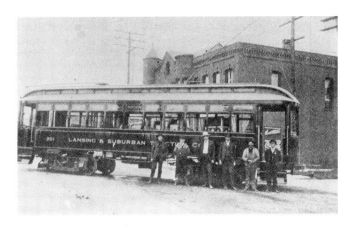

Car 201 of the Lansing & Suburban Traction Company, later renumbered 82 and assigned to Battle Creek. Here 201 is completing a trip from St. Johns and is turning from Cedar Street to run west on Michigan Ave. The photo was snapped in 1904 prior to the change from the Michigan-Cedar connection in favor of the Washington-Franklin trackage which served more of the Lansing and North Lansing business area. *Stoner Collection*

expansion of lines through mid-Michigan.

Even though Commonwealth had established the Michigan United Traction to take over the lease of the MUR, another company (Michigan & Chicago Electric Railway—M&CE) was established to build and operate Commonwealth-owned properties. Then on March 20, 1914, the Michigan Railway was formed to consolidate operation of all Commonwealth holdings. The company said it liked the new name as it represented the direction it was now heading; extending to Chicago was not in the cards.

All the new plans jelled on December 21, 1915, when the MRY announced that one management would operate all lines in mid-Michigan. At that time the company organized the extensive network into divisions: lines from Jackson to Kalamazoo became the Southern; lines from Jackson to Lansing, and their extensions to St. Johns and Owosso, became the Northern. Each city was operated separately with its own superintendent.

The December 1922, *Bus Transportation* ad accompanying this photo carried the following description: "Special 24-passenger Tour-a-Bus body, 88 inches wide, carrying five persons in each seat, (designed) for a 150-inch chassis (looks like a Reo chassis). Perfectly balanced, comfortable, safe and very attractive." The logo on the side reads OWOSSO-FLINT BUS LINE INC. OWOSSO, MICH.
Courtesy Detroit Public Library

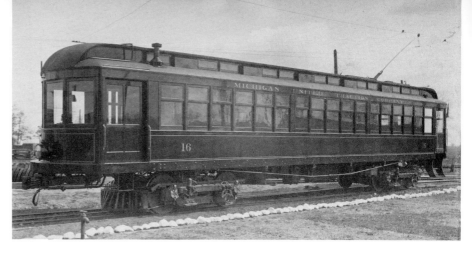

A company photo of car 16, taken at Albion shops, with the Michigan United Traction letterboard, after rebuilding from a 60-63 class car. The refurbishing included installation of multiple-unit controls, radial couplers, 600-1200-volt motors and a baggage compartment.
Schramm Collection

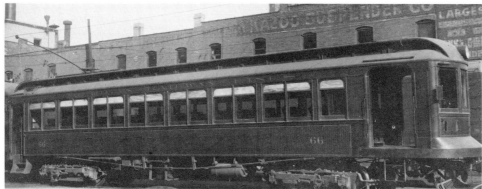

MUR car 66, operating under lease by Michigan Railway, lays over between runs at the Kalamazoo terminal.
Schramm Collection

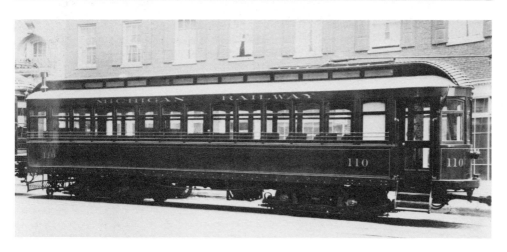

Michigan Railway car 110, with its 47-foot wood body, was built by Jewett in 1902.
Schramm Collection

Michigan Electric Railway Lines was the final name under which these cars operated.
Schramm Collection

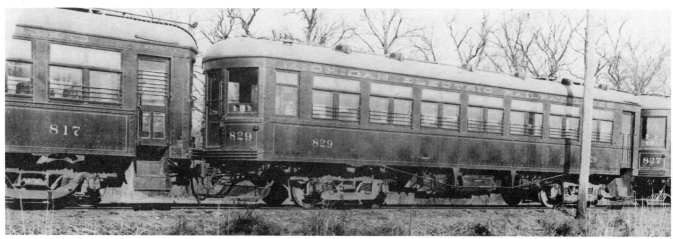

On January 1, 1916, the leases of all the Michigan United properties were transferred to the Michigan Railway.

The Ride Downhill

According to published reports in *Moody's*, MUR's first six months of operation had netted a surplus of $97,000 on a gross of $397,000. Through 1920, bond holders received their interest payments and the company was considered a good investment.

Following World War I, rail traffic began to decline as touring cars and buses began competing for passengers. Automobiles took to the new and improved highways, removing more potential passengers. Suddenly, reduced revenue could not meet the new MR's funding interest payments, and the road defaulted on it bonds.

And that wasn't all. As franchises expired, cities tried to extract even greater financial concessions from the hard-pressed interurbans. The handwriting was on the wall; holding companies decided that it was folly to continue advancing funds to faltering traction subsidiaries.

Justin Whiting was brought in to plan the liquidation of the traction subsidiaries in the interest of the stockholders. His basic plan was to split Commonwealth Power, Railway and Light into two operations with the stockholders receiving equal shares in each of the new companies: Commonwealth Power Corporation and Electric Railways Securities Corporation. During 1921 the lease of the Northern and Southern divisions was terminated and returned to Michigan United Railways; a paper move.

With revenue dropping on some routes very quickly, the bondholders signed a protective agreement on November 8, 1921, prior to reorganization on December 15. A year later, on December 13, 1922, John F. Collins was named receiver. The sale was scheduled for June 30. This receivership did not include the Michigan Railroad's Western or Northwestern divisions.

Another New Company

Reorganization was effected in 1923; the Northern and Southern divisions emerged on August 2, 1923, as the Michigan Electric Railway (MER). President of MER was George R. Cottrelle of Toronto and Vice President-General Manager was John F. Collins.

An example of the tokens used by MUR and Michigan Railway; each city system had its own individualized token. The initials in the center of the tokens represented the following cities: "O"=Owosso, "L"=Lansing, "K"=Kalamazoo, "J"=Jackson and "B"=Battle Creek.

The Jackson train shed sign now says Michigan Electric Railway Co., the final name for this outstate interurban. The Fageol bus became a common sight as Michigan Railway adopted buses at an early date.
Schramm Collection

Small portions of the system began to be abandoned: Grass Lake to Wolf Lake Junction in 1924; Owosso to Corunna in 1926 and Michigan Center to Wolf Lake in 1927.

History soon repeated itself, and the new company could not meet the interest due on its bonds. Since the company could pay its other bills, the owners were allowed to continue operation. In 1928, for the first time, receipts were unable to pay the cost of conducting transportation so this time major lines were removed from electric service: Kalamazoo to Jackson on November 30, 1928; Lansing to St. Johns and Owosso on May 16, 1929, and only two days later cars stopped operating from Lansing to Jackson. Freight continued on some lines and city rail service operated until taken over by other companies and eventually replaced by buses during 1932 and 1933.

Quickly, the company was reorganized as the Michigan Electric Shares Corporation (MESC) on March 20, 1929, with the express purpose of liquidating the interurban lines which belonged to the old Michigan United Railways. After complete abandonment of the rail operations, the MESC closed its books June 19, 1933.

Bus and trucking operations continued. The Southern Michigan Transportation Company, a subsidiary formed in 1925, started a motor truck service to carry high rate freight formerly carried by interurbans, and to provide door-to-door service. In May 1929, the Rapid Transit Company, which operated buses over the old rail routes from Flint to Saginaw, was acquired from bondholders of the Michigan Railroad and consolidated with the Southern Michigan. Eventually, in 1935, the Eastern Michigan Motorbuses took over the Southern Michigan to become the largest intrastate bus company in Michigan.

WESTERN DIVISION

Kalamazoo to Grand Rapids & Battle Creek to Allegan

When the Michigan United Traction Company was formed in 1912, one of the projects scheduled for future construction was an electric line connecting Kalamazoo to Grand Rapids.

As a prelude to this, on May 7, 1913, it was reported that the Michigan and Chicago Electric Railway (a Foote-controlled company) had purchased the Allegan division of the Michigan Central Railroad (the one-time Detroit, Toledo & Milwaukee Railroad) and a private right-of-way into Battle Creek. The company used in acquiring the franchises was the Michigan and Chicago Westbound Railway; this was later changed to Michigan & Chicago Railway Company.

Then on March 20, 1914, with Chicago eliminated as the ultimate destination of the company lines, the operating system became the MRY. It was to form a needed link to the projected Kalamazoo-Grand Rapids line, that the MCRR track between Battle Creek and Allegan was purchased. This line intersected the planned Grand Rapids-Kalamazoo line at Monteith Junction.

Later that year, on November 26, the company formally announced plans to build the Kalamazoo to Grand Rapids line. Prior to this, Foote, now back in the interurban business, had been securing a right-of-way between the two cities.

And what a showcase line it was to be! A high-speed line, and as such, built on 100-foot-wide right-of-way using 80 lb. rail, and maximum curves of 3 degrees with grades of only one percent. Special motors were developed so cars could collect 2400 volts d.c. from a third-rail with over-riding slipper shoes. In towns, over-head pantograph collectors or trolley poles were to be used.

The first terminal in Kalamazoo was the Michigan Traction Building on Portage Avenue. However, construction started on a new terminal at Rose and Water streets, which after many delays and fights, was completed in time for the new service, and the old depot closed. In Grand Rapids the off-street terminal facility was located near city center, easily reached by cars crossing the graceful, arch-span interurban bridge. The freight facility was west of the Grand River and south of Fulton Street.

For the first year the Grand Rapids-Kalamazoo line operated at 2400 volts with only two substations, but continuous problems with arcing forced the company to drop the voltage to 1200. This resulted in additional substations being added along the line.

Two types of cars were designed for use on this division, using the ideas Foote had suggested for the Jackson and Battle Creek line. For limited service, 52 passenger, 67-foot cars with baggage, smoking, coach and parlor compartments were selected. These cars were probably one of the longest, heaviest and most costly interurban cars built up to that time. They regularly operated at speeds in excess of 80 mph. The eight-foot wheelbase on the Baldwin trucks gave a smooth ride. The local cars were of the conventional 61-foot baggage-passenger type.

On November 4, 1914, electricity was first fed to the track, but because the fence protecting the exposed third-rail right-of-way was not finished, the grand opening was delayed until May 5, 1915, when the first promotional trip traveled the entire line. At 9:30 a.m. local newspaper reporters left Grand Rapids for Kalamazoo in President H.H. Crowell's private car. They returned in the afternoon. The one-way trip of 47 miles was made in 42 minutes. On May 11, a special trip was scheduled for mayors and other officials. Service for the public began on both the Grand Rapids-Kalamazoo line and the Allegan-Battle Creek branch on May 17.

The line from Monteith to Battle Creek offered only local service, partially duplicating the nearby Gull Lake branch. After a 2½-mile loop to Gull Lake from the new trackage was placed in service on February 2, 1916, the old Gull Lake branch was abandoned. By 1917 most of the old MCRR Allegan to Battle Creek line had been converted for use by the traction cars.

This interurban line was built late, after the peak years of electric rail system construction. It seemed to be the ultimate in high-speed electric transportation in rural America. Yet, it still was a mixed breed—somewhere between a heavy electrified steam road and an interurban. Photographs of the line reveal its unique construction.

Of course it was built in vain. As it opened, competition was already developing along the roadways parallel to its right-of-way. Steadily decreasing revenues could not support the enormous capital outlay. Control of this division was turned over to the Michigan Railroad in 1919, which operated the line until August 6, 1928, when passenger service was suspended. It was one of the shortest-lived major electric interurban lines in America.

South Bound—GRAND RAPIDS TO KALAMAZOO—Read Down

North Bound—KALAMAZOO TO GRAND RAPIDS—Read Up

MICHIGAN RAILWAY COMPANY

GRAND RAPIDS TO ALLEGAN / ALLEGAN TO GRAND RAPIDS — WESTERN DIVISION

KALAMAZOO TO ALLEGAN / ALLEGAN TO KALAMAZOO

BATTLE CREEK TO ALLEGAN / ALLEGAN TO BATTLE CREEK

Car 804 is sitting next to the Elk's Temple in Battle Creek. This car was not equipped with a pantograph. The crossing gates in back are for Michigan Central Railroad.
Schramm Collection

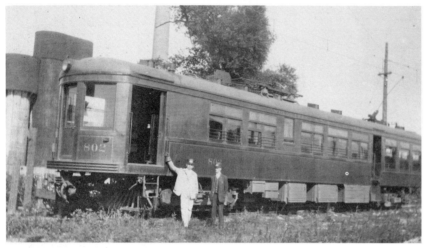

Car 802 at the Battle Creek Terminal yards in 1921. Carl Decker, who later worked for South Shore, is the motorman. Clarence Faber, a local railfan noted, "If a motorman's watch was off over 30 seconds, he did not go to work the next day until the watch inspector okayed it."
Decker Collection

A view looking south toward the Kalamazoo River and city of Kalamazoo.
Lenderink Collection

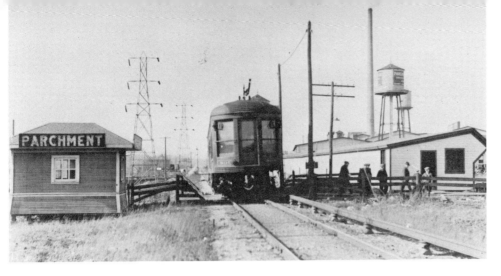

Parlor car 801 has discharged workers for the nearby paper mills in suburban Kalamazoo. The car will now pick up speed and head for Monteith Junction and Grand Rapids. The interurban company used hat checks similar to those used on steam roads, rather than a fare register.

Lenderink Collection

It was a rainy day at Plainwell, judging from the umbrellas in view when this photo was taken.

Lenderink Collection

Cars 802 and 808 northbound at Wayland station, operating under trolley wire. The cars had been joined together at Monteith Junction—one from Battle Creek, the other from Kalamazoo.

General Electric

139

These three photos and their captions appeared on a 1916 Michigan Railway calendar. The first was captioned: "Gauntlet swing bridge (over Grand River), showing overhead construction and special work in Michigan Railway construction."

Below, left: Michigan Railway track view, showing construction and automatic block system for safe operation.

Bottom: Leading to passenger terminal, foot of Lyon Street, Grand Rapids.

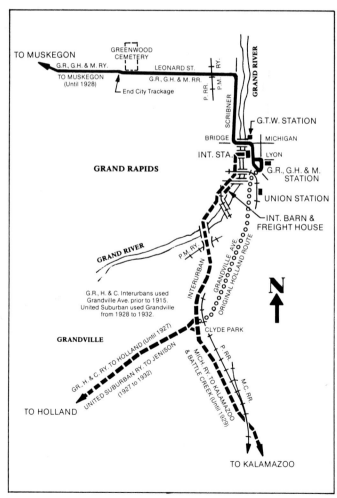

Map of Grand Rapids.

Michigan Railway 810, arriving from Kalamazoo, at Front and Fulton, Grand Rapids, in November 1915. Clarence Faber noted: "Before the private right-of-way and two bridges over the Grand River were completed, the cars used the original GRH&C tracks via Grandville Avenue to reach the temporary terminal at 91 Market Street. There was a temporary layover stub track on the north side of the Pantlind Hotel."

Faber Collection

Car 814 on the upper bridge in Grand Rapids. This structure later became a metered parking lot. Today it serves as a pedestrian bridge to reach the President Gerald Ford Museum.

Faber Photo

The four-track interurban terminal at Grand Rapids shows a mixture of MRR and GRH&C equipment. Photographer Faber noted, "the cars were backed into the terminal, and if the motorman hit the bumper, it meant a 30-day suspension." The terminal was closed in 1929; today this is the site of the Grand Rapids Civic Auditorium.

Faber Collection

The J. G. Brill Co. took this builder's photo of prototype car 800. The car had four compartments; first (forward) was the observation which had seats for eight—five of which were revolving chairs. Next was the passenger section which seated 32, then the smoking section which seated 12. The last (rear) section was the baggage compartment. At 70 tons these were the heaviest cars built for the line. Later this car had its controls moved to the other end and was renumbered 812.

Schramm Collection

St. Louis Car Company built the balance of the large cars, Nos. 802-810 and 814-816, even numbers only. Here is 802 in a builder's photo. The Brill car, 800 (later 812) Faber noted, was of riveted steel smooth-sided panel construction while the flanks of the St. Louis cars had beaded steel (panels scribed to look like tongue-and-groove wood). The underframe utilized fishbelly construction (as seen in many steam road passenger cars). There was chemicalized padding behind the sheathing to insulate the cars.

Schramm Collection

An interior photo of a large car looking forward from the rear parlor section. Faber noted that car 800 had a metal ceiling, while others had a fireproof composition ceiling.

Schramm Collection

CAR NUMBER	BUILDER	BUILT	LENGTH	TRUCKS	MOTORS	CLASS	Notes
800 later 812	Brill	1914	66'10"	D-Baldwin 96-50-A	4-G.E. 239	Pass Parlor	
802,804, 806,808, 810,814, 816	St. Louis	1915	67'6"	D-Baldwin 96-50-AA	4-G.E. 239	Pass Parlor	
801,803, 805,807, 809,811,	St. Louis	1915	61'0"	D-Baldwin 87-40-AT(trl) 96-40-AA(mtr)	2-G.E. 239	Pass	A
900-903	St. Louis	1915	61'0"	D-Baldwin 96-50-AA	4-G.E. 239	Frt Motor	
50,51	St. Louis	1917	53'0"	D-Baldwin 72-25-AT	none	Pass Trailer	B
54-59	St. Louis	1915	53'0"	D-Baldwin 72-25-AT	none	Pass Trailer	B

A—In 1916 801,803,805,809 received Two D-Baldwin 87-40-A trucks and 4 G.E. 254 Motors.
B—Assigned to Western Division during World War I normally used on Northeastern Div.

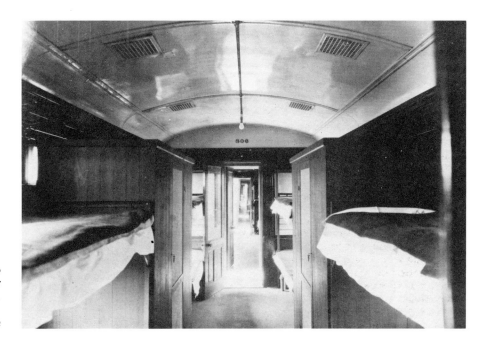

Unable to sell these large cars to other properties, Consumers Power converted them for work service. Number 806 became a bunk car.
Schramm Collection

Car 808's fate was to become a dining (or mess hall) car.
Schramm Collection

A photo of car 807 in service; these 61-foot units provided the local service on the line. Later 807 and 811 were converted for one-man use.

Faber Collection

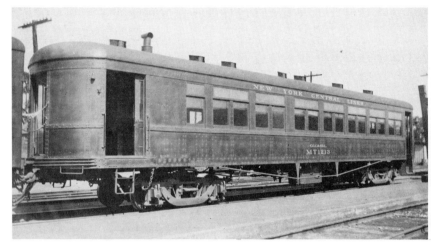

Some of the smaller cars ended up with New York Central, as did No. 1213; its prior Michigan Railway number was 811.

Kremkow Photo

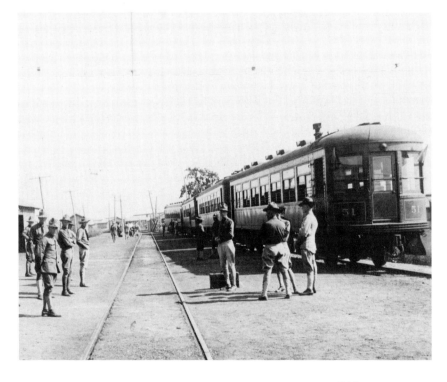

During World War I, Camp Custer was the scene of much army activity. The camp had special tracks to bring in passengers and freight. Car 51 was the second car to bear that number.

Kremkow Collection

NORTHWESTERN DIVISION
Grand Rapids to Holland,
Macatawa & Saugatuck

The Michigan Railway Company officially leased the Grand Rapids, Holland & Chicago Railway January 1, 1916, and named it its Northwestern Division. This division, 42 miles in length, operated 72 miles of electrified double track, mostly on private right-of-way, from Grand Rapids to Holland and the Lake Michigan resorts of Jenison Electric Park, Macatawa Park and Saugatuck. A company ferry carried passengers from Jenison Electric Park to a resort hotel at Ottawa Beach.

The lessors of the Grand Rapids, Holland & Chicago Railway were a combination of Detroit and Holland investors. It is interesting to note the Detroit investors. They included both George and Strathearn Hendrie, and John Winter. The Hendries built the Detroit Citizens' Street Railway (*Detroit's Street Railways, Volume One*), suburban line to Wyandotte and later the interurban line to Pontiac (*When Eastern Michigan Road the Rails, Book One*). John Winter and associates built the Detroit, Rochester, Romeo & Lake Orion Railway, and later the DUR's Flint Division.

While building the line from Lake Orion to Flint, Winter, Oliver Lau and Frank Andrews incorporated the Grand Rapids, Holland and Lake Michigan Railway on February 21, 1900. Their friend, Benjamin S. Hanchett Jr. of Grand Rapids (an officer of the Grand Rapids street railway system), either joined them or asked the Detroit trio to join him in the western Michigan interurban venture. In any case, Hanchett Jr. came into the company as vice-president.

This company acquired the fledgling Holland and Lake Michigan Railway plus the Saugatuck, Douglas & Lake Shore Railway by June 1900. The Holland & Lake Michigan had been chartered June 1897 and built a six-mile line from Holland to Macatawa Beach that opened June 27, 1898. Construction began on the ten-mile line to Saugatuck in the fall of 1898. On July 4, 1899, passenger service to Saugatuck opened to the trestle just north of town.

Officially, the line to Saugatuck was completed on August 19, 1899, and a grand opening celebration marked the occasion. Both resort traction lines worked closely with the Graham & Morton Line's steamships which operated across Lake Michigan between Holland and Chicago.

Construction on the 29-mile Grand Rapids-Holland interurban began October 26, 1900, and continued through the winter. A power plant was established at Jenison and a substation at Zeeland. On July 9 the first cars began operating between Grand Rapids and Jenison. There was not enough local labor for the amount of work which had to be accomplished, and in July a force of 30 men was taken off the Detroit-Flint line construction project at Oxford and brought across the state to complete the GRH&LM. In all, 400 workers were shifted from Oxford, Michigan, to complete the line.

On Saturday, August 31, 1901, the last of the single track of the electric road between Holland and Grand Rapids was laid and the first trip was made on that very day. Stations and buildings were located by John Winter in September after the line was in operation. Waiting rooms and freight depot sites were selected for Vriesland, Zutphen, Jamestown Creamery, Jamestown Center, Hanley, Jenison and Grandville. Zeeland already had a brick passenger, freight station and sub-

Car 9 of the Grand Rapids, Holland & Chicago Railway is seen on a wintry day at the boat docks.
Moore Collection

An early-day connecting bus waits in front of the Saugatuck station.
Moore Collection

station. Many of the stations and buildings followed the plans developed for the Flint line. Regular service from Grand Rapids to Holland began Monday, October 14, 1901, with a "through" fare of 49 cents. By August 1902, a second track to Grand Rapids was completed, making half-hour service possible.

The economic strength of this line was in both freight and passengers. The interurban company serviced its own resort at Jenison Electric Park and the separately-controlled Macatawa Park and Saugatuck. Through passenger cars, known as the *Boat Flyers*, met the boats from Chicago at Macatawa Park. During the summer, commuter limited cars were scheduled to leave the resort in time to arrive at Grand Rapids at the opening of the business day and to return that evening.

Passenger traffic over this line was described as standing room only during the summer and especially on holidays. It was recorded that on July 4, 1905, 10,000 people went to Jenison Park over the interurban line. The company had to purchase additional cars for the crush of the summer passenger traffic. But traffic in the winter months fell off, with the result that the company just barely covered expenses for the year; dividends were rare.

Daily freight runs were scheduled and express cars left Grand Rapids twice a day. Fruit from the Saugatuck area was delivered directly to the Graham & Morton docks. The transfer of perishable and rush freight from the boat docks by interurban to Grand Rapids brought such goods to the city seven hours earlier than from any other port. The company also furnished electric lighting to the Zeeland Brick Com-

pany and to many other industries and homes along its route.

Between 1902 and 1903 lawsuits by the construction company against interurban officials caused a shakeup in the management of the GRH&LM. Strathearn Hendrie became general manager and John Busby, trusted official from the Detroit & Pontiac Railway, became the superintendent. On July 19, 1904, the Grand Rapids, Holland & Chicago Railway was incorporated, with George Hendrie as president of the company and on August 1, 1904, took over the Holland & Lake Michigan Railway. By 1912, the Hendries were making trips to New York looking for a buyer for the interurban company. Early in 1912 Benjamin S. Hanchett regained presidency of the GRH&C with backing by owners of the Grand Rapids Railway, the Commonwealth Power, Railway & Light Company. At the time Hanchett was head of the Grand Rapids Railway.

New money followed new ownership of the GRH&C. Modern steel cars were ordered, tracks replaced, bridges rebuilt, and the branch to Saugatuck rehabilitated into a first class main line. In 1913, work began on a new Chicago boat dock and the rearrangement of the Saugatuck division, which would make it a part of the main line continuing south from Macatawa instead of a branch, connecting at an out-of-the-way junction point. Saugatuck village was a popular resort for Chicagoans who came to the Macatawa boat dock. From there they would ride a car for two miles, then transfer to another car for another ten miles, a trip that might last up to an hour and a half. The Chicago boat would disembark up to 600 persons per trip, making

Grand Rapids, Holland & Chicago car 118 is at Blissveldt Farms on its last trip, November 15, 1926. This was one of the cars reversed and changed for one-man operation.

Stoner Collection

transportation coordination a problem. The new arrangement eliminated the transfer and reduced the travel time to 45 minutes.

The rebuilt line opened in October of 1913, but the company continued to replace ties and ballast during 1914. Low power on this section of track was solved by stepping the voltage up to 1200 volts which was used on other Commonwealth properties. All the new cars ordered had controls to switch from 600 to 1200 volts supplied to the various sections of the line. On May 27, 1915, the new voltage was cut into the circuit.

Commonwealth purchased the Ottawa Beach resort hotel. The interurban company then constructed a ferry, *Ottawa* (with windows that resembled an interurban), to connect the Chicago boat dock with the resort across Black Lake. It went into service May 28, 1914, ready for the summer resort trade.

Over in Grand Rapids a new interurban line was being constructed to Kalamazoo. It featured a private right-of-way into the downtown Grand Rapids Terminal, crossing the Grand River twice within the city. The GRH&C line was crossed near the south Grand Rapids city limits at Grandville Avenue. Shortly after the line was completed in May 1915, the GRH&C switched over to the p/r/w route, thereby avoiding traffic on Grandville Avenue in Grand Rapids. This routing was used until the final abandonment of the Grand Rapids to Kalamazoo line in 1929.

On January 1, 1916, the company was leased to the Michigan Railway (MRY) for operation. The MRY now had the distinction of operating the largest electric system under one name in Michigan with nearly 580 miles of trackage. The GRH&C cars, which had been painted fire department red, were repainted by MRY green with a dark red roof. In 1919 the route became part of the Michigan Railroad (MRR) which then

operated the Northwestern, Northeastern and Western divisions. In the face of declining revenues, the lease of the GRH&C to the MRR was cancelled on January 1, 1924, and returned to the lessor. Again, this was a paper move as MRR officials were still holding office as usual.

By March of 1924 the passenger cars of all five divisions bore a new paint scheme. The green color was retained below the windows, but from the windows up cars were painted a bright orange to make the cars more visible to motorists at road crossings.

As communities improved their streets, interurban companies were required to pave between the rails and so many feet outside of the rails, totally for the benefit of autos and trucks. In Grandville, a court ordered the company to pave between the tracks, but no action was forthcoming on the part of the company.

After dragging the case through the court of appeals, the city took its own action. On Saturday, June 14, 1924, the town marshal placed barricades across the tracks at both ends of State Street, blocking all trains passing through town. Only the mail car was allowed through the blockage because it was conducting federal business.

As the impasse continued, passengers moved from one blocked train to the other by any means possible. The company had pleaded bankruptcy and now waited for a receiver so certificates could be sold. After three days a receiver was appointed and a promise for paving given to the city, so once again the cars were allowed to pass through the city. The paving cost the impoverished interurban about $70,000.

Lacking strong financial backing, the company slipped, as just mentioned, into receivership. Automobile ownership growth and rival bus service cut into rail ridership badly, resulting in abandonment of ser-

The *Ottawa* unloading in 1920. Passengers will now board car 27, waiting in the foreground. In the background is the Ottawa Beach Hotel and the *City of Grand Rapids* heading for Chicago.

Dossin-Great Lakes Museum

Bird's Eye View of Loop, Macatawa, Mich.

Connecting with the Boats

A birds-eye view of the interurban loop at Macatawa.
Schramm Collection

A ground-level view of the boat landing at Ottawa Beach and Macatawa Park. The small ferry in service here was the *Skiddo*, which was later probably replaced by the *Ottawa*.
Schramm Collection

An excellent aerial view of the harbor at Macatawa shows the steamer *Puritan* sitting at the dock. Note the two-car boat train on the pier and the boxcar loading supplies next to the ship.
Moore Collection

The *City of Benton Harbor* was built in 1904 at Toledo, Ohio, by the Craig Ship Building Co. for the Graham & Morton Transportation Co. She was 251.8 feet long. On October 16, 1924, she was sold to the Goodrich Transit Co. In 1936 she became a floating amusement hall until she burned November 24, 1938.
Milwaukee Public Library-Marine Collection

vice west of Jenison on November 15, 1926. The only bidder at the receiver's sale in 1926 was a Chicago scrap dealer who purchased the property for $227,500. He sold the right-of-way to Consumers Power Company for transmitting power and scrapped the track west of Jenison. Besides placing 100 men out of work, the communities along the route lost a total of $150,000 a year in taxes. The modern auto, bus and truck won again.

Under an independent company (United Suburban Railway) with 700 investors, service continued from Jenison to Grand Rapids, 8 miles. Operations began on July 27, 1927, just eight months after the Holland cars quit.

When the Kalamazoo to Grand Rapids line was abandoned, the route into downtown over the interurban bridge was unavailable and cars began using the original route over Grandville Avenue, looping on downtown streets. Equipment was all second-hand and included five ex-Maine cars, one former Grand Rapids city car, and one car from the Windsor area.

But it didn't work out. Soon, the Grandville Avenue city car line was abandoned and the Jenison cars ran only from Jenison to the end of Grandville Avenue. Bus service was offered over the abandoned city car line, but was not satisfactory due to passengers having to transfer. On June 25, 1932, all rail service ended to Jenison.

THE STEAM DIVISION

Kalamazoo to South Haven

Since early 1901, Samual J. Dunkley, promoter of the steamship line operating between South Haven and Chicago, had been promoting an interurban line from South Haven to Kalamazoo under the name The Kalamazoo, Lake Shore & Chicago Traction Company, incorporated April 12, 1905. Other interests, such as the Graham-Morton Steamship Company, were also busy promoting a separate line from Benton Harbor to Kalamazoo calling it The Kalamazoo & Lake Shore Traction Company. This tended to confuse both newspaper reporters and officials of the communities along the route of the proposed traction line.

"City of Grand Rapids," G. & M. Line, Macatawa, Mich.

The *City of Grand Rapids*, built in 1912 at Cleveland, Ohio, for the Graham & Morton Co., was the largest (at 291 feet) and considered the most luxurious of the lake passenger ships. It was sold to Goodrich Transit and became its flagship. She was purchased by the Cleveland and Buffalo Steamship Co. in 1946 and scrapped in 1952.
Milwaukee Public Library-Marine Collection

The *City of Chicago* was built in 1890 at West Bay City for the G&M line. On September 1, 1914, while on a St. Joseph-to-Chicago trip, she caught fire, but all 230 passengers and crew arrived safely. She was then taken to Manitowoc, rebuilt and renamed *City of St. Joseph*. In 1924 she was sold to the Goodrich Lines and by 1935 was converted to a barge.

Milwaukee Public Library-Marine Collection

City of Holland, built at Saugatuck, Michigan, in 1893, was renamed *Melbourne* in 1912. In 1919 she became *Clarence E. LaBeau* and was used just for freight service. She burned on the Maumee River at Toledo on July 11, 1922.

Schramm Collection

After delays in securing needed franchises, work started temporarily in South Haven on June 6, 1905, but continous financing difficulties of the KLS&CT forced an alternate routing. First, the "Calico Grade," a roadbed constructed before the Civil War, connecting Paw Paw with Lawton, was purchased.

Meanwhile, the Michigan Central Railroad was relocating and double-tracking its line between Kalamazoo and Mattawan. On September 27, 1905, the MC sold the original trackage for $80,000 to the Dunkley's group, giving the traction company a private right-of-way from Kalamazoo to Mattawan. The same agreement allowed the KLS&CT to share the Michigan Central's right-of-way from town center in Kalamazoo to the beginning of the MCRR's new track alignment (now portions of Stadium Boulevard) and from Mattawan to Lawton. The problem of crossing the MCRR tracks to get into Lawton was solved by use of a highway underpass midway between the two towns.

On May 5, 1906, service began between Kalamazoo and Paw Paw. Unable to electrify the line as originally planned, Dunkley re-incorporated June 6, 1906, as the Kalamazoo, Lake Shore & Chicago Railway Company (KLS&C) to operate with steam. The nickname more commonly used was "Fruit Belt Line."

Meanwhile, back on May 6, 1903, the Pere Marquette Railroad (PMRR) had purchased the South Haven & Eastern Railroad (SH&E) with the intention of shortening its route to Chicago. This trackage included two separate lines: Paw Paw Railroad (first train November 9, 1867), and the Toledo & South Haven Narrow Gauge Railroad (incorporated February 2, 1876). They became the South Haven & Eastern Railroad on May 23, 1894, and standard gauged in 1898.

Pere Marquette's plans included the acquisition of the Chicago, Kalamazoo & Saginaw Railroad (CK&S) connecting Kalamazoo with Woodbury on the PMRR main line to Detroit. Therefore, the PM would only have to build a connecting line from Lawton to Kalamazoo. But the CK&S would not sell out to PMRR, which resulted in giving up plans for the short cut. At this time the Dewing family of Kalamazoo was involved in the CK&S as well as promoting the Dunkley traction line. Later the CK&S was leased to the Michigan Central. Its expansion plans thwarted, the PM in 1906 leased the SH&E to the KLS&C. The "Calico Grade" portion, which duplicated the Paw Paw to Lawton portion of the SH&E, was then abandoned.

The line's entrance into Kalamazoo, after much debate with city officials over franchises and route, was extended parallel to the MCRR tracks to a new depot at West Main Street. Here passengers could make connections with city streetcars on the Main Street line.

Arrogantly, the MCRR refused a rail connection in Kalamazoo, which limited the KLS&C line to package shipments and less than full car loads (LCL). With this extreme limitation, and business not up to expectations, the line was soon put up for lease.

George Moore, like William Boland, envisioned electric lines operating throughout mid-Michigan. And Moore was on the way to make it a reality rather than a dream. The *Detroit Free Press* on April 20, 1911, reported that Moore had taken over the KLS&C. His plans included a third-rail line to both South Haven and Benton Harbor.

Moore envisioned limited cars running from Detroit to Benton Harbor and boats to Chicago. But not much happened and the company continued to operate the line to South Haven by steam. By the end of the year Moore's company changed management; the plan to build to Benton Harbor was never completed.

When the five-year lease on the property expired on May 31, 1916, the original owners returned to operate it as a steam road. In 1923 the SH&E portion of the route was returned to the PMRR, who continued to operate the line from Paw Paw to South Haven, but abandoned the Paw Paw to Lawton portion. The original KLS&C trackage from Lawton to Kalamazoo was then abandoned on August 7, 1923. On July 3, 1929, all property was liquidated, and the right-of-way from Kalamazoo to Mattawan was sold to American Telephone & Telegraph Company.

Connections with the Benton Harbor-St. Joseph Railway & Light Company cars were made at Paw Paw Lakes. Here KLS&CRy 35 meets BHSJR&L 74.
Sumner Collection

Here is the Kalamazoo depot of KLS&CRy. Development of any through freight service was doomed by a lack of interchange arrangements with MCRR.
Lenderink Collection

The *City of South Haven* enters the South Haven harbor. Built in 1903 at Toledo, Ohio, by the Craig Ship Building Co., for the Dunkley-Williams Co., she was sold in 1918 to the U.S. Navy. By 1920 she was renamed the *City of Miami* and owned by the Havana & America S.S. Corp. In 1922 or 1923, she was sold to the Crosby Transportation Co. and renamed the *E. G. Crosby*. She operated between Milwaukee and Grand Haven or Muskegon until 1925 or 1926, then was removed from service and laid up until she burned December 3, 1935.

Milwaukee Public Library-Marine Collection

KALAMAZOO, LAKE SHORE & CHICAGO RY.

		5	3	1	Oct 29 1916	8	2	4		
		PM	PM	AM	Lv Amer. Exp. Ar	AM	AM	PM		
......	......	*6 45	†3 00	†7 45	0	KALAMAZOO..	6 50	10 55	4 40	......	......
......	......	6 68	3 15	7 59	5	....Oshtemo.....	6 38	10 40	4 27	......	......
......	......				7	....Brighton....	*6 35			......	......
......	......	*6 04	*3 23	*8 05	8	......Rix.....	*6 32	10*35	*4 18	......	......
......	......				9	....Walker.....	*6 30			......	......
......	......				10	....Eassom.....				......	......
......	......	6 15	3 38	8 15	13	...Mattawan...	6 22	10 25	4 10	......	......
......	......	6 20	3 45	8 20	15	....Newbre ...	6 16	10 20	4 05	......	......
......	......	6 25	4 00	8 25	17	....Lawton....	6 10	10 15	4 00	......	......
......	......	6 65			22	Ar..Paw Paw..Lv	†6 00	10 05	3 50	......	......
......	......	PM	4 10	8 40		Lv..Paw Paw..Ar	AM	AM		......	......
......	......				25	....Barrison....				......	......
......	......	*4 22	*8 50	27	..Lake Cora..	*9 55	*3 38		......	......	......
......	......	4 32	9 00	31	...Lawrence ...	9 43	3 28		......	......	......
......	......	4 47	9 15	38	Ar..Hartford...Ar	9 30	3 15		......	......	......
......	......	4 52	9 30		Lv..Hartford...Ar	9 15	3 15		......	......	......
......	......	*5 08	*9 42	43	....Toquin....	*9 00	*1 10		......	......	......
......	......	5 15	9 50	47	....Covert....	8 52	1 10		......	......	......
......	......	*5 21	*9 55	50	...Packard....	*8 43	*1 03		......	......	......
......	......	*5 25	*9 59	52	...Fruitland...	8 39	12*59		......	......	......
......	......	5 35	10 10	55	SOUTH HAVEN	†8 30	12†50		......	......	......
		PM	AM		Ar Lv	AM	PM			

Goodrich
Transit
Company

Goodrich Steamer Alabama, Muskegon, Mich.

The *City of Indiana* was built in 1890 at Manitowoc for the Goodrich Transportation Co. This photo shows the ship prior to lengthening, which occurred in 1916. She was condemned in 1928, and about 1936 she was scrapped.
Milwaukee Public Library-Marine Collection

Two views of the *Alabama*; above at Muskegon, at right taken July 20, 1941, at Sturgeon Bay, Wisconsin. The ship was built in 1910 at Manitowoc, Wisconsin, for the Goodrich Co. which operated it until 1933. Various owners operated it until 1946, and about 1964 it was rebuilt into a barge.
Milwaukee Public Library-Marine Collection

154

Northern Michigan Transportation Company

The *Illinois* was built in 1899 at Chicago for the Northern Michigan Transportation Co. From 1922 until 1932 the Goodrich Line owned the ship, after which she had various owners and ran on various routes until scrapping in 1947.
Milwaukee Public Library-Marine Collection

Indiana Transportation Company

The *Theodore Roosevelt* was built in 1906 at Toledo for the Indiana Transportation Co. Considered the fastest of the lake ships, she was a navy training ship during World War I. She was 275.6 feet in length and could carry 3500 day passengers. Operating under various owners (including the Boblo Boat Company for one season) through the years, she was scrapped in 1950.
Milwaukee Public Library-Marine Collection

Freight and Work Equipment

A 1915 view of freight motor 902 and train, northbound on the private right-of-way adjacent to the Michigan Railway freight house, at the corner of Front and Fulton streets in Grand Rapids.

Hague Collection

Pantograph-equipped No. 902 leads a southbound stock train at Gull Lake Junction in 1915.

Company Photo

A freight unit in service on the high-speed line.

Lenderink Collection

An early freight motor is at Parma.

Schramm Collection

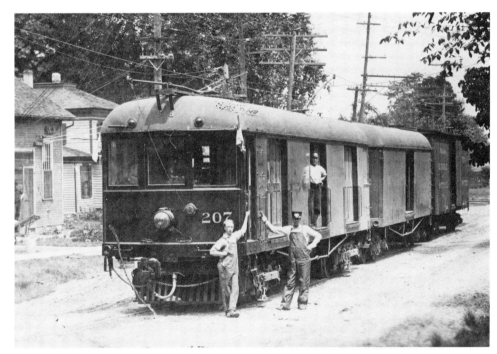

Built in 1911 by McGuire-Cummings, number 207 was part of a six-unit order of these double-ended box motors. This view is in front of the Augusta depot and substation.

Schramm Collection

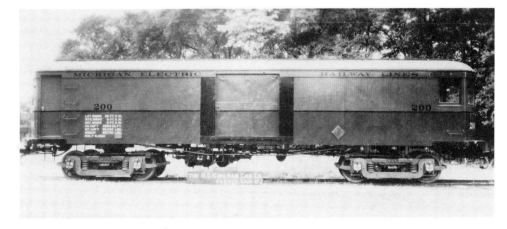

Box motor 200 was one of two built in 1924 by the Kuhlman Car Company. It was sold in 1929 to the Northern Ohio Interurban Company.

Schramm Collection

This Kalamazoo terminal view shows the nearly filled freight yard. Note the large snow plows on the box motors, which were used to clear the line.

Krambles Collection

Michigan, No. 1000, the business car of Michigan Railway, at the Taylorville shops in Albion.

Schramm Collection

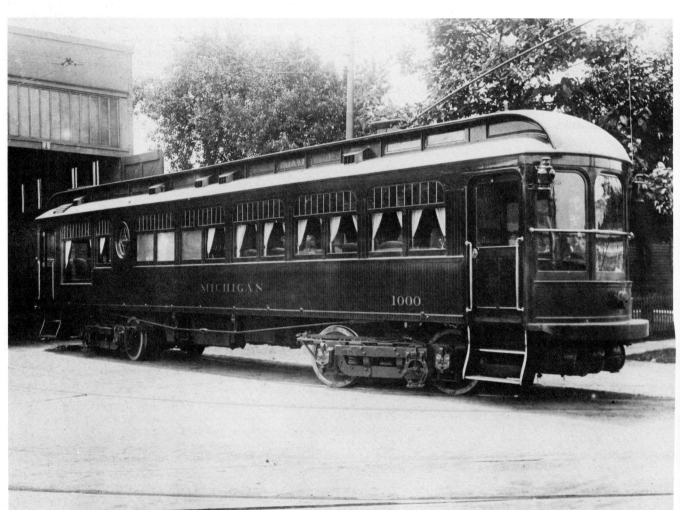

158

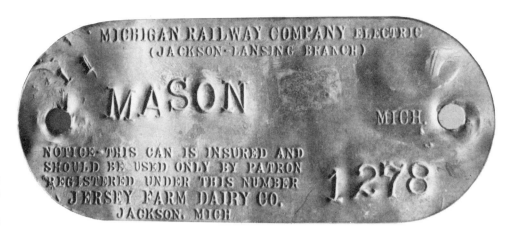

A metal tag, which was permanently attached to the milk cans.

Schramm Collection

GRGH&M freight motor 113 was a rolling advertisement for interurban freight service.

Ferriss Collection

We are looking west at Michigan Railway's main shops at Taylorville located just west of Albion.

Faber Collection

One picture *is* worth a thousand words. A westbound Greyhound bus is parked in front of the joint Greyhound-Intertown depot in Wayne, sometime during the mid-1950s. Note the newer pavement in the center of Michigan Avenue where the interurban track had been. The station is now a restaurant. *Wayne Historical Society*

7

INTERURBAN AND SUBURBAN BUS SERVICE

A FEW HARDY SOULS operated primitive motor buses prior to the paved roads, using truck chassis outfitted with seats to transport passengers. Others used vehicles with large and ungainly wheels to negotiate the deep rutted roads in an early attempt to provide bus service to outlying areas. As the state began paving the major roads from Detroit to nearby cities, a new interurban competitor came on the scene, the touring car. Many were operated by individuals, some of whom formed owners' associations.

An early company on which we found data was the Detroit Rapid Transit Company, linking Detroit to Ann Arbor, Flint, Port Huron, Wyandotte and Grosse Ile. It filed for incorporation on March 19, 1921, under provisions of Act 232 of the Public Acts of 1903, and sought authority to issue $5,000 in capital stock. The purpose was to operate a system of automobile transportation. By August 9, 1921, it had sold $3,850 in stock and purchased five automobiles. It then requested approval to increase the stock to $500,000, and to issue and sell at that time $60,000.

In November 1921, it began operations and issued its first timetable. On February 16, 1922, the company requested an increase of $50,000 in stock and indicated to the state it had purchased 13 cars for passenger service. Twenty-two automobiles were obtained to carry freight and personal property.

The February 1922, *Bus Transportation* magazine reported the company was operating fourteen 6-66 Paige passenger cars and eighteen 3½-ton Paige and Reo Speed Wagons for freight. By May 1922, it reported service between Ann Arbor and Detroit was suspended when the MPUC prohibited the company from carrying more then six passengers per vehicle.

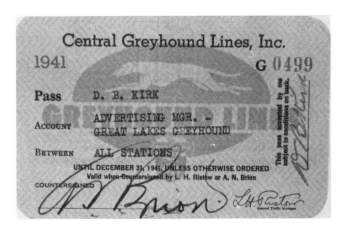

After taking over Highway Motorbus Company, People's Motor Coach continued to operate under its name until 1928. Here's coach 272-6P in a photo dated March 9, 1927. It was an ACF model 508-2-B3; its chassis serial number was 21304. This ACF design was patterned after the Fageol Safety Coach.

Schramm Collection

In January 1922, another potential competitor was the Highway Transportation Company. It planned to operate a belt line going out Michigan Avenue, to Wayne, to Northville and back to Detroit via Grand River Avenue. A second line was to go out Michigan Avenue to Ypsilanti and Ann Arbor. This firm planned to use four 23-passenger bus bodies on Commerce truck chassis. Detroit city officials wanted HTC to turn back at the city limits, saying the streets were already congested with buses and interurbans.

A statewide chart of buses and touring cars as of November 1922, showed Detroit to Ann Arbor served by 15 touring cars and no buses. A quote from an interesting article stated, "The electric interurbans have been the victims of the private touring car competitor more than that of bus transportation. There are several routes, most of them originating from Detroit, where passenger cars are being operated by individual

owners." This information and chart came from the *Bus Transportation* issue of December 1922.

Buses Replace Touring Cars

The Highway Motor Bus Company (this company name also often appeared as one word, "Motorbus") filed for permission to incorporate and issue $25,000 in stock on March 4, 1922. Even though we do not know when actual operations began, the company was an early property taken over by the DUR bus system. After the incorporation of Peoples Motor Coach on September 14, 1924, the DUR quickly expanded its bus lines.

On October 1, 1924, the first bus line began from Detroit to Wyandotte, Trenton and Grosse Ile. Then on November 10, 1924, Ann Arbor newspapers were reporting the Peoples Motor Coach would take over the Highway Motor Bus Company the following week.

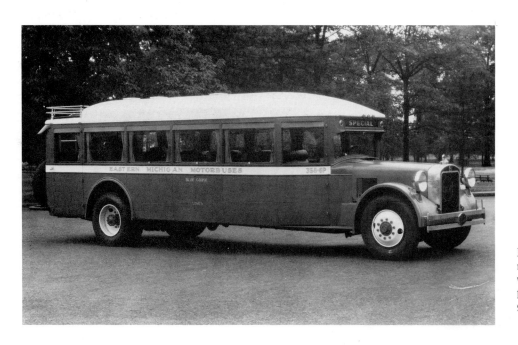

In 1929 twelve of these ACF model 508-12-P12s, equipped with Hall-Scott engines, were purchased by Eastern Michigan Motorbuses.

Schramm Collection

DETROIT—YPSILANTI—ANN ARBOR—JACKSON SCHEDULE

Effective June 18, 1927.   Light Figures A. M. Dark Figures P. M.   **Subject to change without notice**

STATIONS		WEST BOUND FROM DETROIT TO JACKSON

STATIONS		E			E		E		E			E		E		E		E			E		E			E			E		E	E	E
Detroit	Lv	7 30		8 30	9 30	9 55	10 30		11 30		12 30		1 30	1 55	2 30	3 30		4 30	5 30	5 55	6 30	7 30		8 55	9 30	11 30							
Ypsilanti	"	8 50		9 50	10 50	11 15	11 50	12 50	1 15		1 50	2 50	3 15		3 50	4 50		5 50	6 50	7 15	7 50	8 50		10 15	10 50	12 50							
Bon Air	"	9 00		10 00	11 00	11 25	12 00	1 00	1 25		2 00	3 00			4 00	5 00		6 00	7 00	7 25	8 00			10 25	11 00	1 00							
Ann Arbor	Ar	9 10		10 10	11 10	11 35	12 10	1 10	1 35		2 10	3 10	3 35		4 10	5 10		6 10	7 10	7 35	8 10	9 10		10 35	11 10	1 10							
Ann Arbor	Lv		9 40						1 40				3 40					5 40		7 40			9 40										
Lima Center	"		10 05						2 05				4 05					6 05		8 05			10 05										
Chelsea	"		10 15			12 05			2 15				4 15					6 15		8 15			10 15										
Sylvan	"		10 25			12 15			2 25				4 25					6 25		8 25			10 25										
Grass Lake	"		10 40			12 30			2 40				4 40					6 40		8 40			10 40										
Leoni	"		10 45			12 45			2 45				4 45					6 45		8 45			10 45										
Jackson	Ar		11 05			1 05			3 05				5 05					7 05		9 05			11 05										

STATIONS		EAST BOUND FROM JACKSON TO DETROIT

STATIONS		E		E		E		E		E		E		E		E		E		E
Jackson	Lv			7 40		9 40		11 40		1 40		3 40		5 40		7 40			
Leoni	"			8 00		10 00		12 00		2 00		4 00		6 00		8 00			
Grass Lake	"			8 05		10 05		12 05		2 05		4 05		6 05		8 05			
Sylvan	"			8 20		10 20		12 20		2 20		4 20		6 20		8 20			
Chelsea	"			8 30		10 30		12 30		2 30		4 30		6 30		8 30			
Lima Center	"			8 40		10 40		12 40		2 40		4 40		6 40		8 40			
Ann Arbor	Ar			9 05		11 05		1 05		3 05		5 05		7 05		9 05			
Ann Arbor	Lv	6 40	7 10	7 40	8 40		9 40	10 40	11 40	12 40	1 40	2 40	3 40	4 40	5 40	6 40	7 10	7 40	8 40	10 30
Bon Air	"	6 50	7 20	7 50	8 50		9 50	10 50	11 50	12 50	1 50	2 50	3 50	4 50	5 50	6 50	7 20	7 50	8 50	10 40
Ypsilanti	"	7 00	7 30	8 00	9 00		10 00	11 00	12 00	1 00	2 00	3 00	4 00	5 00	6 00	7 00	7 30	8 00	9 00	10 50
Detroit	Ar	8 20	8 50	9 20	10 20		11 20	12 20	12 50	1 20	3 20	4 20	4 50	6 20	6 50	7 20	8 20	8 50	10 20	12 10

E or F—Denotes Trips Traversing Ecorse Road or M-23 from Ypsilanti to Detroit.   All other trips traverse Michigan Avenue or M-17.   *—Sundays and Holidays only.

HIGHWAY MOTORBUS CO.   OTHER CONNECTIONS ON REVERSE SIDE.   **PIERCE MOTORBUS CO.**
A. L. DRUM, RECEIVER   *On Signalling Buses at night do so with a Lantern, Flash-Light or Flare.*

ANN ARBOR—Board of Commerce Inn.   JACKSON—M. E. R. Interurban Station   DETROIT—Union Bus Terminal, 502 Grand River Ave. W.
Phone 3589   207 Francis Street   Phone Randolph 4180—4181

A June 18, 1927 bus schedule. Note the company spelling of Motorbus—it has been found in the *Russell Bus Guide* either as one or two words.

The line continued to operate under the old name until reorganization in 1928 as Eastern Michigan Motorbuses.

Buses replaced electric interurbans as early as 1925. The interurban line from Ypsilanti to Saline was abandoned on September 27 of that year and was replaced by buses on October 15, 1925—the DUR's first known interurban replacement. On January 1, 1926, the Detroit to Ann Arbor bus line was extended from Ann Arbor to Jackson. Then a new route to Ann Arbor was started, using the newly-paved Ecorse Road. The route used Fort Street, Oakwood Boulevard and Ecorse Road to Ypsilanti, then on Ann Arbor-Jackson Road to Jackson. On October 23, 1926, Pierce Motor Company started competing service on Ecorse Road, but by June 18, 1927, Peoples Motor Coach had purchased Pierce Motor at a cost of $32,000. The two routes continued to be operated from Detroit to Ann Arbor. One used Michigan Avenue, the second route to Jackson used the former Pierce connection to Ann Arbor then on the Ann Arbor-Jackson Road to Jackson.

Eastern Michigan Motorbuses

Peoples Motor Coach continued to grow while the rail system shrank. When the DUR was reorganized in September 1928, as the Eastern Michigan System, Peoples Motor Coach became Eastern Michigan Motorbuses. On October 5, 1928, the MPUC approved the name change of all companies, including subsidiaries such as Highway Motor Bus, to EMM with the payment of a $16,537 fee. The fee covered the licensing of the 141 buses the company now owned, of which 13 were assigned to the Detroit-Jackson line.

The onset of the Great Depression did not spare the buses. On November 7, 1931, the Eastern Michigan System, which included both rail and bus lines, went into receivership. Two receivers were appointed; A.L. Drum, who was president of EMS, and the Detroit Trust Company. Two complaints had been filed; one by Detroit Edison for $3,725 in unpaid electric bills and supplies. The second was by U.S. Rubber Company, totaling $7,832 for bus tires.

From the DUR's first bankruptcy on March 10, 1925, up to late 1931, only one bus operation had been discontinued. Port Huron city officials refused to give EMM a cost-plus contract to continue operating buses after the streetcars stopped running on January 28, 1930. EMM did continue running buses there until a new company, Carpenter's Rapid Transit Company, took over on June 15, 1930.

During receivership, all remaining rail interurban operations were discontinued by May 31, 1934. Streetcar lines in Pontiac were dropped on November 15, 1931, and the replacement bus lines met the same fate on September 22, 1932. On June 17, 1933, the Ann Arbor city bus lines were relinquished.

Receivership for Eastern Michigan Motorbuses ended on August 31, 1934, but not for the Eastern Michigan Railways. The only remaining rail operation, Flint City Lines, continued until April 5, 1936.

Eastern Michigan Railways was reorganized by bondholders, and on August 5, 1938, was incorporated as the Eastern Michigan Transportation Corp. The EMR owned all the capital stock, 400,000 shares, of EMM, Flint Trolley Coach, Inc., and various properties in Detroit and Flint.

As a part of the reorganization, a foreclosure was filed on December 6, 1938, with the sale taking place February 9, 1939. The amount received was $2,000,020, the minimum amount the court would allow. The court noted if sold separately, the EMM stock would bring at least $1,250,000. Sale was confirmed February 27, 1939, and purchase price was payable in stock of the Eastern Michigan Transportation Corp. (EMTC). Greyhound owned $1,380,500; constituting approximately 41% first mortgage bonds, and $323,500, constituting 7% adjustment mortgage bonds. Under reorganization Greyhound received 39%, Pacific Michigan 30%, with the balance going to other bondholders.

Curiously, one such bondholder was the Department of Street Railway. In the commission minutes dated March 7, 1940, it was recorded that the DSR claim against EMR was $33,000 for use of city car tracks, and EMTC sent DSR notice it would receive 1/10 share in stock for each $100 unit of its claim. For any balance of less that $100 the DSR would receive 3% cash settlement.

Actually, the DSR was offered $200 for its share by the EMTC local manager. But the DSR held out and decided to take the stock, a wise decision. The claim was finally settled, per the commission minutes of October 2, 1942, when DSR accepted $1,566.71. Also ap-

proved was the sale of 33 shares of stock for $14 per share; this was the balance due the DSR for maintaining interchange facilities until November 8, 1931.

The Hound Noses In

From 1935 until Greyhound's takeover in 1941, expansion continued. One takeover that greatly affected this corridor was in 1935 when EMM took over the Southern Michigan Transportation Company's intercity bus lines. Southern Michigan had its beginnings on June 27, 1925, with routes from Kalamazoo to Jackson and Jackson to Lansing.

Then on July 10, 1925, the Rapid Transportation Company filed for incorporation for a route from Bay City to Flint. On March 2, 1929, the Michigan Electric Shares Corporation was incorporated as a result of reorganization of the Michigan Electric Railway. It now controlled the city streetcar lines in Battle Creek, Jackson, Kalamazoo and Lansing, along with the city bus lines and interurban bus routes.

The bus lines were operated by the Southern Michigan Transportation Company, which in May 1929, took over the Rapid Transportation Company from bondholders of the Michigan Railroad Company. It now controlled 203 miles of bus routes. On January 31, 1935, Eastern Michigan completed the purchase of Southern Michigan Transportation Company.

The other large EMM takeover was Great Lakes Motor Bus Company, which had many miles of routes but few buses. This company was formed in 1931 and operated from Detroit to Sault Ste. Marie. On July 31,

Detroit—Ypsilanti—Ann Arbor—Jackson Schedule
EASTERN TIME

Effective October 11, 1928   Light Figures A. M.   Dark Figures P. M.   Subject to change without n

STATIONS											WEST BOUND FROM DETROIT TO JACKSON														
	X	E			E			E			E			E			E	△		△E	†E		E		
DETROIT........Lv.	7 30	7 55	8 30	9 30	9 55	10 30	11 30	11 55	12 30	1 30	1 55	2 30	3 30	3 55	4 30	5 30	5 55	6 30	7 30	7 55	8 55	9 30	11 30		
YPSILANTI........"	8 50	9 15	9 50	10 50	11 15	11 50	12 50	1 15	1 50	2 50	3 15	4 00	5 00	5 25	5 50	6 50	7 15	7 50	8 50	9 15	10 15	10 50	12 50		
Bon Air........"	9 00	9 25	10 00	11 00	11 25	12 00	1 00	1 25	2 00	3 00	3 25		5 25		6 00	7 00	7 25	8 00	9 00	9 25	10 25	11 00	1 00		
ANN ARBOR........Ar.	9 10	9 35	10 10	11 10	11 35	12 10	1 10	1 35	2 10	3 10	3 35	4 10	5 10	5 35	6 10	7 10	7 35	8 10	9 10	9 35	10 35	11 10	1 10		
ANN ARBOR........Lv.		9 40			11 40			1 40			3 40			5 40			7 40			9 40					
Lima Center........"		10 05			12 05			2 05			4 05			6 05			8 05			10 05					
Chelsea........"		10 15			12 15			2 15			4 15			6 15			8 15			10 15					
Sylvan........"		10 25			12 25			2 25			4 25			6 25			8 25			10 25					
Grass Lake........"		10 40			12 40			2 40			4 40			6 40			8 40			10 40					
Leoni........"		10 45			12 45			2 45			4 45			6 45			8 45			10 45					
JACKSON........Ar.		11 05			1 05			3 05			5 05			7 05			9 05			11 05					

STATIONS							EAST BOUND FROM JACKSON TO DETROIT												
				E		E		E		E		E		E			△E		
JACKSON........Lv.				7 40		9 40		11 40		1 40		3 40		5 40			7 40		
Leoni........"				8 00		10 00		12 00		2 00		4 00		6 00			8 00		
Grass Lake........"				8 05		10 05		12 05		2 05		4 05		6 05			8 05		
Sylvan........"				8 20		10 20		12 20		2 20		4 20		6 20			8 20		
Chelsea........"				8 30		10 30		12 30		2 30		4 30		6 30			8 30		
Lima Center........"				8 40		10 40		12 40		2 40		4 40		6 40			8 30		
ANN ARBOR........Ar.	X			9 05		11 05		1 05		3 05		5 05		7 05		△	9 05	†	
ANN ARBOR........Lv.	7 10	7 40	8 40	9 10	9 40	11 10	11 40	1 10	1 40	2 40	3 10	3 40	4 40	5 10	5 40	6 40	7 10	7 40	8 40	9 10	9 30
Bon Air........"	7 20	7 50	8 50	9 20	9 50	10 50	11 20	11 50	12 50	1 50	2 50	3 20	4 00	4 50	5 20	5 50	6 50	7 20	7 50	8 50	9 2.	10 40
YPSILANTI........"	7 30	8 00	9 00	9 30	10 00	11 00	11 30	12 00	1 00	1 30	2 00	3 00	3 30	4 09	5 00	5 30	6 00	7 00	7 30	8 00	9 00	9 30	10 40
DETROIT........Ar.	8 50	9 20	10 20	10 50	11 20	12 20	12 50	1 20	2 20	2 50	3 20	4 20	4 50	5 20	6 20	6 50	7 20	8 20	8 50	9 20	10 20	10 50	12 10

X—Mondays and Saturdays only.   †—Sundays and Holidays only.   △—Saturdays, Sundays and Holidays only.
E—Denotes Trips Traversing Ecorse Rd. or U. S. 25 and M-17 from Ypsilanti to Detroit.

An October 11, 1928 bus schedule shows increased service.

1937, Eastern Michigan gained control of Great Lakes Motor Bus. On Septembr 27, 1938, agreement was reached for EMM to purchase all assets, assume all liabilities and dissolve the company.

Eastern Michigan was now the state's largest intrastate bus company. In 1940 it operated lines from Detroit and Port Huron to Grand Rapids, Toledo to Sault Ste Marie. It had a network of 1,410 highway miles; annually its coaches traveled 9,605,642 miles, carrying 9,894,595 passengers. It delivered 1,750,000 lbs. of newspapers; carried 2,000,000 lbs. of package express and 30,000 lbs. of government material. The charter business for 1940 amounted to 203,024 passengers.

At this time Greyhound was poised to become a major player in Michigan's bus sweepstakes, but its first attempt hit a snag. In September 1939, Greyhound was denied approval by the ICC in its attempt to take over Eastern Michigan. The reason given was "lack of competition between Detroit and Battle Creek other than one railroad which owns a substantial interest in Central Greyhound." An earlier opinion noted that Central Greyhound was jointly owned by Greyhound Corp. and the New York Central, each holding half the voting stock.

Greyhound was already playing a major policy-setting role, and Eastern Michigan Motorbuses routes and schedules were set up to augment Greyhound through these years.

Finally, approval was received and on April 1, 1941, Greyhound took over Eastern Michigan. On June 11, 1941, Great Lakes Greyhound Lines, Inc. was formed. Today, Greyhound operates this corridor using expressways and Michigan Avenue via Wayne and Ypsilanti through Ann Arbor to Jackson. Here the line splits, with one route via Kalamazoo and Benton Harbor to Chicago; and the second via South Bend to Chicago.

Southern Michigan Transportation Company purchased ACF's model 508-12-B11 in 1929. Number 35 here has the name *Austin Blair* on each side. These early buses were named after well-known Michigan persons including state officials.
Motor Bus Society Inc.

This earlier model bus, operated by Southern Michigan by 1925, is probably a White. The November 1925 *Bus Transportation* captioned it, "Type of parlor car bus now being operated over the highways of Michigan."
Detroit Public Library

The Garwood Buses

Two different Garwood buses. Top: Coach 640-8P model DFI was operated by Great Lakes Motor Bus Co. which ran between Detroit and Sault Ste. Marie. Below is coach 611-8E model CFI, purchased in 1937 by EMM. Both buses were powered by Ford V-8 engines.

Motor Bus Society, Inc.

An interior view of a Garwood bus. The center aisle is lower, allowing more headroom; this was due to the rear engine. These early streamlined buses were designed by Bill Stout who was also famous for his airplane designs.

Schramm Collection

166

The
A.C.F. Buses

The ACF buses were popular with both Peoples Motor Coach and Eastern Michigan Motorbuses. Both of these buses were model H-9-Ps. The upper, 589, was purchased in 1937; the lower, 626, was purchased in 1938. Note the difference in the paint schemes.

Motor Bus Society, Inc.

An interior view of the ACF coaches shows its comfortable seating.
Motor Bus Society, Inc.

The Victory Coaches

WORLD WAR II turned Detroit into the living embodiment of Franklin D. Roosevelt's description of the U.S. as a whole: The Arsenal of Democracy. Old factories quickly became jammed to capacity; new factories were built. And all these workers had to be carried by public transit to and from the employment centers. Many new plants were built away from existing public transit.

One such factory was Henry Ford's giant Willow Run bomber plant, built in a cornfield four miles from Ypsilanti and 27 miles from Detroit. One of the area's early expressways (the Ford) was built to connect Detroit and the plant.

As late as August 1941, the plant was still only a blueprint. But by June 1, 1942, there were 16,000 employees at work, with 500 being added weekly. The ultimate work force was to be 60,000.

Willow Run workers would be drawn from an area of 400 square miles including 122 towns and villages. This area was divided up and a network of 23 bus routes established. Additionally, the DSR provided express runs from Detroit (after serving a waiver of its statuatory ten-mile limitation). Service was started on April 15, 1942, with two Short way and two Greyhound routes serving the plant. By September 1942, Greyhound had 35 coaches assigned to service Willow Run.

Greyhound started planning for this heavy movement of workers in June of 1941. With gas and tire rationing a possibility and replacement parts becoming scarcer, the increasing need for public transit was apparent. Greyhound wanted a crowd-swallowing vehicle, and after obtaining a car haulaway trailer, had it rebuilt for passenger service by Baker Body Co. of St. Louis. After testing the vehicle and receiving approval for its use from the ODT and other regulators, Greyhound obtained additional units.

On April 12, 1943, the first haulaway trailers began running between Ann Arbor and Willow Run. By August 1943, there were 35 in service on additional routes from Detroit to Wyandotte, Willow Run and Pontiac, and from Flushing to Flint.

These Victory Coaches, as they were called, carried 45 seated and 50 standee passengers. Their longitudinal seats had no springs, but were padded. The exit was in the rear, while the entrance was near the front. The trailer-bus carried a crew of two; a driver up front and collectorette, who handled the fares. The latter position was filled by a woman who reported directly to the accounting department. All were guaranteed employment for the duration plus six months.

Three large *Victory Coaches* are loading at Willow Run. Though not popular with riders, they did move great amounts of workers to and from the war plants.
Motor Bus Society, Inc.

This was another one of the *Victory Coaches*, with its crew of two, posing in Wyandotte. The trailer was numbered TB-25 and the tractor 6980.
Dworman Photo

In 1940, with Greyhound controlling Eastern Michigan Motorbuses, the last order went to Yellow Coach (GMC). Shown here with a Jackson destination sign is 24-passenger 702, model PG 2901.

Motor Bus Society, Inc.

Suburban Operations

As was the case with the other avenues radiating from Detroit, Michigan Avenue developed both intercity and suburban bus services. As previously detailed, the intercity routes were quickly taken over by Peoples Motor Coach, leaving the local and suburban services to the Detroit Motorbus Company (DMC).

There may have been a local bus service in the Dearborn area prior to the start of the DMC local service in 1925. Today, Dearborn encompasses two communities, the western part being the original "old" Dearborn. Here is where a military post was once located; nearby is Greenfield Village and the Henry Ford Museum. The eastern portion originally was Springwells, later renamed Fordson. The giant Ford Rouge plant is in this section.

DMC received approval to organize on February 3, 1919, from the MPUC and then filed articles of association with the secretary of state. On April 30, 1919, authority to sell stock was granted with a provision that the following had to be stated on each stock: "The ordinances of the city of Detroit under which the company will operate, provided that any license issued there under, shall be subject to renewal or revocation or alteration of the ordinance." With this restriction in place of the usual franchise guaranteeing a certain number of years' operation, stock was found difficult to sell.

At an earlier meeting, DMC's directors resolved that they would not begin operation without at least 50 buses. After six frustrating months of attempting to sell its impaired stock, the organizers considered abandoning the project. But they felt there was a need for augmented public transit in Detroit after the long 30-year "traction war" which was just ending. So, during February and March 1920, the company was reorganized.

169

The First Buses Arrive

In September 1919, the company requested Fifth Avenue Coach Company of New York City to send a bus, along with a crew to drive and repair it. On September 21, 1919, bus 702 arrived in Detroit. It made its first trip on Woodward Avenue from Grand Circus Park to Jefferson. The event was a media attraction with police escorts and movie cameras recording the trip. The bus continued giving free trips around the downtown area until the spring of 1920.

The first buses purchased were all double-deckers built by Fifth Avenue. They were of two types; the 500 series with right hand drive and 700 series with left hand drive. The buses seated 48 and featured open upper decks, which were not precisely suited to Detroit's climate. After several attempts, a way was found to partially enclose them to protect passengers during bad weather. Then there were Detroit's low bridges, which meant lowering the chassis on the first bus models.

The first revenue service began June 11, 1920, on the East Jefferson line from Water Works Park to Grand Circus Park at Woodward and Adams. DMC started with eleven buses on an eight-minute headway, which was soon reduced to four minutes as additional buses arrived.

Detroit's bus service during the first years expanded rapidly, as noted in the following report dated May 28, 1926.

Year	Miles Operated	Route Miles	Passengers	Buses Oper.
1920*	623,355	13.5	2,335,475	22
1921	2,489,571	18.3	9,135,605	52
1922	3,547,946	22.7	14,322,026	74
1923	4,922,543	42.6	19,457,436	98
1924**	8,147,828	48.6	29,586,367	104
1925**	11,378,672	182.1	35,913,031	NA

On January 1, 1925, the DSR began its own bus operations, establishing a motor coach division. During the first year it expanded operations rapidly throughout the city. By the end of the year it was operating 18 bus lines and had in service over 150 small Dodge-Graham 21-passenger buses.

DMC To The Suburbs

With the DSR in the bus business, DMC's situation within the city limits became tenuous. Thus, the DMC began extending operations beyond the city limits. Unable to obtain a city franchise, or any assurance of remaining on Detroit's streets, DMC continued on a day-to-day basis. Suburban operations expanded through acquisitions, the DMC taking over Grosse Pointe Bus Company, Detroit, Northville and Milford

Coach Company, Renne Motor Transit Company, Brightmoor Transit Company, and routes to River Rouge, Redford, Dearborn, Big Beaver and Pontiac. The Grosse Pointe takeover and subsequent operations by Lake Shore Coach Lines was covered in *When Eastern Michigan Rode the Rails, Book 2*.

Most of these companies ran west or north of Detroit. The Big Beaver and Pontiac lines were sold to Martin Bus Company, which operated them until taken over by SEMTA in 1975. The Brightmoor and Redford lines were lost when the area they served was annexed to Detroit.

By the end of 1925 DMC was operating buses to Wayne, having taken over this route from Renne Motor Transit. Judging from photos of their equipment, Renne had been running to Wayne since 1923. On February 11, 1925, RMT filed "articles of association" with the MPUC, following that up on February 25, 1925, filing for approval to sell $50,000 in stock. After the takeover, this line became DMC route number 18. Later the line was extended to Belleville.

The line to Northville ran via Seven Mile Road, and the Plymouth route utilized Plymouth Road. This allowed more of a direct service to downtown Detroit than was possible by the interurban which ran from Northville via Wayne to downtown Detroit. This had much to do with the rail line's early demise.

Local Dearborn Service

The Springwells *Independent* on July 10, 1925, reported the city council's approval for Detroit Motorbus to build a garage on Ford Road near Miller Road, to be completed by October 1. These were the years of great

Shown after the Greyhound takeover is an ex-EMM (ACF model H-9-P) coach now repainted in Greyhound colors, in 1942 or 1943 in Ypsilanti. *Motor Bus Society, Inc.*

This photo was taken at Plymouth Road and Southfield in 1920. It is not known where or how the Frischkorn Company made connections with other lines.
Collections of Henry Ford Museum and Greenfield Village

expansion in Dearborn and surrounding areas due to the building of the Ford Rouge plant. Now the DMC could compete with the DSR rail and bus lines in serving this new facility. At the same meeting on July 10, 1925, the DSR received approval to use Warren, Michigan and Coolidge (Schaefer) to reach the plant.

On April 18, 1927, the DMC began operating from Warren & Coleman to the Ford plant during shift changes. By March 1, 1928, the DMC had in operation three new lines; one from Michigan and Division (Greenfield) Road to Ford Road, to Western Avenue and then to downtown Detroit via Michigan; one from Warren south into Fordson (Dearborn), and a line on Tireman from Wyoming to Division (Greenfield) Road. On January 1, 1932, this was taken over by the DSR.

DMC's position in Dearborn solidified on December 17, 1929, when it received a council resolution allowing it to operate up to 30 coaches on Dearborn streets. For this privilege it would be taxed $25 per year. This resolution was still in effect as late as February 1946.

Detroit was another matter. The Motor City was decidedly unfriendly and on January 1, 1932, the city of Detroit forced the DMC out of business entirely. DMC lines inside Detroit were taken over and became part of the DSR system. DMC suburban lines were parceled out to two separate companies under new names. The eastern suburban routes to the Grosse Pointe area went to the Lake Shore Coach Lines, Inc.

The western suburban routes to Dearborn, Wayne, Northville and Plymouth were retained by DMC for a brief period until on February 16, 1932, Dearborn Coach Company took over operations. C.A. Britt, who

had ten years with DMC, became president; while George Hind, who came with the first bus in 1919, and had started with Fifth Avenue in 1913, became vice-president.

By 1934 the company was operating 200 route miles in Dearborn on five lines. Sixty buses were owned with 55 buses in daily operation. Most came from the old DMC, but it is not known whether any were double-deckers. In 1933 they averaged 2,900 daily passengers; the following year it was 3,200.

In addition to Dearborn local routes, DCC provided service to the Ford Rouge Plant and to downtown Detroit. In 1934 the daily average of Ford workers carried was 1800; the average to Detroit was 2310.

In June 1935, Dearborn Coach filed with the MPUC to transfer a portion of its certificate to Lincoln Park Coach Company. Involved was the Fort Street line from Lincoln Park to the Ford plant, and the State Street line from Ecorse to Dearborn. The Lincoln Park operation appears to have been a subsidiary of Dearborn Coach and a small garage was maintained on Southfield Road in Lincoln Park.

With the approach of World War II, labor troubles increased. In June 1941, Dearborn Coach signed a closed shop agreement with Local 1265 of the Amalgamated Association of Street, Electric Railway and Motor Coach Employees of America. After that date strikes and walkouts seemed to become a yearly occurrence.

According to Bert Jasper, later president of the transit company, Dearborn Coach was sold in August 1946, to David Broderick. Britt resigned as president on August 27 and was succeeded by Broderick.

Not surprisingly, the company grew during the war years; in 1941 it operated 4,173,000 revenue miles; by

This 1923 bus, probably on a Reo chassis, was operated by Renne from Detroit out Michigan Avenue to Wayne. The photo was taken as an advertisement for Budd Wheel Corp.
Manning Brothers Historical Collection

1945 it topped seven million and carried over eight million passengers. During the war 87 buses were purchased; however, 77 had to be scrapped due to parts shortages. By 1947 DCC had 145 buses in operation, including 43 new 29-passenger Fords and ten 39-passenger GMC's. A joint passenger terminal was built in Wayne on Michigan Avenue.

Company shutdowns due to strikes became a cause for greater concern. On August 19, 1948, the Dearborn city council approved a jitney ordinance and 160 striking bus drivers promptly applied for jitney licenses. When the strike ended after 14 days, there were 167 jitneys operating in Dearborn.

Then in 1949, the Dearborn council advertised for another company to take over bus operations in Dearborn. The only reply came in September from Great Lakes Greyhound, which declined the invitation. In July 1949, the council drafted a tough new jitney ordinance which provided that if regular bus service was interrupted one week or more, the transit company's license to operate in Dearborn would be revoked.

Sure enough, in 1949 there was a 55-day strike, which, when finally settled, resulted in a paltry 1½ cent hourly wage increase. In October 1950, the operator's name was changed to Intertown Suburban Lines Corporation (Michigan); known as Intertown Suburban. According to a company flyer the new name was chosen to reflect the new lines and expanded services provided. It also noted the buses were to be painted in new colors of blue and gray.

In August 1954, Bert Jasper became president of Intertown Lines. Eventually, in March 1960, the American Transit Company of St. Louis, took over management. Jasper, however, remained as president, a post he held until Southeastern Michigan Transpor-

tation Authority (SEMTA) purchased the company.

During a lengthy Intertown strike from January 8 to February 18, 1962, the DSR extended its lines into Dearborn to provide some service. On February 19, 1962, the Metropolitan Transit, Inc., took over, and operated the lines until SEMTA took over on January 1, 1974. The Lincoln Park garage was not re-opened after the 1962 strike and service resumed with 60 buses, which later grew to 80 buses.

During these years bus service was gradually curtailed, and to quote Jasper "when SEMTA came about, it was the very thing we were looking for. It was a godsend." Now with SEMTA providing service, Bert Jasper, who started with DMC as a bus driver shortly after arriving from Scotland, could now enjoy his long planned and many times postponed retirement.

Local Buses

The main route out Michigan Avenue was the 18-mile Wayne line. Other routes included Cherry Hill and Garden City. The Wayne line used two inbound and outbound routes inside the city of Detroit. Some were marked "via Michigan Avenue," and ran on that street all the way. Most of the buses carried "via Lafayette-West Grand Blvd." markings, and turned off of Michigan at the Boulevard, went south to Lafayette and turned east there to reach downtown. In the 1950's Fort Street was used instead of Lafayette.

Cadillac Square was the principal loading area in downtown Detroit. Over the years both sides of the square were used. When the north side was utilized, loading was adjacent to the Family Theatre. Later, when the south side was used, outbound buses left downtown on Congress Street in order to return to Fort Street. Inbound buses were not permitted to pick

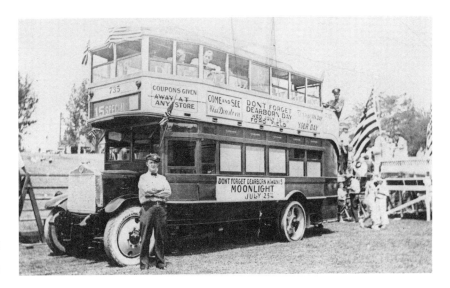

Detroit Motorbus 735 has ads showing scheduled events in and for Dearborn.
Bidigare Collection

THE expansion of the Detroit Motor Bus Co.'s service into Detroit's suburbs during 1925, as shown by this map of routes over which buses are now traveling, partly explains why America's fastest-growing city won that honor.

Not a single suburban line was in operation a year ago. Buses on routes which sprang into existence since May now cover 400,000 miles a month in the suburbs. Added to the 600,000 miles covered monthly by buses on city routes, the total for 300 buses now in service is 1,000,000 miles a month.

Nearly one-third of the total number of buses was added during 1925. And of the 98 new buses put into service since 1924, 80 are six-wheelers. Because of the increased efficiency gained in the use of the six-wheel type, it is the plan of the company to buy only this type in adding to its equipment, according to W. F. Evans, president.

Patronage is increasing steadily on all the suburban routes, the company announced Saturday. The latest additions are the Big Beaver route via Rochester road to Roches-

and Canton Center road to Plymouth; Redford route over the Six Mile road to Redford.

Two routes expected to be opened in 30 days are the Belleville between Wayne and Belleville, and the Canton Center, between Plymouth and Canton on the Canton Center road.

Application has been made for a franchise to run buses on with Woodward avenue, between Detroit and Pontiac. Other suburban routes include the Kercheval, Grosse Pointe, Birmingham, Northville, Wayne and Ford factories. The latter connects the Highland Park and Springwells plants of the Ford Motor Co.

To provide for further expansion the company is building a bus garage and a 400,000-gallon, underground, gasoline storage plant in Springwells and has purchased a site for another garage near Wayne. When the Springwells storage plant is completed, the bus company facilities will provide for storage of 1,000,000 gallons of gasoline.

The city routes are the Jefferson avenue; Cass avenue and Second

boulevard; Cass avenue and Grand boulevard; Lafayette boulevard; West Grand boulevard and Lafayette; John R street to Ford factory; John R and and Grand boulevard, and the Grand boulevard.

The earliest morning bus starts out at 5:43 a. m.; the last evening bus leaves the Windsor ferry at 1:02 a. m. Hourly service all day is furnished on the suburban lines with 15-minute service during rush hours.

ROCHESTER

PONTIAC

BIG BEAVER

OAKLAND HILLS COUNTRY CLUB

BIRMINGHAM

MAPLE ST.

CLAWSON

PROPOSED ----
PRESENT ——

ROYAL OAK

ELEVEN MI. ROAD

8 MILE ROAD

NORTHVILLE
SANITARIUM

SEVEN MILE ROAD

SIX MILE ROAD

FORD PLANT

PLYMOUTH

PLYMOUTH ROAD

GRAND RIVER

PURITAN

TIREMAN

MICHIGAN

FORD ROAD

DEARBORN

FORD PLANT

CANTON ---- WAYNE

BELLEVILLE   DETROIT MOTOR BUS CO. LINES

Ex-Detroit Motorbus 452 was still being operated by the Dearborn Coach Company when this January 20, 1937 photo was taken. It was a Safeway six-wheel bus built in 1925 at Philadelphia.
Manning Brothers Historical Collection

Like the DSR, Dearborn Coach purchased some of these small Ford buses with body by Union City Body Company, Union City, Indiana.
Dearborn Historical Commission

Another local system to purchase Garwood buses was Dearborn Coach Company. Here 302 is serving the Michigan Avenue route in 1936. Behind it, up the street, is an Eastern Michigan bus. This Garwood Model C used a rear-mounted Ford V-8 engine.
Collections of Henry Ford Museum and Greenfield Village

174

Dearborn Coach 817 has a winged emblem on its side.
Collections of Henry Ford Museum and Greenfield Village

Dearborn Coach 825 is at Outer Drive and Michigan passing St. Joseph's Retreat on its way to Detroit.
Collections of Henry Ford Museum and Greenfield Village

This photo of the world-famous Ford Rotunda features a number of Dearborn Coach Co. vehicles in varying paint schemes. The Rotunda, originally built for the 1933 Century of Progress Exposition in Chicago, was later moved to Schaefer Road in Dearborn, where it served many functions. It was destroyed by fire on November 9, 1962.
Collections of Henry Ford Museum and Greenfield Village

up any passengers inside Detroit, outbound they could not discharge passengers within the city. By 1961 the downtown stop had been changed to Michigan and Shelby.

In East Dearborn a number of local or feeder buses connected with the main line at Bingham Street, two blocks east of Schaefer. These locals included such names as Coleman, Steadman, and Salina. Here a connection could be made to reach Fort Street buses of the Lincoln Park division. In West Dearborn the heavy transfer point was Monroe Street, where North Loop, West Loop, Oxford Loop and South Loop locals served the residential areas.

Here, a connection to the Lincoln Park buses was possible. At Telegraph Road, the Garden City line split off to the north and went across Ford Road and eventually wound up in Wayne, with the direct Wayne line continuing on Michigan Avenue.

For a number of years a separate company, called Inkster Service Lines, Inc., met the main line at Inkster Road. Three Ford buses, painted cream with red trim, numbered 10, 20 and 30, were used on this loop line which served the south side of that community.

Wayne County General Hospital (Eloise) was another transfer point. From here a shuttle bus marked Nor-Wayne passed through a large housing development and met the main line again at the Wayne terminal.

DSR Service

When Henry Ford decided to move his major operations from Highland Park to the Dearborn Rouge plant, the DSR was faced with the necessity of major routing changes. Previously all main traffic was north-south, with the Ford plant on the north (in Highland Park) and downtown Detroit on the south. Now it would be east-west with extensions and new lines built to serve the plant. Rail lines would carry the heavy traffic at the outset, but soon buses would augment the service, carrying Detroit residents to work and home.

On June 30, 1930, the Coolidge bus line started tripper service along Coolidge, Michigan, and Miller Road to Ford Rouge gate #4. Beginning on June 22, 1931, and operating all days the plant was operating, service was given from the Woodward terminal in Highland Park to the Rouge plant gate #3.

Thus, the DSR became a major factor in Dearborn's public transit. In 1932, the DSR reported it was carrying 90,000 passengers in Dearborn by rail and bus.

Northville And Plymouth

One of the early companies on record in this area was the Outer Belt line which started in 1922 with four buses and operated from Pontiac to Walled Lake with a 60 cent fare. Then on May 23, 1925, the MPUC received an application to organize the Outer Belt Transit Lines and seeking permission to sell $35,000 in common stock. By 1926 the company was advertising in the *Plymouth Mail* and was operating from Mt. Clemens to Ann Arbor via Plymouth.

On July 4, 1927, Peoples Motor Coach purchased the line and operated it with four buses. On April 15, 1928, the Mt. Clemens to Pontiac portion was dropped, and by December was being run by the Pontiac-Mt. Clemens Coach Line. The Pontiac-Farmington-Northville-Plymouth-Ann Arbor portion of the line was operated by Greyhound until the early 1950's.

Valley Coach Lines operated the line from July 11, 1951, until March 22, 1952, when Bee Line took over. From February 1, 1979, until April 10, 1987, the line was operated by Tower Bus Lines, Inc. During its final years only a single round trip was made daily. A schedule in effect February 23, 1976, showed Bee Line again operating from Pontiac to Mt. Clemens, which remained part of the route until the end.

Additional bus service to Plymouth and Northville was provided by Detroit Motorbus in 1925. The Detroit, Northville and Milford Coach Company was purchased to obtain the Northville route. How Plymouth rights were obtained is not known. The first mention we found was in the *Plymouth Mail* on July 29, 1921. An advertisement appeared, offering a 50 cent one way fare, 90 cent round trip to downtown Detroit. Scheduled were four round trips daily. The name used in the advertisement was the Detroit-Plymouth Bus Company.

These routes had the advantage of going directly into downtown Detroit. The Northville line used Seven Mile Road and Grand River, while the Plymouth route used Plymouth Road and Grand River. After reorganization, Dearborn Coach briefly operated both lines, but decided shortly to sell them. Little data has been found on the operation of these two routes after the sale. We have a schedule, effective September 6, 1946, for the Plymouth Coach Company. It may have been the successors to the Dearborn Coach Company.

Plymouth Coach Company operated the Plymouth line until 1948 when Deluxe Stages took over. As of 1987, Deluxe still operated franchise service in the area. The Coverdale & Colpitts 1968 study for SEMTA noted that this operator offered one regularly scheduled route from Detroit to the House of Correction near Plymouth on Sundays only. The balance of its business was principally charter. Perhaps for this reason, Deluxe was not purchased by SEMTA.

The history of Northville Coach Company, likewise, is obscure. The first schedule we have is number 9, effective November 1, 1946. Northville Coach Lines was still operating to Northville in 1968. The Coverdale & Colpitts study listed it as operating 18 buses

Intertown coach 181 is sitting by the Ford World Headquarters on Michigan in Dearborn.
Bidigare Collection

LINCOLN PARK DIVISION		
ZONE 1 TICKET 15695		AM / PM
N	E	S	W

FROM	TO	FARE
CICOTTE APPLEWOOD	CICOTTE APPLEWOOD	10
GODDARD DIX	GODDARD DIX	
DETROIT	DETROIT	15
ALLEN OAKWOOD	ALLEN OAKWOOD	20
ALLEN OUTER DR.	ALLEN OUTER DR.	
ECORSE FELHAM	ECORSE FELHAM	25
GODDARD Mortinview	GODDARD Mortinview	30
ECORSE TELEGRAPH	ECORSE TELEGRAPH	
ECORSE MIDDLEBELT	ECORSE MIDDLEBELT	35
FORT SOUTHFIELD	SOUTHFIELD	40
FORT OAKDALE	FORT OAKDALE	
FORT EUREKA	FORT EUREKA	45
SOUTHFIELD JEFFERSON	SOUTHFIELD JEFFERSON	50
DIX OUTER DR.	DIX OUTER DR.	
MICH. MONROE	MICH. MONROE	55
FORDS	FORDS	E
FORT OAKWOOD	FORT OAKWOOD	
FORT OUTER DR.	FORT OUTER DR.	

DEARBORN COACH COMPANY
INTERTOWN LINES SYSTEM
COURTESY—SERVICE
1LS/D-66-RB-

INTERTOWN SUBURBAN

TRANSFER 12406

N	E	S	W

FROM LINE				TO LINE			
1	2	3	4	1	2	3	4
5	6	7	8	5	6	7	8
9	10	11	12	9	10	11	12
13	14	15	16	13	14	15	16
17	18	19	20	17	18	19	20
21	22	23	24	21	22	23	24
25	26	27	28	25	26	27	28
29	30	31	32	29	30	31	32
33	34	35	36	33	34	35	36
37	38	39	40	37	38	39	40

A - M	P - M	E

ZONE					
1	2	3	4	5	6
7	8	9	10	11	12

ILS D-58-RD-480M 1-51
ELLIOTT TICKET N. Y.   UNION PRINTERS

METROPOLITAN TRANSIT

N	E	06210	S	W

	1		L I N C O L N P A R K DIV.		6		21
1		2			5		22
2							23
3	WEST BOUND				4	EAST BOUND	24
4					3		25
5		5			2		26
6		6			1		
7	CROSS TOWN	1	2	3			27
8		4	5	6			28
9	ALLEN PARK	1	2	3			29
10		4					30
11	L. P. LOCAL	1		3			31
12	FORDS		M	S			32
13	LINCOLN PARK						33
14							34
15	MELVINDALE						35
16							36
17	MORTENVIEW						37
18							38
19	JIM DALY ROAD						39
20	A.M.		P.M.				E

177

Renne Motor Transit bus 105 was a Yellow Coach model 733. Little is known of this company's operations, except that during 1937 it received certificates to operate between Wayne and Ypsilanti, Ypsilanti and Detroit and also Wayne and New Boston.
Motor Bus Society, Inc.

and serving the northwestern portion of Detroit. In 1964 this company took on the DSR when it planned to expand service in the suburbs and receive more federal funding. In fact, DSR plans to extend its Seven Mile Road line to a shopping mall at Middlebelt Road were thwarted when the Northville Coach Lines went to court. This action not only stopped the planned expansion here, but also in other areas, when the court ruled the DSR was a common carrier and had to obey rules the same as any other operator.

Significantly, NCC's suit nullified a statewide vote in 1940 which had exempted the DSR from certain rules governing privately-owned common carriers. Northville Coach, since 1968, has been taken over by Shortway lines and a portion of its former route was operated by SEMTA until 1983.

Since 1978, SEMTA has operated a Park & Ride route from this area to downtown Detroit during the rush hours.

SEMTA is Created

With privately-owned bus systems generally on the ropes, in 1967 the Southeastern Michigan Transportation Authority was created to provide public transit for the counties of Wayne, Macomb, Monroe, Oakland, St. Clair and Washtenaw. Later, Livingston joined the first six to make it a seven county authority.

SEMTA has a mandate, but no muscle. Afraid of offending tight-fisted constituents, Michigan legislators created the framework for an enduring public transit solution—but left out the most important ingredient—funding.

Failure to provide taxing authority to pay for promised service improvements has to this day stymied SEMTA plans. One such promise is rail rapid transit for Detroit, long planned and dreamed of—especially in the Woodward corridor. As of 1987 nothing had

been done, even though on October 5, 1976, President Gerald Ford approved a $600 million federal commitment to build a system.

In fact, ground has been lost. All commuter rail service to Detroit from both Pontiac and Ann Arbor has vanished. Recently SEMTA, which had taken over the Pontiac service from the Grand Trunk Western Railroad, sold the last of its rail equipment. The final scheduled run from Pontiac was on October 14, 1983; however, a court order forced operation until the following Monday.

The Ann Arbor commuter train was operated under contract with Amtrak, which operated the *Executive* from 1975 until January 13, 1984. Its replacement was a SEMTA bus in the morning; in the evening the 5:25 p.m. Chicago-bound Amtrak train sufficed. Later Michigan Trailways operated the morning bus, subsidized by SEMTA. Finally on June 30, 1986, even that service was terminated when the subsidy was dropped, due to lack of funds.

Another problem in creating SEMTA was the failure to build it around Detroit's major in-city transit property, the Detroit Department of Transportation (the onetime Department of Street Railway). Instead a new authority was created, with very limited funding, which began purchasing the suburban companies. First purchased was Lake Shore Coach Lines, Inc. on September 1, 1971; then Pontiac Municipal Transit on July 2, 1973; Metropolitan Transit on January 1, 1974; Great Lakes Transit on April 1, 1974; followed by Martin Lines on March 20, 1975. All of these systems were weak sisters.

The one large property serving the city of Detroit and accounting for over 80% of the daily ridership, still is not part of the system. This city versus suburban stand-off was brought about by the ridiculous way the authority was created. Had the state legislature fol-

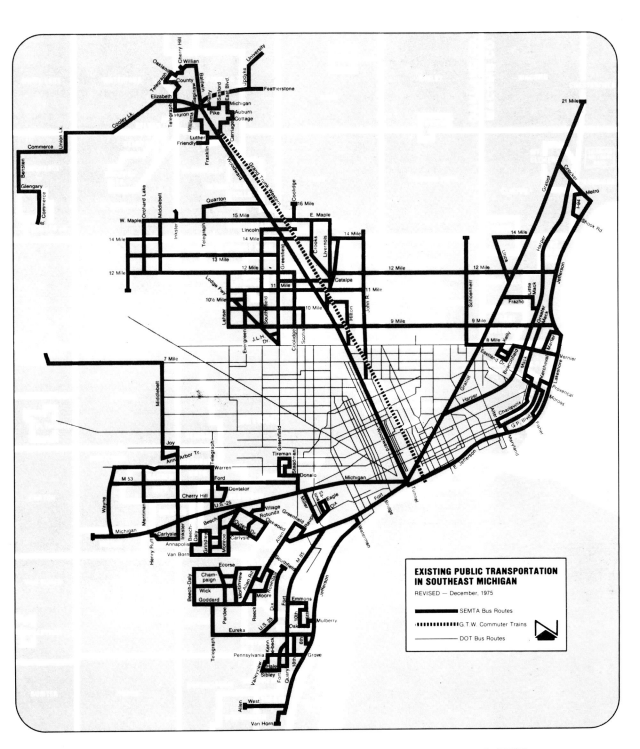

EXISTING PUBLIC TRANSPORTATION
IN SOUTHEAST MICHIGAN

REVISED — December, 1975

━━━━━ SEMTA Bus Routes

┅┅┅┅┅ G.T.W. Commuter Trains

───── DOT Bus Routes

𝄐	019508	SEMTA Wayne Division				Connector Transfer–10¢					
Date Valid			**Month Valid**			**Tour Identification Number**				**To Linehaul: Good for Travel to Zone Punched**	**To Connector: Good for Travel to Additional Zones Punched**
1 2 3 4 5 6 7 8			Jan May Sept			1 2 3 4 5				1 5 ★	0 3
9 10 11 12 13 14 15 16			Feb Jun Oct			1 2 3 4 5				2 6	1 4
17 18 19 20 21 22 23 24			Mar Jul Nov			6 7 8 9 0				3 7	2
25 26 27 28 29 30 31			Apr Aug Dec			6 7 8 9 0				4 8	

179

THE ■ People Mover℠

DETROIT IN MOTION

SCHEDULE

The People Mover operates seven days a week. To ride, you pay 50¢ at any of the fare collection gates, located in each of the 13 People Mover stations. If you are using a People Mover Fast Pass, simply insert card into the cardreader at the People Mover turnstile. You'll be admitted automatically. Elderly and handicapped: For fare information, call 962-RAIL.

OPERATING HOURS

Monday-Thursday	7 a.m.-11 p.m.
Friday	7 a.m.-Midnight
Saturday	9 a.m.-Midnight
Sunday	Noon-8 p.m.

Operating hours are adjustable for special events.

ROUTE

The 13 People Mover stations are connected by 2.9 miles of track. Average wait time between vehicles is approximately 3 minutes. Round trip is 14 minutes.

1. Times Square
2. Michigan Ave.
3. Fort/Cass
4. Cobo Hall
5. Joe Louis Arena
6. Financial District
7. Millender Center
8. Renaissance Center
9. Bricktown
10. Greektown
11. Cadillac Square
12. Broadway
13. Grand Circus Park

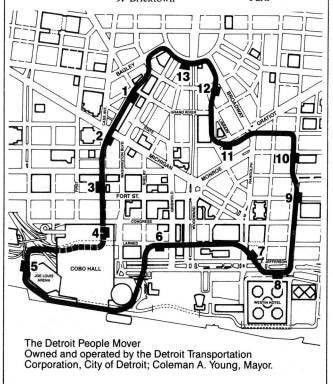

The Detroit People Mover
Owned and operated by the Detroit Transportation Corporation, City of Detroit; Coleman A. Young, Mayor.

---

lowed the lead of other states in creating SEMTA, it would have done so by expanding the DSR. Now the successor operation, D-DOT continues to serve the city, and SEMTA, suburbia. Until this stand-off is terminated, and a single authority created, public transit in the Detroit area will continue to lag far behind the rest of the nation.

The People Mover

Detroit's quest for rail rapid transit over the years has been most elusive. The one plan—and an improbable one at that—that did become a reality began as a SEMTA study by 1975. This study suggested a people mover, subway and/or monorail. It resulted in President Gerald Ford approving a $600 million federal commitment on October 5, 1976, to build a rapid transit system in Detroit. At that time the people mover was a minor part of the package and was estimated by SEMTA General Manager Thomas Lipscomb to cost $30 million.

By May 1979, the route was approved by the SEMTA board. Then in June 1981, the first engineering contracts were awarded to the Urban Transportation Development Corporation of Toronto for the people mover. Funding was approved by Congress in April 1982. Groundbreaking took place on October 31, 1983.

But a steady stream of construction difficulties by 1985 pushed the estimated cost of completion to over $200 million, a cost the Urban Mass Transportation Administration refused to fund.

Under pressure, SEMTA and D-DOT had to transfer funds earmarked to purchase needed buses to cover the cost of the over-runs. There were other problems, including faulty construction which resulted in parts of the structure having to be replaced. Realignment of the route caused additional costs.

By October 1985, an embarassed SEMTA was forced to turn the project over to the City of Detroit to complete and operate the system. Under the city's direction, the people mover was completed by the promised date and operations began on July 31, 1987.

Unusual in modern city transportation is the use of linear induction motors in the 12 vehicles. Each unit can carry 34 seated and 66 standee passengers and can travel at an average speed of 20 mph with a top speed of 32 mph. The cars are similar to those in use in Vancouver, B.C., and in suburban Toronto.

Downtown Detroit, at last, saw a rebirth of rail transit. The question of whether the people mover is a true transit tool—or a toy—is still open.

This flyer, issued on opening day, explains the operation of the People Mover.

Car 11 is being shifted by the Unimog in the maintenance
control facility located at the Times Square Station.
Detroit Department of Public Information

Northeast-bound cars 03 and 11 are passing Cobo Hall and
Arena heading for Station No. 6 in the financial district.
Detroit Department of Public Information

This postcard view of the Detroit-Windsor Tunnel shows two of the first order of model 40 Twin Coaches passing the International Boundary.
Schramm Collection

Coach 24 was photographed on the last day of bus operation by the Detroit and Windsor Tunnel Company. The modern entrance on the Detroit side was rebuilt to accommodate the adjacent Ren-Cen complex.
Van DeGrift Photo

The Auto Tunnel Bus

Detroit has not only a highway bridge and railroad tunnel connecting it with Windsor, Canada, but since November 3, 1930, also an auto tunnel. The Detroit and Canada Tunnel Co. operated its own fleet of buses for commuters until February 1, 1982. When the ICC and Windsor City Council refused to grant a fare increase from 50 cents to 75 cents to help cover increased operating costs, the company decided to drop the service. Ridership had dropped as more and more commuters drove their cars through the tunnel.

To provide a commuter service for Windsor residents, who make up the largest group of customers, Transit Windsor took over operations on February 1, 1982, and were charging a 75 cent fare.

Two Ford plant tour buses, which operated within the plant and to neighboring facilities. Right: This Ford AA model has a Union City body. Opposite Page: This bus was later sold to White House sightseeing tours and operated in Washington, D.C.
Collections of Henry Ford Museum and Greenfield Village

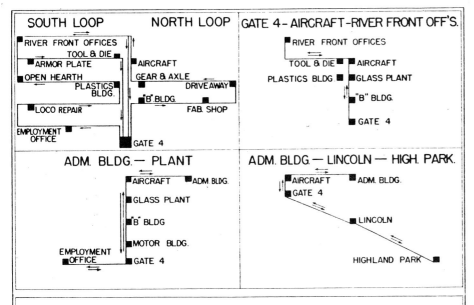

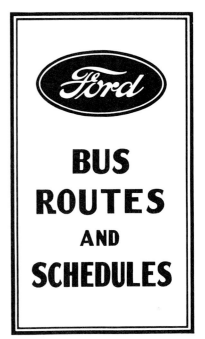

SOUTH LOOP   **NORTH LOOP**   **GATE 4 – AIRCRAFT – RIVER FRONT OFF'S.**

ADM. BLDG. — PLANT   **ADM. BLDG. — LINCOLN — HIGH. PARK.**

INTRAPLANT BUSES

NORTH LOOP: 15 MINUTE SERVICE AT ALL POINTS. LEAVES GATE-4 EVERY QUARTER HOUR.

SOUTH LOOP: 15 MINUTE SERVICE AT ALL POINTS.

GATE-4-AIRCRAFT-RIVER FRONT OFFICES: 10 MINUTE SERVICE IN EACH DIRECTION.

EMPLOYMENT OFFICE: 10 MINUTE SERVICE.

THERE IS 5 MINUTE SERVICE IN EACH DIRECTION ALONG ROAD 4.

INTERPLANT BUSES

ADM. BLDG. – ROUGE PLANT: 15 MINUTE SERVICE IN EACH DIRECTION.
     BUSES LEAVE ADM. BLDG. AND GATE-4, TRAVELING IN OPPOSITE
     DIRECTIONS EVERY QUARTER HOUR.

ADM. BLDG.– LINCOLN– HIGHLAND PARK: ONE HOUR SERVICE IN EACH DIRECTION.
     BUSES LEAVE ADM. BLDG. AND HIGHLAND PARK ON THE HOUR,
     AND LINCOLN IN BOTH DIRECTIONS ON THE HALF HOUR.

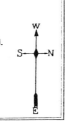

Map of Ford Bus Routes.

In 1949, New York Central locomotive 2360 was scooping up water at the Four Mile Lake pan east of Chelsea. Track pans filled the locomotive tender while the train continued to roll, thereby assuring fast operating schedules.

Stoner Collection

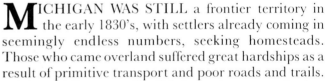

8

RAILROADS ACROSS THE STATE

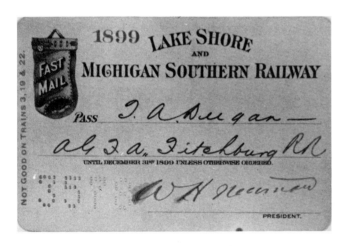

MICHIGAN WAS STILL a frontier territory in the early 1830's, with settlers already coming in seemingly endless numbers, seeking homesteads. Those who came overland suffered great hardships as a result of primitive transport and poor roads and trails.

Meanwhile, a new English invention was poised to capture the imagination of people around the world; the *Rail-Road*. This marvel of the age allowed all-year, all-weather travel. It reduced shipping costs greatly, and speeded up the movement of merchandise. Michigan knew a good thing when it saw it, and prior to becoming the 26th state on January 26, 1837, no less than 21 charters were issued to construct railroads. Two of the four early lines that survived the severe shortage of capital for construction were eventually built clear across Michigan.

Investors in both Adrian and Port Lawrence (Toledo) received a Michigan charter on April 22, 1833, authorizing $100,000 in capital stock with the stipulation that when $50,000 was sold, the corporation would exist. (Toledo was considered by Michigan to be within its border until December of 1836 even though Congress gave the area to Ohio June 15, 1836.) On May 20, 1834, the Erie & Kalamazoo Railroad, named after the two planned terminals (Lake Erie and the Kalamazoo River) was incorporated.

The press recognized the potential importance of railroads early. The *Detroit Journal and Currier* on January 7 and 14, 1836, printed a two-part story on railroads. These articles must have fired the imagination of the investing population because shortly afterwards the Detroit & St. Joseph Railroad was able to sell its stock and begin building. Many other Michigan railroad projects were quickly formed, but the group in southern Michigan was already building.

Construction of the E&K began in late 1835, according to the *Journal* of December 12, 1835. Six-inch-square wooden stringers rested on white oak ties initially placed four feet apart, later becoming eight feet apart. The ties were not placed on the ground but on heavy beams.

On August 10, 1836, the *Free Press* reported that the 33-mile Toledo-Adrian line ". . . is now ready for iron. Of the 7,000 tons ordered, 70 tons had arrived and was in the process of being laid." Strap iron rails ⅝-inch thick and 2½ inches wide were nailed to the wooden stringers to support the weight of the steam engine that was on order.

Detroit newspapers continued to carry short notes about the events occurring on the E&K. On August 22, 1836, the *Journal* printed that 12 miles of the line was in operation as of the 18th between the Territorial Road and Palmyra. Operation consisted of a car being pulled by a team of horses that was replaced every four miles along the route. The steam locomotive, on order, was expected to pull greater loads. By fall, the line was in operation to Adrian.

Then on June 20, 1837, the *Toledo Weekly Blade* announced the arrival of the first locomotive. That incident placed the Erie and Kalamazoo Railroad in full operation with steam power between Toledo and Adrian. This was the first locomotive to operate west of New York State. The second locomotive arrived September 29, and went into service October 17, 1837. The company alternated their usage to assure that both were in working order.

Eventually there were four locomotives, named *Adrian*, *Toledo*, *Tecumseh* and *Lenawee*. The first years were profitable; however, in 1839 the land boom ended and bank failures increased. Without the company bank to finance the rail line, the Erie & Kalamazoo Railroad went into receivership. Even though a survey was completed extending the road past Adrian to Marshall, the project never materialized.

The Wildcat Banks

When a railroad wanted to raise cash to build, only four Michigan banks existed. Two were in Detroit and two in Monroe, where the government land offices were located. The Michigan Territorial Council approved an act allowing the Erie and Kalamazoo Railroad to establish a bank on March 26, 1835. This bank and several others authorized at the same time were capitalized at $100,000, and allowed to circulate three times that amount of paper money.

The Adrian bank opened in August of 1836 and furnished money to construct the road. The Territorial Council continued to approve the establishing of additional banks with permission to print and circulate their own money. By 1837 there were 19 banks operating, and on March 15, 1837, the act was further liberalized. But the easy money didn't last long. On July 11, 1836, President Andrew Jackson issued his famous "Specie Circular" to decrease speculation and rein in the banks. It decreed that after August 15, 1836, all payments for public land had to be made in specie. This created a severe shortage of specie throughout the country.

In New York, banks suspended specie payments on May 10, 1837, and Detroit banks followed a week later. By 1839 the banks were broke, and with declining receipts, the Erie & Kalamazoo went bankrupt in 1840.

Meanwhile, another railroad got off to a sputtering start. Planned to operate from Detroit to the St. Joseph River, the Detroit & St. Joseph Railroad was chartered June 29, 1832. The route was surveyed in 1834 by Colonel Berrien, but by 1837 nothing was complete and no trains were operating. In fact, when the state finally purchased the line, $102,000 had been spent, and only 30 miles of right-of-way cleared between Detroit and Ypsilanti. Rolling stock consisted of one locomotive, one passenger car, and parts for six freight cars.

Michigan Takes Over

On March 21, 1837, Michigan, like Ohio and Indiana and later Illinois, started a program of internal improvements which included canals and railroads. This program was to be funded by the sale of public lands and Michigan's share of the federal surplus now that it was a state. Three railroads were proposed to cross the state; the Michigan Southern from Monroe to New Buffalo, the Michigan Central from Detroit to the St. Joseph River, and the Michigan Northern from Palmer (St. Clair) to the Grand River.

When the state chartered these early railroads, they retained the right to take them over at a later date. By January 2, 1838, Governor Mason, in his report to the legislature, reported that the Detroit and St. Joseph Railroad had been purchased to form the Michigan Central. The date of sale of property and transfer of franchises was April 22, 1837.

Because the Michigan Southern Railroad was to bypass the town of Tecumseh, a special state fund was created to support construction of a line from Palmyra through Tecumseh and Clinton to terminate in Jacksonburgh. Bending to a cry for lower freight rates and great political pressure, the Palmyra and Jacksonburgh Railroad Company was incorporated March 28, 1836.

The line was to connect with the Erie & Kalamazoo at Palmyra, the Michigan Southern east of Adrian

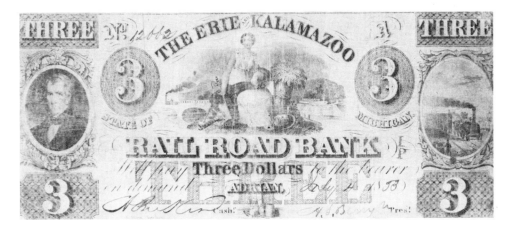

The lack of banking institutions in the Michigan Territory resulted in the Erie & Kalamazoo Railroad establishing its own bank to finance the railroad. This three-dollar bill was issued by the Erie and Kalamazoo Railroad Bank.
Johnson Collection

(Lenawee Junction), and the Michigan Central at Jacksonburgh (Jackson). Duly, the P&J opened to Tecumseh on August 9, 1838 and then to Clinton, using horsepower. The line reached Jackson in July 1857. The Erie & Kalamazoo was responsible for operation of this branch until 1844, when the state legislature purchased it and turned the line over to the Michigan Southern.

The River Raisin & Lake Erie Railroad was chartered March 28, 1836, and opened in 1838 with impressive but impractical plans. It was to run from LaPlaisance Bay to Monroe and Dundee, then to Blissfield, where it would connect with the Erie & Kalamazoo. But a shortage of funds kept the tracks from advancing beyond Monroe. At LaPlaisance Bay a warehouse was built, and in Monroe, Toll's Dock was built at East Front Street along the Raisin River.

This 3.5-mile railroad was built of wooden rails and laid across the marsh on pilings. The motive power was provided by horses, and there were two cars—one for freight and the other for passengers. The idea was to make Monroe a port to rival Toledo. However, when the canal was built across the marsh to straighten out the river, the railroad was abandoned and the warehouse moved to Monroe.

Building Public Railroads

It was always the favorite railroad of the politicians, and Michigan Central somehow received special consideration when scarce material and supplies were needed. The state pushed work on this line, and on February 5, 1838, it reached Ypsilanti, where a celebration was held. The first train, pulling two cars, left the Detroit depot located at Campus Martius, later the

This 1870s drawing depicts the first Erie & Kalamazoo Baldwin locomotive, *Adrian*, in 1837. The passenger car was named *Pleasure Car*. To ride this car from Toledo to Adrian, including 50 pounds of baggage per passenger, the charge was 12 shillings. Usually freight (burden) cars were included on all trains. These were built in the company shops using wheels and axles purchased in the East.
Henning Collection

187

After the state completed the line from Monroe to Adrian, this advertisement was used to promote its use. Note the cost—$400,000—in state funds. **Johnson Collection**

site of the city hall. The trip took 3 hours, and after many speeches, the ceremonial train began its return trip.

Unfortunately, the new-fangled locomotive made it only to Dearbornville where horses were pressed into service to continue the trip back to Detroit. By May 17, 1838, two trains a day were leaving for Ypsilanti, (at 6 a.m. and 1:30 p.m.). The *Free Press* on May 21 reported the company was averaging an income of $400 a day.

Work continued at a slow but steady pace and the railhead reached Ann Arbor on October 17, 1839; Dexter on June 30, 1841; Jackson on December 29, 1841; Albion on June 25, 1844; Marshall on August 12, 1844; Battle Creek on November 25, 1844; and Kalamazoo on February 2, 1846.

Even though the railroad's income was greater than its day-to-day expenses, funds were lacking to pay interest on loans and pay for needed up-grading of the equipment and track. The state, unable to fund its

internal improvements such as railroads and canals, passed an act on March 28, 1846, to sell its railroads back to the private sector.

Earlier, the state had to deal with its southern rail route, which, unlike the Central, was not completely surveyed. It was decided to use Monroe as the eastern terminal. The first step was the purchase by Michigan of the River Raisin & Lake Erie Railroad for $32,500.

The plan was for passengers to disembark from ships at LaPlaisance Bay, use the railroad into Monroe, and then change to the Southern. To connect the two railroads, a short, .38-mile extension to the end of the Michigan Southern track at First and Harrison was built. With $350,000 backing the Michigan Southern Railroad, ground was broken May 21, 1838, at Monroe. The line was then built from Monroe west to Adrian, reaching there on November 23, 1840. It reached Hudson on May 27, 1843, and Hillsdale on September 25, 1843.

Sadly, the Southern was always considered a step-child to the Central, at least as long as the state controlled both lines. Hand-me-down locomotives came from the Central. But, the citizens of Monroe were proud of their railroad and tried to protect it from the Central when both built westward. Wing, in his *History of Monroe County*, relates that the Central, needing strap iron rail, sent orders to the Southern to give up its rail. The party sent to procure the rail could not find any.

After a lengthy search up and down the line, the men returned empty handed. A group of Monroe citizens had loaded the rail on flatcars during the night and shipped it out of town, where it was then camouflaged in a gully beside the track.

According to company figures, the Southern, after reaching Hillsdale, began to earn more income than the Erie & Kalamazoo. Although the Michigan Southern rail line was drawing settlers into its territory and supplying farmers with cheap transportation to the eastern markets, the state sold the line on November 30, 1846, to local interests for $500,000.

Unlike the Central, the Southern was not always profitable. At the time of the sale the rolling stock consisted of four locomotives, three 4-wheeled passenger cars and a few freight cars. The small engines were so light that in wet weather the tracks had to be sanded so they could pull up any grades. Locomotives *Hillsdale* and *Tecumseh* were purchased to counter that problem.

The state required the Southern to build across to Michigan's west shore within three years. The route was to follow the state survey to Coldwater, where it could be altered, but must stay in Michigan.

The Southern also had to complete the Jackson branch within the same three years. None of these conditions was met, but, like the Central, the railroad was completed to Chicago.

At first, the offices of the road were located in Monroe, home to major promotors of the line. To encourage ships sailing from Buffalo to use Monroe rather than Toledo, the port dockage fee was reduced. Monroe was growing in importance and population. Still, however bright the future looked, the main gateway to the west was to be Toledo on the Erie & Kalamazoo line.

Hard times in Michigan in the 1840's caused the new railroad considerable financial problems and delayed further construction. After the rail line reached Hillsdale on September 25, 1843, the only extension was five miles to Jonesville. It was financed in 1850 by the citizens of Jonesville so they could be on a rail line. Variations of this form of local financing put many a bend in a rail line as the company inched along towards its destination.

Not surprisingly, the millions of dollars needed to develop early rail lines were not available locally, so investors outside of the state were sought. Hence, both the Michigan Southern and the Erie & Kalamazoo lines came under the control of George Bliss of Springfield, Massachusetts. As with the Central, eastern interests now had taken control of another Michigan line.

Bliss had become a Michigan Southern stockholder in 1847. In 1848 he purchased the Erie & Kalamazoo, and a year later was elected director of the Michigan Southern. Thus, the two lines were effectively brought under the same operating management.

With this merger accomplished, the main terminal point of the railroad was shifted to Toledo, and the track from Monroe to Adrian became a branch line. George Bliss, who had built the Boston and Maine Railroad, now began a building program that would take him clear across the state, into Indiana and terminate the Michigan Southern in Chicago. He began by regauging the 4'-10" gauge Erie & Kalamazoo track to the standard 4'-8½".

Crossing the State Line

Stockholders of the Buffalo & Mississippi Railroad visited New York City in the spring of 1849 to secure help in building a railroad to LaPorte, Indiana, after being rejected by the Michigan Central. Their success resulted in the formation of the Northern Indiana Railroad. E.C. Litchfield, the largest stockholder of the Michigan Southern, teamed up with Bliss to be elected to the Northern Indiana Railroad board of directors in May 1850.

This was the official beginning of a gigantic building program in which the Michigan Southern line was built from Jonesville to the Michigan-Indiana state line near Elkhart. The Northern Indiana continued from there to LaPorte and on to Bailey Town (Burns Harbor). Meanwhile, the Buffalo & Mississippi Rail-

The Mail Carrier of 100 years ago.

Catching and delivering the Fast Mails on the

LAKE SHORE & MICH. SOUTHERN RY.
The unrivaled Passenger Route.
NO FERRY TRANSFERS, NO DELAYS.
Secure Tickets by this popular thoroughfare.

This advertisement touted the through passenger and fast mail services of the Lake Shore & Michigan Southern Railway. *Johnson Collection*

road, being built from Michigan City to Chicago, was part of the complete project under the supervision of Bliss. Within two years deals were made, surveys completed, land purchased, rights-of-way graded and 132 miles of track laid. Fifteen hundred men were employed on the railroad project from Jonesville to Chicago. The final link from LaPorte to Bailey Town was completed May 22, 1852, thus making a through rail line from Toledo to Chicago.

First trains rolled into Coldwater on December 10, 1850; Sturgis on March 1851; and to the state line near White Pigeon, 15 miles from Elkhart on July 1851. To skirt the requirement that it construct a rail line to Michigan's west shore, Bliss used the Northern Indiana Railroad charter to build from the state line near White Pigeon to LaPorte, Indiana. The railhead reached South Bend on October 4, 1851, and LaPorte on January 9, 1852.

At the same time, the company, using the charter of the Buffalo & Mississippi Rail-Road, constructed a rail line from Michigan City due west along the south shore of Lake Michigan, passing through Ainsworth (South Chicago) in February of 1852. Then, using trackage rights on the Chicago, Rock Island & Pacific Railroad, the line entered Chicago on February 20, 1852. On paper it looked as though the Southern had beaten its arch rival, the Central, by about three months. But, there existed a rail gap of 15 miles between Michigan City and LaPorte, Indiana. While waiting to close the gap, the Truesdel and Roberts' stagecoach line was hired to carry passengers between the two communities.

The *Chicago Daily Journal* of February 20, 1852, recorded it thusly, as the first train from the east arrived in Chicago;

> The Cars—First Train—the Cars came in this morning over the Southern Michigan Road, for the first time, at half past ten o'clock and rung the bells and sounded the whistle according to established precedent. Their arrival was welcomed by hundreds of persons, and Captain Swift's Artillery proclaimed it in notes that shook the welkin. It was indeed a triumphal entry, and one of the victories of the Age of Iron and Steam.
>
> Therefore, until further notice, the cars will leave this city for the east . . . at two o'clock P.M.
>
> George M. Gray Esq. Agent, may be found at the Railroad Office in the Tremont Building.

The Gap Is Closed

During this period, the rivalry among cities vying to obtain a railroad was intense—especially so between Michigan City and LaPorte. Bliss soon felt the wrath of Michigan City residents toward him and toward LaPorte. And all because he had drawn a straight line west from LaPorte intersecting the Buffalo & Mississippi Railroad on the shore of Lake Michigan at Bailey Town, thus bypassing Michigan City.

Because of bad weather and lack of iron rails, this diversion was not completed until May 22, 1852, when the first "through" train arrived in Chicago from Tole-

do. This put an end to the Truesdel and Roberts horse stage over the 12-mile plank road connecting the Michigan City railhead with the main line at LaPorte and the overnight stop in LaPorte to catch the next day 7 a.m. train to Toledo. Up to now, New York City and Chicago had at best been 5½ days apart. With completion of the rail line to the east, travel time shrank dramatically.

At the same time Bliss was completing the interlocking directorship between the Northern Indiana, Buffalo & Mississippi, and Michigan Southern, Michigan City residents were giving assistance to the Michigan Central to cross the state line and build to their community. Later Bliss was known to tell listeners that he bypassed Michigan City because it would have added 13 miles to the line.

Expansion fed expansion, and the Michigan Southern soon tied its main terminal town, Toledo, with Detroit, giving the MS access to all three lake port cities. Service was opened to the Detroit & Milwaukee's Detroit depot in July 1856, and operated under lease as the Detroit, Monroe & Toledo Railroad.

After the company officially changed its name to Michigan Southern & Northern Indiana Railway (1855), a new direct link between Elkhart and Toledo was constructed in 1858. This new route, called the *Air Line*, became the main line for the New York Central while the *Old Road* was slowly downgraded by the NYC into a sleepy branch line. Its last passenger train ran November 19, 1956, and eventually was cut-up in piecemeal abandonments or sell offs. Presently, Conrail operates the west end, Hillsdale County Railroad the center, and Lenawee County Railroad the eastern section, with no connection between the latter two lines. The five-mile Tecumseh-Clinton portion of the former Jackson branch is being operated by the Southern Michigan Railroad, a railfan group. The remain-

LS&MS engine 529, built during the 1880s.
Schramm Collection

ing trackage which included the Erie & Kalamazoo from Blissfield into Toledo is abandoned, except for a short distance out of Toledo to an Ottawa Lake grain elevator.

The *Air Line*, on the other hand, is today's double-track, high density Conrail New York-Chicago main line, though none of it is in the state of Michigan. Commodore Vanderbilt gained control of it in 1869, adding to his ownership of the New York Central. Thus, he now controlled a through line between New York and Chicago. This also gave the NYC access to Detroit from Toledo on the Detroit, Monroe & Toledo Railroad trackage.

Taking the MCRR Private

The state sold the Michigan Central for $2 million to a group of investors led by James F. Joy of Detroit. A charter was approved March 28, 1846, and a stock issue of $5 million authorized. The stipulations mandated completion to the west Michigan shore within three years, a new route into Detroit, moving the downtown depot, and rebuilding the line with 60 pound T-rail. Shortly, on September 24, 1846, the state gave possession of the line to the Michigan Central Railroad. On May 30, 1848, the new downtown Detroit depot opened for business at West Jefferson and Third Street.

Under state ownership the goal had been to build three railroads across the state to open up new areas for development. Now under private ownership with its large capital investment, the goal would be to maximize profits. So, the Western terminus would not be the undeveloped shores of Lake Michigan, but Chica-

go, which was soon to emerge as a major railroad center. During the years that railroads were being constructed, stagecoaches met the trains at the end of the line and carried the passengers westward. The *Detroit Gazette* on May 22, 1843, reported "the fare to Jackson is $2.50 and stages leave Jackson for the west upon arrival of the train allowing passengers to reach Chicago two days less than by steamboat."

After the railhead reached Marshall, it became a 36-hour trip. One could leave Detroit by rail at 8 a.m., reach Marshall at 3:30 p.m.; then began a 22-hour, 90-mile stagecoach trip to St. Joseph. Here a steamboat took 6 hours to deliver the passenger in Chicago, 69 miles away. On February 2, 1846, the rail line was completed to Kalamazoo.

Railroad war clouds began to form now as both the Central and Southern came under the control of eastern capital. Each began to look toward the frontier city of Chicago. At first, the Michigan Central Railroad seemed to be interested in the Ohio and Mississippi River area. But after the State of Illinois began an internal railroad improvement plan financed by influential eastern investment houses and the famous land grant act of September 20, 1850, Chicago suddenly became the goal of every railroad building west. In 1846, only one railroad connected with Chicago and it ran west. The Central laid its tracks southwest toward New Buffalo, forcing the Southern further south into Indiana.

While the Southern's railhead remained in Hillsdale, the Central pushed its rails to Niles (October 1, 1848) and to New Buffalo (April 23, 1849). Now, during the lake shipping season, the stagecoach ride was

The depot at Hillsdale served over 22 passenger trains a day during the great days of train travel. From Hillsdale, a division point, one could board through cars to New York City, Chicago, Lansing, Jackson, Ft. Wayne, Ypsilanti and Detroit.

Breck Collection

191

This multi-story structure was Michigan Central's Ypsilanti depot as it appeared in 1865. Today a red brick single-story building remains, even though no Amtrak trains stop here.

Stoner Collection

eliminated. A large dock was constructed at New Buffalo to serve the transshipping of passengers and freight for Chicago.

Across the border in Indiana, another drama was occurring. As far back as 1835 a railroad was formed under the name Buffalo & Mississippi (B&M). This line was to run from Toledo to the Mississippi and Ohio rivers, and even though orator Daniel Webster turned the first shovel of dirt and purchased lots in Michigan City, the line did not construct any meaningful trackage.

It was not until 1848 that the project was able to attract enough funding to build a line. An agreement was signed on February 8, 1848, with the Michigan Central to allow use of the B&M right-of-way from the Michigan state line to Michigan City.

Stockholders of the B&M were suddenly aware that their new road might soon become a pawn in the battle of the rival Michigan Central and Southern railroads to reach Chicago. Factions began to choose sides. Some favored a deal with the Southern, but an agreement had already been made with the Central—if the MCRR got busy.

On August 24, 1849, the B&M told the Central that it must be in Michigan City by November 1, 1850, or lose its rights to get into town on B&M rights-of-way. Meanwhile, the Central agreed to purchase (on April 24, 1851) a southern Indiana line, the New Albany & Salem (Monon), for $500,000 with the stipulation they must build tracks from New Albany to Michigan. Then the NA&S charter would allow the MC to build from Michigan City to Chicago.

Early locomotives received names as well as numbers. Here is Michigan Central's *Persian*, built in 1856.

Henning Collection

With hours to spare, the Central's tracks crossed the state line and arrived at Michigan City October 29, 1850.

This done, the Michigan Central began to build across northern Indiana toward Chicago. Newspapers for this period of time are fragmented and the story is incomplete until the tracks arrived in Chicago over the right-of-way of the Illinois Central which had just been chartered (February 10, 1851). Ground was broken in Chicago December 23, 1851, for the Illinois Central Railroad, and tracks completed to Kensington on May 20, 1852. On May 12, 1852, J. Brooks was requesting from the city officials permission to build tracks from the south city limits to near a park in downtown Chicago. A locomotive and work train was reported in downtown Chicago on May 21, 1852, by the *Chicago Journal*. Then this piece of great news appeared in the *Journal* on the 24th:

Chicago and Detroit are now within twelve hours travel of each other. Today, two daily trains are to be started each way upon the Michigan Central Railroad, the morning train to connect with the New York and Erie Railroad line of Steamers, and the evening train will connect with the North Shore Line boats, at Detroit, and with Ward's line of Steamers running from this city to ports on the west shore of Lake Michigan.

The two trains from this city, morning and evening, respectively, start at half-past eight in the morning, and at nine in the evening. The former arriving in Detroit at nine in the evening, and connecting with the steamboats to Dunkirk and Cleveland. The latter at half-past nine in the morning, and connecting with the line of steamboats which run in concert with the Buffalo and Albany Express train on the Central New York line of railroads.

It will be noticed that neither of the evening trains stop at any but the regular stations.

The trip from Chicago to New York, can now be made in *one sixth* of the time formerly requisite, and when too, it was claimed under the head of *accelerated* velocity in comparison with locomotives in earlier times.

Two locomotives with numbers and names were *Queen*, numbered 200 and built about 1870, and *Admiral*, numbered 124, built in 1871.
Stoner Collection

193

Early Railroad Ships

PRIOR TO COMPLETION of rail lines linking Michigan to the east, or west to Chicago, steamboats shuffled passengers from shore to shore along the Great Lakes. Service was slow but relatively luxurious.

Two major railroad-owned shipping routes developed on Lake Erie, one of which was along the lake's south shore, the other along the north shore. Because of clean air and smooth riding, it is easy to see why traveling by boat was a lot less tiring than by either railroad or stagecoach, but it held dangers in the form of storms, breakdowns or accidents.

The following boat lists have been compiled by Gordon Bugby, a historian on Great Lakes ships.

South Shore Service

Year-Route	Remarks
1848 Buffalo to Monroe	
Baltimore	both owned in Monroe
Southerner	
1849 Buffalo to Toledo and Monroe	
Baltimore	As announced pre-season,
Southern	actual service may have
Benjamin Franklin	differed.
DeWitt Clinton	
Julius D. Morton	
Anthony Wayne	
1850 Buffalo-Dunkirk-Cleveland-Toledo-Monroe	
Troy	Dunkirk was now terminus
Superior	of New York & Erie Railroad.
1851 Buffalo-Dunkirk-Cleveland-Toledo-Monroe	
Baltic	Up to this date all steamers
Hendrick Hudson	used were probably chartered.
1852 Buffalo-Dunkirk-Monroe	
Southern Michigan	
Northern Indiana	Both owned by Arthur Edwards.
Empire State	Earliest 300 footer on lakes; purchased by MS&NI
1853 Buffalo-Toledo	
Southern Michigan	
Northern Michigan	Both purchased in June from Edwards by MS&NI
Empire State	
1854 Buffalo-Toledo	
Southern Michigan	
Northern Indiana	
Empire State	
1854 Dunkirk-Sandusky-Toledo	
Keystone State	Owned by General Charles
Niagara	Reed of Erie, and serving
Louisiana	N.Y. & Erie R.R. terminal.
1855 Buffalo-Toledo	
Southern Michigan	
Northern Indiana	
Empire State	Retired end of year engines placed in *Western Metropolis*.

1855 Dunkirk-Toledo	
Keystone State	
Niagara	
Empire	Not a Reed boat, was first ship in U.S. Registry of over 1000 tons.
1856 Buffalo-Toledo	
Southern Michigan	
Northern Indiana	Burned July 17, 1856, off Point Pelee, 30 lives lost.
Western Metropolis	Began service August
1857 Buffalo-Toledo	
Southern Michigan	
Western Metropolis	
City of Buffalo	Began service July
St. Lawrence	Chartered until *City of Buffalo* ready.

Late in August 1857, the MS&NI sold the ships to a third party to avoid attachment at Buffalo for railroad debts. In 1857 there was another depression.

1858 Buffalo-Toledo (No Service)	
1853-1857 Buffalo-Cleveland	
Crescent City	
Queen of the West	
1858 Buffalo-Cleveland (No Service)	
1859-1862 Buffalo-Cleveland	
Western Metropolis	Ran in connection with
City of Buffalo	Cleveland & Toledo R.R. and MS&NI
1853-1854 Buffalo to Sandusky	
Mississippi	For the Mad River and
St. Lawrence	Lake Erie Railroad.

North Shore Service

Year	Ship	Owner	Notes
1847	*Canada*		Both Canadian
	London		registry
1848	*Canada*		Both Canadian
	London		registry
	Pacific	Ward	
1849	*Hendrick Hudson*		Briefly-midseason
	Canada	Ward	Ward purchased *Canada*, replaced *Hendrick Hudson*
	Atlantic	Ward	Begin service on 5/28
	May Flower	MCRR	Began service on 5/28
1850	*Atlantic*	Ward	
	Ocean	Ward	
	May Flower	MCRR	
1851	*Atlantic*	Ward	
	Ocean	Ward	
	May Flower	MCRR	Stranded December
1852	*Atlantic*	Ward	Lost 8/20/52
	Cleveland	Ward	Replaced *Atlantic*
	Buckeye State	Phillips	
	Ocean	Ward	
	May Flower	MCRR	Replaced by *Caspian* in spring.
	Caspian	Ward	Early season.

1853	*Buckeye State*	Phillips	
	Ocean	Ward	
	May Flower	MCRR	
1854	*Buckeye State*	Phillips	to mid-year
	Ocean	Ward	to mid-year
	May Flower	MCRR	Wrecked Nov.
	Plymouth Rock	MCRR	Started 7/12
	Western World	MCRR	Started 7/7
1855	*Western World*	MCRR	
	Plymouth Rock	MCRR	
	Buckeye State	Phillips	Replaced *May Flower*
1856-7	*Western World*	MCRR	
	Plymouth Rock	MCRR	
	Mississippi	MCRR	Purchased

Steamers operated by General Charles Reed between Detroit and Dunkirk, N.Y., in connection with the Michigan Central and N.Y. & Erie railroads.

1851 Dunkirk-Detroit
Niagara
Keystone State
Queen City
Empire (Replaced Queen City in June)

1852 Dunkirk-Detroit
Niagara
Keystone State

1853 Dunkirk-Detroit
Niagara
Keystone
Queen City

1854—no Detroit service; steamers go on Dunkirk-Toledo route.

Lake Michigan Service

Mr. Bugbee has also prepared a list of steamers of Eber Rock Ward and Samuel Ward running on Lake Michigan in connection with the Michigan Central railroad:

Year-Route	Remarks
1841 St. Joseph-Chicago	
no service yet	train reached Jackson December 29.
1842 St. Joseph-Chicago	
Huron	Two stages each way between Jackson & St. Joseph

Year-Route	Remarks
1843 St. Joseph-Chicago	
Huron	Replaced in September
Champion	by *Champion*. Stage Jackson to St. Joseph 26 hours, 120 miles. Boat St. Joseph to Chicago 69 miles, 6 hours
1844 St. Joseph-Chicago	
Champion	Train to Marshall, Aug. 16—100 miles, 8-hour trip. In 1836 this was a 2-day trip.
1845 St. Joseph-Chicago-Milwaukee	
Champion	
1846 St. Joseph-Chicago-Milwaukee	
Champion	Trains to Kalamazoo January 31.
1847 St. Joseph-Chicago	
Detroit	Replaced by
Champion	*Champion* in July
1848 St. Joseph-Chicago	
Sam Ward	Trains to Paw Paw in June,
Pacific	Niles in October.
1849 New Buffalo-Chicago-Milwaukee	
Sam Ward	Train to New Buffalo in April.
Pacific	Boats for Chicago met PM train.
Detroit	—for Milwaukee the AM train.
Julius D. Morton (chartered)	No more summer stage.
1850 New Buffalo-Chicago-Milwaukee	
Sam Ward	By November track
Pacific	reached Michigan
Detroit	City
Canada	
Julius D. Morton (chartered)	
1851 New Buffalo-Chicago-Milwaukee	
St. Louis	
Sam Ward	
Pacific	
Arctic	
1852-Chicago-Milwaukee	
Pacific	

(In May 1853, Captain Clement purchased the Chicago-Milwaukee-Sheboygan steamers *Arctic* and *Traveler*)

A rare item was this cover carried by the *May Flower* in June 1850.

Johnson Collection

The *Southern Michigan*, sister ship to the *Northern Indiana*, was built in 1852 by Bidwell & Banta at Buffalo, New York. She was 300.9-feet-long and operated from 1852 until her burning on July 17, 1856. Dismantled in 1863, her engines were placed in the *Thomas Cornell*.

Dossin Great Lakes Museum

The *Atlantic* began service on May 28, 1849. She was owned by the Wards and operated until lost on the lakes, August 20, 1852.

Courtesy of the Great Lakes Historical Museum

DAILY LINE BETWEEN DETROIT AND BUFFALO.

IIGAN CENTRAL R.R.

NEW YORK CENTRA

S T E A M E R S,

WESTERN WORLD.	PLYMOUTH ROCK.	MAY FLOWER.
C. C. STANARD COMMANDER.	G. E. WILLOUGHBY COMMANDER.	T. T. HODSON COMMANDER.
aves Buffalo Mondays and Thursdays.	Leaves Buffalo Tuesdays and Fridays.	Leaves Buffalo Wednesdays and Saturd
" Detroit Tuesdays and Fridays.	" Detroit Wednesdays and Saturdays	" Detroit Mondays and Thursda·

HROUGH TICKETS TO ALL IMPORTANT POINTS BETWEEN THE ATLANTIC AND MISSISSIPPI, CAN BE PROCURED AT ALL THE PRINCIPAL RAIL ROAD, AN
STEAM BOAT OFFICES, EAST AND WEST, AND ON BOARD THE STEAMERS.

This 1854 ship advertisement shows the six-day-a-week service between Detroit and Buffalo. Two of three ships, *Plymouth Rock* and *Western World*, were sisters and went into service that July. The third, *May Flower*, was wrecked that November. The *Plymouth Rock* was built in 1854 by J. Englis at Buffalo, New York. The passenger and freight side-wheeler was 335.1 feet long. It was operated by Michigan Central until 1857, then in 1863 it was converted into a drydock.

Dossin Great Lakes Museum

The *May Flower*, built by Michigan Central at Detroit, began operating May 28, 1849, to Buffalo. It was wrecked in November 1854.

Courtesy Dossin Great Lakes Museum

MICHIGAN CENTRAL RAIL ROAD COMPANY'S
STEAMER MAY FLOWER,

Rails to Michigan City

MICHIGAN CITY, Indiana, became the battleground in the quest of Michigan Central and Michigan Southern to reach Chicago. Written into the Central's charter was the stipulation that only with permission was the Southern allowed to build less than five miles away from the Central's tracks. As both lines crossed the state to the shore of Lake Michigan, the Central turned south toward Niles near the Indiana border, before reaching New Buffalo on Lake Michigan. Using the five-mile separation tactic, the Central expected to stop the Southern at Niles, but the Southern reacted by routing its tracks into Indiana.

Meanwhile, a group of investors from Michigan City and La Porte, Indiana, held title to a paper railroad, the Buffalo & Mississippi Railroad (B&M). Ground was turned in 1837, but lack of funding halted construction. According to the Michigan Central Agreements Book, B&M officials struck a deal in 1848 which allowed the Central to use the B&M right-of-way from the Michigan border to Michigan City, Indiana. It was made official on August 24, 1849. The agreement also allowed the Central to connect to the B&M main line that would be built from Chicago through Michigan City to La Porte. About this time the B&M was offered for sale to the Central for $50,000, but the Boston office of the company turned it down.

Other B&M stockholders, unhappy over these events, held a meeting with officials of the Southern. As a result, B&M, using Southern funding, constructed the rail line from Michigan City to Chicago.

The Central, now having second thoughts about stopping at Michigan City, purchased $500,000 worth of stock in The New Albany & Salem Railroad Company (NA&S was later known as the Monon line) on April 24, 1851, for which the Central received the rights to build tracks from Michigan City to the Illinois border. NA&S used most of the funds to complete the line from Michigan City to Lafayette, Indiana.

The *Free Press* on October 29, 1850, reported, "Michigan Central began operating to Michigan City, today. The station house at that place is the handsomest building on the road." According to the Agreements Book, NA&S was to share all passenger depots at Michigan City at no cost to its own company. This undated photo shows the first depot on the left while NA&S located a freight house on the right. In 1907 the third depot was constructed, and it is still in place but used as a restaurant; Amtrak uses a small shelter.
Schramm Collection

An Amtrak train from Detroit to Chicago crosses the South Shore electric tracks. By the time this photo was taken, the Monon tracks to southern Indiana sharing this right-of-way had been removed. Behind the camera a few yards was the site of the B&M crossing to Chicago. Only the B&M trackage between the Illinois state line and Burns Harbor remains of the main line from Michigan City to Chicago.
Henning Photo

The Michigan Central scheduled trains from Detroit westward daily except Sunday at 9 a.m. and daily at 5:30 p.m.

Eastern Connections by Boat

As railroads developed and competed increasingly with the steamboats, the Combination, which controlled shipping on Lake Erie, shifted operations from Detroit to Toledo in 1845. This meant that only through steamers heading for Chicago via lakes Huron and Michigan would stop at Detroit. Those boats were scheduled to arrive after the daily westbound trains had departed. The fares from Buffalo to Detroit was set at seven dollars while to Toledo it was four dollars.

The Ward Line attempted to compete with the Combination along the south shore of Lake Erie, but after its ship *Champion* was mobbed in Cleveland, Ward moved it to Lake Michigan.

Competition soon arrived on Lake Erie aimed at the Combination. In 1842 the Canadian steamer *Kent* was placed in operation from Buffalo to Detroit by the North Shore Line with only a stop at Port Stanley, Ontario. This made it nearly an across-the-lake express run. In 1845 the *London* was added to the line, but on August 11, 1845, they collided and the *Kent* was sunk.

In 1846 the state of Michigan sold the Central to private interests, and a new superintendent, John W. Brooks, arrived from the east. He oversaw the building of Detroit's new waterfront depot and wharf. He also wanted reliable sailings from Buffalo to Detroit free from the control of the Combination.

Lake Erie's North Shore Line continued to grow, as the *Canada* was added in 1847. The two steamers made four sailings each week from each terminal. But, Brooks wanted the Ward Line to increase sailings to six a week by adding its vessel *Samuel Ward* to the fleet serving the Central. This would mean a daily sailing every day except Sunday. But Ward couldn't manage it, and Brooks decided to build his own ship. Using a portion of the Detroit depot, a shipyard was established and the *May Flower* built. On May 28, 1849, she set sail for Buffalo, and the MCRR was in the steamboat business.

Rail Connections East

These ships were great in summer, but during the winter, when the lakes froze up, the connection to the east remained with stagecoaches across Canada. An all-weather system was needed.

The entry of Western Ontario into the railway age was protracted. In 1834 the legislature of Upper Canada gave the London & Gore Railway a charter granting the right to construct a line from London to Burlington Bay, and the use of navigable waters of the Thames River and Lake Huron. The charter was allowed to lapse until 1845, when it was renewed and amended. The new name was the Great Western Railway Company and the route was from the Niagara River to the Detroit River.

Although groundbreaking was in London on October 23, 1849, construction was delayed, and the first train did not operate from Hamilton to Niagara Falls until November 1853. On December 15, 1853, the first train arrived in London from Hamilton.

Then on January 17, 1854, the first train arrived in Windsor from Niagara Falls. The *Dart* and other passenger ferries provided connections with Detroit for the many visitors crossing the Detroit River to celebrate. A holiday was declared in Detroit, and along the waterfront and up Woodward Avenue, fire companies and uniformed citizens militia were out in force. The first train arrived at 4 p.m. with the second at 5 p.m., both announced by booming cannons.

On the eastern end of the line a bridge was built to cross the Niagara River, which opened in 1855 for traffic. At the west end, ferries, such as the *Union*, were placed in service. These early ferries carried no cars but pushed barges for an occasional transfer of cars. However, there was no real need to handle cars since the gauges of the railroads were different.

Indeed, the Canadian government, fearing a future U.S. invasion, had forced the Great Western to build a 5'-6" gauge, thus preventing interchange with the U.S. roads. Soon, however, common sense prevailed and in 1864, iron for a third rail was purchased for the line from the Suspension Bridge (Niagara Falls) to Windsor. On December 3, 1866, a test was made as far as London, and by 1867 the line completed to Windsor.

With the ferry *Great Western*, which had begun service January 1867, and equipped to handle railroad cars, freight could now be shipped across Eastern Canada without breaking bulk. It was not until 1873 that the gauge was changed throughout to the standard 4'-8½".

Another railroad to enter the east-west market was the Canada Southern, which planned to build from Buffalo to Chicago, bypassing Detroit to the South. In Canada the name Canada Southern was used for the line from Buffalo to Gordon Station, 1.2 miles north of Amherstburg. To cross the Detroit River, the Canada Southern Bridge Company was formed on September 23, 1873. It combined the Detroit River Railway Bridge & Tunnel Company (Canada) and the Detroit River Railroad & Bridge Company (U.S.).

The idea of building a bridge over the main channel was fought by the shipping interests. Construction of a tunnel was abandoned so a car ferry was ordered to connect Gordon Station with Stoney Island. Projecting from Stoney Island, a 900-foot bridge crossed to Grosse

Great Western

In later years the housing was removed from the *Great Western*, leaving the tracks exposed to the weather. In this view, she is shown sailing under the Grand Trunk Railway banner.

Dossin Great Lakes Museum

The *Great Western* was built in 1866 at Walkerville, Ontario. This early photo shows her original appearance, with the tracks enclosed.

Dossin Great Lakes Museum

Michigan Central

WITH THE CANADA SOUTHERN RAILROAD established in Windsor in 1884, the car ferry *Transport* was shifted there for crossing to Detroit. In the first year of ferry operation, she was joined by a similar new sidewheeler, *Michigan Central*. Four years later, in 1888, the new steel *Transfer* replaced the older wooden vessel. It featured a propeller for ice breaking assistance in addition to her paddlewheels.

The final addition in 1904 to this Michigan Central fleet was the large propeller carferry *Detroit*. It was to be the prototype of twentieth century river ferries. However, the Michigan Central fleet was transferred to the Wabash Railway when the underwater tunnel between Detroit and Windsor was ready.

As of 1987, barges ply the river for Grand Trunk-Canadian National, Norfolk Southern and the CSX. But their days might be numbered; plans were underway to enlarge the rail tunnel to accommodate the oversize boxcars that presently must use the car barges.

Railroad Car Ferries

Here *Transport* is crossing the Detroit River in 1918. It was carrying the American Red Cross across the river, according to the note on the back of the photo. Whether those are returning wounded soldiers was not recorded.

Manning Brothers Historical Collection

The *Michigan Central* was built in 1884 at Wyandotte, Michigan, by the Detroit Dry Dock Co. It foundered off Drummond Island on October 27, 1926; then its engines were removed.

Dossin Great Lakes Museum

Locomotives 162 and 163 are entering the tunnel with a freight train bound for Windsor in 1953. The ex-Michigan Railway car on the left, now MT-9, is a section crew car.

Dworman Photo

Ile, then a four-span bridge led to the mainland. This short line totaled 3.6 miles in length between Gordon Station and Slocum Junction near Trenton.

On the U.S. side, the Chicago & Canada Southern Railroad was formed to build a line to Chicago. It was built only as far as Fayette, Ohio, by 1873, although surveyed to Chicago but never completed because of the poor money market. A branch line built under the name of the Toledo, Canada Southern & Detroit Railroad opened service September 1, 1873, between Toledo and Grand Trunk Junction in Detroit. While the company was independent of Vanderbilt, the trains used the Brush Street Depot of the Detroit & Milwaukee Railroad.

In September 1873, the wooden car ferry *Transfer I* was put into service. It was a side-wheeler, 244 feet in length and could carry 21 cars on its three tracks. The center of the railroad's activities was on Grosse Ile, where the roundhouse and repair shops were located.

Problems arose in the winter when the ferry was unable to cross due to heavy ice. The 1874-5 winter was especially bad, and by December 17 crews were attempting to blow a path with nitro-glycerine. The *Transit* was brought down from Detroit to assist; however it was lighter, and soon found unsuitable.

Old Man Winter could not be defeated. Express trains were taken off, freight and perishable goods were then sent by Great Western through Windsor-Detroit or sledded across the ice from Gordon to Grosse Ile. The Windsor *Daily Star* reported on this condition for over two weeks. It also noted that the Windsor Board of Trade was pressing for the building of a Canada Southern line from Essex Center to Windsor where a winter crossing would be easier.

In 1876 Commodore Vanderbilt purchased the Canada Southern, which was by then bankrupt. He had also purchased controlling stock of the Michigan Central, and by 1877 named Samuel Sloan as president. In 1880 the iron car ferry *Transport* was added to supplement the *Transfer*. A new line was built from Essex Center to Windsor and operations began December 31, 1883. This spelled doom for the Grosse Ile crossing, which was only occasionally used until 1888, and when the *Transfer I* was found unseaworthy, it was entirely abandoned.

The bridge between Stoney Island and Grosse Ile was removed in two stages; the first being in 1905, with the remainder in 1913. As Grosse Ile became a residential area, the line became a commuter run to Detroit, and operated as such until January 9, 1924. The bridge between Grosse Ile and the mainland was sold along with the remaining track, to the Wayne County Road Commission. It was rebuilt as a highway bridge and is still in use today. The brick depot on the island, the only remaining railroad building, is now the home of Grosse Ile Historical Museum.

At Last—a Crossing

Crossing the Detroit River by rail had been an impossible dream for years. Sailing ships objected to bridges, and tunnel technology was not fully developed to overcome construction difficulties. On May 1, 1871, railroad entrepreneur James F. Joy made application to Detroit's council for permission to use certain streets as tunnel approaches. He received approval on August 1, 1871. On September 14, ground was broken in the Detroit and Milwaukee Railroad depot yard opposite St. Antoine Street. By January 31, 1872, the shaft was completed for a distance of 108 feet beneath the surface of the river. Work continued until 1873, then was stopped due to finding high amounts of sulphur and quicksand—much more than Joy's engineers could deal with.

Work on another tunnel began downriver at Grosse Ile on April 21, 1879. This tunnel was being pushed by Vanderbilt, who now owned the line. This made Detroit business interests unhappy at the prospect of losing through railroad business on a new route which ignored Detroit completely.

Where to put the tunnel? The state legislature, on May 27, 1879, approved bills allowing the use of Detroit's Belle Isle. The bill provided $200,000 for the purchase of the island, and $500,000 to build a bridge or tunnel. The bill also provided for the electorate to vote on the building of railroad facilities. The issuing of bonds to raise the necessary funds had to be approved by the Board of Estimates, and on June 30, they approved the island's purchase. So, on September 25, Belle Isle was purchased and became a park. But no railroad was built there. Detroit's electorate in November 1880, voted 58,040 to 37,340 against building the railroad facilities.

Detroit and Windsor were finally connected after the turn of the century. On July 1, 1910, the Detroit River tunnel began passenger operation between the two cities. On September 15, freight service was started. The 8,376-foot tunnel ended the many years of rail tie ups that even a fleet of ten-car ferries often could not unsnarl. This meant Detroit finally had a continuous high-speed rail connection with the east coast—an impossible dream come true.

The tunnel made the old Detroit depot at 3rd and West Jefferson obsolete, since the passengers would no longer arrive at the river's edge from the car ferries. To reach this depot now, trains from the east would have to reverse themselves upon leaving the tunnel. And so was built a new passenger terminal at a cost of $7 million, of which $2,500,000 was spent on the station and office building. The new Michigan Central Station opened December 26, 1913, earlier than scheduled, due to a fire in the old station. It was located 2,600 feet west of the tunnel portals at Michigan and Fifteenth Street. There were 11 through passenger tracks passing under the train shed, plus 7 additional freight tracks on the same elevated structure.

Business was still expanding; the Michigan Central alone was estimated to handle an average of 5,000 passengers daily in Detroit. On special days and holidays the estimate was 9,000. The old station had been estimated to have handled 75 trains with a total of 544 cars daily.

Changing Patterns

When first built, railroads gave citizens living along the line access to nearby towns and far away places. Then came the interurbans which offered more frequent service, lower fares and could stop anywhere along the line to pick up or discharge passengers. This made huge inroads on the railroads' local passenger traffic; however, they still retained the long-distance traveler. Interurban lines such as the DJ&C operated only to Jackson and part time to Kalamazoo, while the MCRR (which paralleled it) continued on to Chicago without change of cars.

Even as local passenger traffic was being lost, Michigan's railroads continued for a while to expand their long-distance markets. The Pennsylvania Railroad finally arrived in Detroit during the 1920's. The B&O offered its first passenger service between Detroit and Washington on June 13, 1920. An earlier arrival was the Canadian Pacific Railway which built a line from London, Ontario, to Detroit in 1890, then used Michigan Central tracks to provide through passenger service from Montreal to Chicago, via Toronto and Detroit. In later years the CPRR also used the Michigan Central tunnel under the Detroit River.

During the Great Depression of the 1930's all forms of transportation suffered declining levels of business—passenger as well as freight. The interurbans such as the DJ&C and DUR did not survive, but the local traffic did not return to the railroads. The automobile and bus, using the many miles of new concrete highways, took over. As the railroads lost the local trade they began closing stations and reducing service to cut operating costs.

Long-distance travel still posed profit potential even if volume was reduced—or so the railroads thought. During the mid-1930's, to hold the long-distance traveler, new "name" trains were installed stressing comfort and speed. In 1936 the *Mercury* began service on the New York Central from Detroit and Cleveland. Later another *Mercury* was put on between Detroit and Chicago offering a scheduled running time of 4½ hours, and in those days the train was on time. Another

new name train on the MC/NYC Detroit-Chicago run was the *Twilight Limited*. In 1937 a morning train between Detroit and Chicago was added and named the *Michigan*.

The timetables advertised these trains as ". . . a fine hotel on wheels." Likewise, service to the east from Detroit to Boston and New York boasted name trains such as the *Wolverine, Detroiter, The Niagara, North Shore Limited, Trans-Atlantic Limited* and the *DeWitt Clinton*. In the reverse direction names like the *Frontiersman, Number Forty-Five* and *The Chicagoan* raced over the rails of the Michigan Central.

These new streamliners indeed brought travelers back to the rails, but World War II brought the deluge. This fast increase in railroad use by the public (and the U.S. government) strained rail facilities to the limit. All during the war the railroads struggled on, wearing out their equipment and the roadbeds.

After the war railroads made attempts to retain their wartime passengers with new and better equipment, by changing from steam to diesel locomotives, streamlined cars and fast schedules. Rather late in the game, the New York Central put on a new lightweight train between Detroit and Chicago named the *Aerotrain*. This train seated 320 and made the trip in 4 hours and 20 minutes, on a non-stop schedule. (In 1852 the fastest train took 12 hours to make the same trip between Detroit and Chicago.) Going into service on April 29, 1956, *Aerotrain* was not successful in attracting new riders and was taken off. Whatever the attractions of speed, *Aerotrains* small, bus-like cars rode terribly and passengers stayed away in droves.

Rail passenger service was further injured by the new interstate highway network which began to be built in the 1950's. When the I-94 freeway between Detroit and Chicago was completed in 1961, the NYC was then operating only five daily passenger trains between those points. By the mid-1960's Detroit's large rail terminal was becoming deserted. It was closed January 5, 1988; a small temporary depot nearby is being used.

Another factor detrimental to railroads was a government desire to improve airline travel by providing new and larger airports for the airlines, while railroads still had to provide their own depots and pay high taxes on them. Contract carrying of U.S mail was transferred from railroads to airlines, which meant many trains which had held their own only with mail contracts were soon abandoned.

The wonder is that any rail passenger service still exists, but it does, thanks to Amtrak, which in 1987 operates two daily trains in the Detroit-Chicago service, with a third running Friday through Sunday. The schedule has been lengthened to 5½ hours for the 279-mile trip.

The westbound *Mercury* is at
Central Avenue in Detroit on
November 7, 1948, headed by
locomotive 5426.
                Novak Photo

Captured at Jackson, New York Central's
first-rate *Mercury* is heading for Chicago.
By the early 1960s this name train had
been retired.

                Woodard Collection

Bay City Junction, February 21, 1952. In
the distance can be seen the Detroit depot
tower; the next track shows the rear of the
Mercury just arriving from Chicago.
                Novak Photo

The westbound *Twilight Limited*, No. 31, was photographed west of Wayne Junction on September 6, 1948.
Novak Photo

The short-lived Great Lakes Aerotrain, with engine 1001, is at the yard, east of Miller Road. It had just arrived from Chicago.

Novak Photo

To cut costs, New York Central operated units such as motor car M-205, shown here pulling two coaches; this view may have been taken on the Grand Rapids branch. A motor unit such as this may have been used with a passenger trailer in the mid-1930s for commuter service between Ann Arbor and Detroit.
Stoner Collection

This view was taken at Kalamazoo on May 22, 1971, shortly after Amtrak took over the line. The ex-Penn Central engine badly needs a paint job, but at least the author was able, for the first time in years, to purchase food and drink on the train.

Ken Schramm Photo

The United Aircraft turbo made a Michigan visit in 1971. Here it sits under the trainshed in Detroit on September 7, 1971.

Ken Schramm Photo

On an August 1974 Sunday afternoon the *Preamble Express*, forerunner of the *American Freedom Train*, sits in the nearly empty yards adjacent to the Michigan Central depot in Detroit.

Ken Schramm Photo

The Detroit-Chicago corridor received French-built Turbos late in the 1970s. Here, one is loading in Ann Arbor on its way to Detroit.

Andrews Photo

Detroit to Ann Arbor Commuter

A westbound commuter train operating between Detroit and Jackson on June 25, 1949, has just passed Lonyo Road in Detroit. The buildings at right are part of the westbound classification yards.

Novak Photo

This Ann Arbor commuter was caught on film at Ypsilanti on April 2, 1974. Once a busy depot with 20 mainline trains stopping per day, the one commuter train was all that remained.

Ken Schramm Photo

The *Executive*, which replaced the Budd car in 1975, operated from Detroit to Jackson. It operated until January 13, 1984, when funding from SEMTA and the State of Michigan was eliminated.

Andrews Photo

This gallery of postcard views shows depots along the MCRR route from Detroit to Niles.

MCRR's third Detroit depot was designed by L. W. Eiolitz. It was both a head-end depot and a transfer point to the railroad's steam ships.

Top right: Ypsilanti, the original division point. Although not in use, this building is still standing, but the upper floors have been removed.

Middle right: Ann Arbor. Designed by F. H. Spier, this station featured separate waiting rooms for men and women. Presently, the depot is Chuck Muer's "Gandy Dancer" restaurant.

Chelsea. This rural, wooden depot still stands. The last train to use it was the "Michigan Executive."

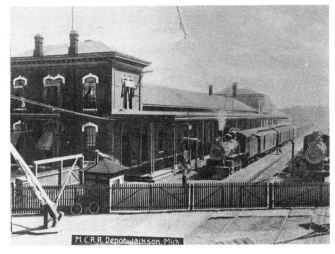

Above: Battle Creek. Designed in 1887 by Rogers and McFarlane, it still stands, but trains now stop at a new transportation center.

Above right: Jackson. This Civil War style depot has been restored.

Michigan Central Depot, Marshall. Mich.

Marshall. An unusual depot which at an early date was moved across the tracks. It has since been razed.

M. C. R. R. Train, Niles, Mich.

Niles. Built in the 1890s under the direct supervision of chief engineer J. D. Hawks, who later built the DYAA&J. The building is still in use.

ROSTERS

INTERURBANS OF THE DETROIT UNITED RAILWAY SYSTEM

The following roster is in DUR-assigned numerical order which corresponds to the order of division takeover:

7000-7008 — Wyandotte	7250-7291 — Rapid Railway
7051-7062 — Orchard Lake	7500-7519 — DM&T
7101-7112 — Pontiac	7750-7787 — DJ&C
7151-7164 — Flint	

Subsequent purchases and assignments did not follow this order.

The data has been gathered from many sources: 1. Remaining DUR records at the Burton Historical Collection, Detroit Public Library and Schramm collection. 2. Data compiled by Clarence Faber, Clarence Woodard and Sid Ferriss. 3. Additional data made available by Harold Cox and Roy Benedict. When there was conflicting data on dimensions, motors, etc., the earliest DUR data was used. The DUR began using inventory cards in individual envelopes in 1908. Every time motors, controllers or trucks were exchanged for another type, the inventory card would note the change. Only a selective set of cards have been discovered, but they give insight into the problem of conflicting data.

CAR NUMBER	BUILDER	ORDER NUMBER	DATE DELIVER	TRUCKS	MOTORS	CONTROL	WEIGHT	SEATS	BODY LENGTH	LENGTH OVERALL	WIDTH OVERALL	DIVISION ASSIGNED
7000-7008[1]	Det. Cit Railway	—	1899	DT-Dupont	2-Steel 34	K-14	35,800	45	33'2''	44'5''	8'5''	Wyandotte
7051-7062	Kuhlman	50	1900	DT-Dupont	4-West 38B	—	—	—	40'0''	51'0''	—	Orchard Lake
7063-7072	Niles	—	1910	DT-Bald 78-25A	4-West 317	GE K 36B	—	—	41'10''	53'7''	8'3¾''	Flint
7073-7076	Niles	—	1912	DT-Stand C-80	4-West 303	GE—M	81,100	50	45'10½''	58'5''	8'8''	DM&T
7077-7083	Niles	—	1912	DT-Stand C-80	4-GE 205	—	64,920	53	41'10½''	52'7½''	8'9''	Flint
7084-7093[2]	Niles	—	1913	DT-Stand C-80	4-West 303	—	—	50	45'10''	58'4''	8'7¼''	DM&T
7094	Niles	—	1913	DT-Stand C-80	4-West 303	—	—	50	45'10''	58'4''	8'7¼''	Flint
7095-7096	Niles	—	1916	DT-Stand C-80	4-West 303	GE—M	83,000	50	45'7''	58'3½''	8'10¼''	Flint
7101-7112	Kuhlman	—	1897	DT-Brill 27	2-Steel 34	K-14	34,100	40	34'0''	45'0''	8'6''	Pontiac
7113-7122	Cincinn.	800	1907	DT-Bald	4-West 93A	K-14	56,350	45	36'2''	46'4''	8'9½''	Pontiac
7123-7126	Niles	460	1910	DT-Bald 78-25A	4-West 317	GE K-36B	56,350	45	36'2½''	46'4''	8'8''	Pontiac
7127-7128	Niles	—	1912	DT-Bald	4-West 317	—	—	—	36'3''	46'5''	—	Pontiac
7129-7131	Niles	—	1913	DT-Bald	4-West 317	—	—	—	36'3''	46'5''	—	Pontiac
7132-7139	Kuhlman	625	1916	DT-Stand C-60	4-West 557A	W-HL	—	54	42'10''	55'0''	8'6''	Pontiac
7140-7147[3]	Kuhlman	626	1916	DT-Stand C-60	Trailer	—	—	60	42'10''	55'0''	8'6''	Pontiac
7151-7158	Kuhlman	—	1900	DT-Peck.	2&4 West 56	—	—	54	33'7''	43'7''	—	Flint
7159-7164	Jewett	—	1901	DT-Peck.	4-Steel 34	—	—	—	34'5''	45'1''	8'4''	Flint
7250-7255	Barney & Smith	—	1896	DT-B&S	2-Walker 75	K-14	42,000	30	31'5½''	41'0''	8'6''	Rapid
7256-7259	Barney & Smith	—	1896	DT-B&S	2-West 76	K-13	—	—	31'6½''	39'10''	8'6''	Rapid
7260-7263	Barney & Smith	—	Prior 1899	DT-B&S	2-West 76	K-13	42,000	48	31'6''	39'8''	8'6''	Rapid
7264-7267	Barney & Smith	—	Prior 1899	DT-B&S	2-West 76	K-13	38,850	51	34'0''	42'2''	8'6''	Rapid
7268-7273[4]	Barney & Smith	—	1898	DT-B&S	4-West 76	K-14	61,400	53	39'2''	50'6''	8'6''	Rapid
7274-7279	Kuhlman	—	1899	DT-Dupont	4-West 56	L-4	59,900	50	39'10''	51'4''	8'6''	Rapid
7280-7291	At time of takeover these may have been passenger or work car numbers											
7292-7297	Brill	12696	1903	DT-Brill 27-A-2	4-West 76	—	—	—	40'0''	51'8''	—	Rapid

Builders photo of 7790 taken July 1, 1907. *Schramm Collection*

CAR NUMBER	BUILDER	ORDER NUMBER	DATE DELIVER	TRUCKS	MOTORS	CONTROL	WEIGHT	SEATS	BODY LENGTH	LENGTH OVERALL	WIDTH OVERALL	DIVISION ASSIGNED
7298-7304	Cincinn.	500	1906	DT-Bald	4-West 112	West	64,700	53	41'10''	52'7½''	8'8¾''	Rapid
7305-7307	Cincinn.	500	1906	DT-Bald	4-West 112	West	64,700	53	41'10''	52'7½''	8'8¾''	Flint
7308	Niles	—	1912	DT-Stand C-60	4-West C-80	—	—	—	41'10½''	52'7½''	—	Rapid
7309-7310	Niles	—	1915	DT-Stand C-60	4-West 303	GE—A	81,800	50	45'10''	58'4''	8'9''	Rapid
7311-7312	Niles	—	1916	DT-Stand C-80P	4-West 303	GE—M	83,000	50	45'7''	58'3½''	8'10¾''	Rapid
7500[5]	Niles	—	1906	DT-Bald	4-West 121	GE—M	73,460	—	40'4''	51'10''	8'6''	DM&T
7501-7505[6]	Jewett	—	1901	DT-Peck 26	4-West 56	K-14	57,000	46	33'6''	42'10''	8'8''	DM&T
7506-7507[7]	Jewett	—	1901	DT-Peck 26	2-West 56	—	—	—	42'9''	51'6''	8'4''	DM&T
7508-7519	Stephen.	—	1904	DT-Peck MCB	4-West 76 & 86	—	—	—	40'7''	51'0''	8'6½''	DM&T
7520-7521	Niles	—	1916	DT-Stand C-80P	4-West 303	West A.L.M.	83,000	50	45'7''	58'3½''	8'10¾''	DM&T
7522-7529	Jewett	—	1917	DT-Brill 27 MCB	4-West 557A	West A.L.M.	81,880	50	45'5½''	58'3½''	8'10½''	DM&T
7530-7539[8]	Kuhlman	698	1920	DT-Brill 27 MCB3X	4-West 557A	West A.L.M.	83,660	54	45'9½''	58'5''	8'5¾''	DM&T
7540-7545[9]	Kuhlman	699	1920	DT-Brill 27-MCB3X	Trailer	—	57,000	70	49'0''	58'6''	8'5¾''	DM&T
7543[10]	Rbt-DUR	—	1924	DT-Brill 27-MCB	4-West 93A	—	—	—	49'0''	58'6''	8'5¾''	DM&T
7540	Rbt-DUR	—	1927	D-Brill 27-MCB	4-West 577A	West ALFC36	83,660	54	49'0''	58'6''	8'5¾''	DM&T
7546-7555	St. Louis	1322	1924	DT-Brill 27-MCB 2	4-GE 275 A	PC-5 Sk	68,700	54	44'3''	56'6''	8'8½''	Flint
7556[11]	St. Louis	1122	1928	—	—	—	—	—	—	53'3''	—	Flint
7750-7764	Numbers assigned Ann Arbor city cars											
7765-7774	Barney & Smith	—	—	DT-B&S	4-West 76	West A.L.M.	68,600	55	41'9''	53'3½''	8'9½''	DJ&C
7775-7780	Barney & Smith	—	—	DT-B&S	4-West 38	L-4	58,400	54	39'2½''	49'5¼''	8'9''	DJ&C
7781	Barney & Smith	—	—	DT-B&S	4-West 38	—	—	—	34'1''	42'5''	—	DJ&C
7782	Barney & Smith	—	—	DT-B&S	4-West 38	K-14	59,120	30	34'8''	45'8''	8'9''	DJ&C
7783[12]	Barney & Smith	—	—	DT-B&S	4-West 38	—	—	—	34'1''	42'5''	—	DJ&C
7785-7787	Barney & Smith	—	—	DT-B&S	4-West 38	K-14	51,000	42	33'0''	44'3''	8'10½''	DJ&C
7790-7794	Kuhlman	353	1907	DT-Bald	4-West 112	L-4	65,400	53	41'10½''	52'7½''	8'11¾''	DJ&C
7795-7796	Niles	—	1916	DT-Stand C-80P	4-West 333	West A.L.M.	83,000	50	45'7''	58'3½''	8'10¾''	DJ&C
8000-8001[13]	DUR	—	1924	DT-Stand C-80P	4-West 303	GE—M	85,700	28	45'10''	58'4''	8'7¼''	Flint
8002[14]	DUR	—	1924	DT-Brill MCB	4-West 303	GE—M	73,460	28	40'4''	51'10''	8'6''	DM&T
8003[15]	DUR	—	1924	DT-Brill	4-West 557	—	—	—	45'9½''	58'5''	8'5¾''	DM&T
8021, 8022, 8024[16]	DUR	—	1924	DT-Stand C-60	4-GE 214	K-34	—	34	42'10''	55'0''	8'6''	Pontiac

Lightweight Interurbans

CAR NUMBER	BUILDER	ORDER NUMBER	DATE DELIVER	TRUCKS	MOTORS	CONTROL	WEIGHT	SEATS	BODY LENGTH	LENGTH OVERALL	WIDTH OVERALL	DIVISION ASSIGNED
3301-3310[17]	Kuhlman	834	1925	DT-Brill 77E-1	—	—	38,080	46	31'6''	43'2''	8'6''	

FOOTNOTES:

1. 7004, 7006, 7007, rebuilt as funeral cars.
2. 7084, 7087, rebuilt, renumbered 8000, 8001.
3. Three motorized, renumbered 8021, 8022, 8024.
4. Org. Shore Line cars.
5. Official car used for overnight travel.
6. Originally seven cars, two converted to express cars.
7. Open-bench cars for Monroe Piers.
8. After burning 7536 rebuilt, renumbered 8003.

9. Two were motorized.
10. Had observation platform in deluxe service.
11. Built 1916 for Grand Rapids, Grand Haven and Muskegon.
12. Originally trailers.
13. 7084 and 7087 rebuilt.
14. 7500 rebuilt.
15. 7536 rebuilt.
16. Three of 7140-7 series trailers rebuilt.
17. Rebuilt as city cars.

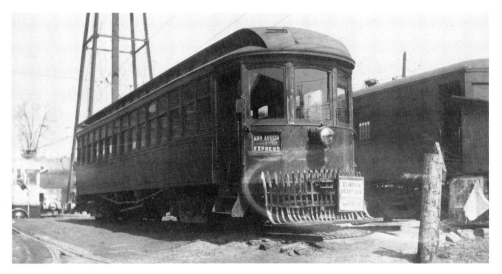

7791 at the Detroit interurban freight house at Monroe and St. Aubin.

Kremkow Photo

ANN ARBOR CITY CARS

DUR Number	Prior Number	Builder	Date Received	Trucks	Motors	Seats	Body Length	Length Overall	Notes
7750	100	Kuhlman		ST-Brill	2-West 12a	40	20'0"	29'8"	8 bench-open car Out of service 9/20/16
7751	101	Kuhlman		ST-Brill	2-West 12a	40	20'0"	29'8"	8-bench-open car Out of service 9/20/16
7752	102	Kuhlman		ST-Brill	2-West 12a	40	20'0"	29'8"	8 bench open car Out of service 4/9/13
7753	103	Kuhlman		ST-Brill	2-West 12a	40	20'0"	29'8"	8 bench open car Destroyed 9/1/16
7754	104	Kuhlman		ST-McGuire	2-G.E. 800	40	20'0"	29'8"	8 bench open car Detroyed by students Halloween
7755	105 or 106			ST-McGuire	2-West 12a	25	18'7"	27'7"	6 window closed car Converted line car 12/3/12
7756	107	St Louis		ST-McGuire	2-G.E. 800	23	18'-7"	28'-3"	6 window closed car Converted line car 12/3/12
7757	108	St Louis		ST-McGuire	2-G.E. 800		18'-0"		6 windows Scrapped 1907
7758	109	Niles		ST-Dupont	2-G.E. 800		20'0"	29'8"	7 window closed car Destroy Oct. 1923
7759	110	Niles		ST-Brill	2-G.E. 800		20'0"	29'8"	7 window closed car Destroy i/10/16

Above cars in service at time of D.U.R. take-over in 1907.

CAR GROUP	BUILDER	DATE DELIVERED	TRUCKS	MOTORS	SEATS	BODY LENGTH	LENGTH OVERALL	NOTES
441-455	Stephenson	1895	ST-Dupont	2-G.E. 800	25	20'20"	31'5"	Arrived from Flint 1913-448 Sent to Detroit by 1922-448 Arrived from Flint 1916-453 as one-man car Destroyed 10/20/20-453 Arrived from Flint 1921-as one-man cars 444, 445, 447, 449 450, 455
386-391	Brill	1895	ST-Brill	2-West 68	34	20'0"	30'8"	Arrived from Detroit 1913- 386, 387, 388, 390, 391, also 389 rebt as one-man car Destroyed 1915-387, in 1919-390 Sent to Detroit by 1922-386,389
272-275	Jackson & Sharp	1895	ST-Dupont	2-West 68	25	21'0"	32'7"	Arrived from Flint 1914-272, 273 Arrived from Detroit 1914—274 Sent to Detroit by 1922-273, 274
301-385	Stephenson	1895	ST-Dupont	2-West 68	26	22'0"	31'2"	Arrived from Detroit 1921-306, 335, 349, 385

In 1925 all remaining Ann Arbor streetcars were destroyed when replaced by buses.

A note regarding the following bus rosters. We are attempting to provide bus fans the material we have gathered on the various bus companies and their equipment. In volume 2 of this series we included the SEMTA roster which was the most available since it is presently operating. In this volume we are including the Ann Arbor system followed by the Detroit Motorbus and their descendant companies, Lake Shore Coach Lines, Dearborn, Intertown and Metropolitan lines. In future volumes we plan to include the DUR's Peo-

ples Motor Coach and Eastern Michigan Motorbuses roster.

These rosters are not complete but at this time represent all the information we have been able to find. Hopefully it will assist future bus fans as to what was operated during these early years. Most data came from what company records we found or newspapers. Also, major contributors were John Hoschek, librarian for the Motor Bus Society, and Bernard Drouillard, member of the Bus History Assn.

ANN ARBOR CITY BUS COMPANIES AND THEIR ROSTERS

RECEIVED	COACH NUMBERS	NUMBER COACHES	BODY BUILDER	SERIAL NUMBER	CHASSIS BUILDER	SERIAL NUMBER	MODEL	SEATS	NOTES
PEOPLES MOTOR COACH COMPANY (2/1/25-10/4/28)									
1925	—	12	Yellow Coach	—	Yellow Coach	—		29	
Starting 1925	—	18	—	—	Reo	—	—	21	Replaced Yellow Coaches on a 3-for-2 basis.
EASTERN MICHIGAN MOTORBUSES (name change only) (10/5/28-6/7/33)									
1931	—	12	—	—	—	—	—	—	5 were reported in service on 1/13/33.
ANN ARBOR TRANSPORTATION CO. (7/24/33-7/20/36)									
1933	20-24	5	—	—	Ford	—	—	10	

RECEIVED	COACH NUMBERS	NUMBERS COACHES	BODY BUILDER	SERIAL NUMBER	CHASSIS BUILDER	SERIAL NUMBER	MODEL	SEATS	NOTES

ANN ARBOR CITY BUS CO. (7/21/36-4/30/43)

RECEIVED	COACH NUMBERS	NUMBERS COACHES	BODY BUILDER	SERIAL NUMBER	CHASSIS BUILDER	SERIAL NUMBER	MODEL	SEATS	NOTES
1936	—	2	—	—	—	—	—	20	For temporary summer service also used an 8-passenger station wagon, 5-passenger sedan.
9/1936	14-19	6	Fitzjohn	6256, 6255, 6257, 6258, 6260, 6259	Ford	3213098, 3212981, 3213706, 3208001, 3213833, 3212332,	35Z	17	
8/1939	20-21	2	Fitzjohn	6720, 6721	Ford	5154347, 5182166	35Z	17	
1941	—	2	Union City Body Co.	—	Ford	—	19-B	27	
1942	—	—	Union City Body Co.	—	Ford	—	29-B	27	

RECEIVED	COACH NUMBERS	NUMBER COACHES	COACH BUILDERS	SERIAL NUMBER	MODEL	SEATS	NOTES

ANN ARBOR CITY BUS, INC. (Subsidiary of Greyhound) (5/1/43-4/6/57)

RECEIVED	COACH NUMBERS	NUMBER COACHES	COACH BUILDERS	SERIAL NUMBER	MODEL	SEATS	NOTES
1943	Began operations with above 12 coaches						
1947	—	12	GMC	—	—	29	—

ANN ARBOR TRANSIT, INC. (4/12/57-6/12/59)

RECEIVED	COACH NUMBERS	NUMBER COACHES	COACH BUILDERS	SERIAL NUMBER	MODEL	SEATS	NOTES
1957	See note	12	Checker-Transit	—	—	31	Used DSR buses—Ann Arbor added dash and number to DSR numbers—7613, 7638, 7645, 7647, 7650, 7657, 7718, 7720, 7738, 7740, 7754, 7758. Built 1950.

CITY BUS CO. OF ANN ARBOR (9/1/59-5/1/63)

RECEIVED	COACH NUMBERS	NUMBER COACHES	COACH BUILDERS	SERIAL NUMBER	MODEL	SEATS	NOTES
1959	001-007	7	Divco-Wayne	—	—	21	
—	0017	1	Divco-Wayne	—	—	21	
—	0018	1	Wayne	—	—	—	Wayne conventional

PUBLIC BUS CO. (5/8/63-1/4/64)

Leased buses from City Bus Co. of Ann Arbor

CITY BUS CO. OF ANN ARBOR (1/13/64-5/22/68)

Began with their same 9 buses above.

RECEIVED	COACH NUMBERS	NUMBER COACHES	COACH BUILDERS	SERIAL NUMBER	MODEL	SEATS	NOTES
1964	—	7	—	—	—	24	

ANN ARBOR CITY TRANSIT (7/15/68-1/31/69)

RECEIVED	COACH NUMBERS	NUMBER COACHES	COACH BUILDERS	SERIAL NUMBER	MODEL	SEATS	NOTES
1968	—	6	GMC	—	—	32	
—	—	10	Ford	—	—	—	Vans

ANN ARBOR TRANSPORTATION AUTHORITY—A.A.T.A. (5/7/69 to date)

RECEIVED	COACH NUMBERS	NUMBER COACHES	COACH BUILDERS	SERIAL NUMBER	MODEL	SEATS	NOTES
1969	—	11	GMC		TDH-4512		Two came from Metroplitan Transit, Inc. #175, 177 serial 1279, 1281.
1969	20-21	2	Ford	39603, 39604	E32GHF	10	
1970	1-5	5	GMC	007-011	TDH-3301	28	In 1972 re #101-105.
1970	22	1	Ford	35076	E22GHF	10	
1970	30-33	4	GMC	546-549	T6H-4512A	45	In 1972 re #230-233.
1970	6-12	7	GMC	094-100	TDH-3301A	33	In 1972 re #106-112.
1972	42	1	Highway	25130	TC-31	25	Built in 1971.
1972	43	1	Highway	25202	TC-31	25	
1972	201-203	3	GMC	141-143	T6H-5306A	53	Used from Buddy's Trans. Co. #704-706 built 1969.
1972	302-304	3	Ford	27985, 27988, ?	B60CCP	60	
1972	305	1	GMC	1832	TDH-5105	51	Used from DSR #1336—built 1956.
1972	234-235	2	GMC	1178, 1176	TDH-4519	45	Used from Burlington Rapid Transit #106, 104 built 1966.
1972	306-307	2	GMC	12186E, 12979E	SV4016G	40	School bus body—built 1966.
1973	23	1	Dodge	35423	B35BE3X	16	
1973	24	1	Dodge	091160	B35BE3X	12	
1973	25-26	2	Dodge	125568, 114142	B35BE3X	12	
1974	27-36	10	Dodge	B -	B35BE3X	12	
1974	236-238	3	GMC	878, 875, 877	TDH-4519	45	Used from Danville Traction & Power Co. #172, 169, 171 built 1965.
1974	—	1	Mercedes-Benz	—	0309	16	Leased for dial-a-ride; burned shortly after receival.
1974	240-250	11	GMC	1175-1185	T6H-4523A	40	
1975	37-65	29	Dodge	—	B35BE5X	12	
1975	421-425	5	Dodge	—	B35BE6X	H	Handicap.
1975	501-507	7	Dodge	—	B35BE5X	H	Handicap.
1976	66	1	Dodge	095976	B35BE6X	12	
1976	251-253	3	GMC	2189-2191	T6H-4523A	40	
1977	67-74	7	Dodge	—	B35BE7X	12	
1977	508	1	Dodge	020957	B35BE6X	12	
1979	301-307	7	Grumman	91395-91401	35096-6-1	38	Ex-E.M.U.
1980	113-114	2	GMC	191-192	TDH-3302A	33	
1980	430-436	7	Dodge	—	Fortabus	12	
1981	308-321	14	GMC	BV 811717-BV 811730	T70604	37	•
1981	437-439	3	Chevrolet	—	—	—	
1982	322-326	5	Flxible	CDO94495-CDO94499	40096-6N	46	
1985	327-332	6	Flxible	FDO96527-FDO96532	40096-6T	46	
1986	601-604	4	Ontario Bus	—	Orion II	16	
1986	441-445	5	Dutcher	97007-97011	—	6	
1987	333-338	6	GMC	HV824812-HV824817	T70606	36	
1987	605-608	4	Ontario Bus	—	Orion II	16	

DETROIT MOTORBUS ROSTER

RECEIVED	COACH NUMBERS	NUMBER COACHES	BODY BUILDERS	SERIAL NUMBER	CHASSIS BUILDER	SERIAL NUMBER	MODEL	SEATS	NOTES
9/1919	702	1	Fifth Ave.	—	Fifth Ave.	—	L	48(1)	Double-deck, left-hand drive.
5/1920-6/1920	501-513	13	Fifth Ave.	—	Fifth Ave.	—	A	48	Double-deck, right-hand drive.
8/1920-9/1920	514-520	7	Fifth Ave.	—	Fifth Ave.	—	A	48	Double-deck, right-hand drive.
8/1920	701	1	Fifth Ave.	—	Fifth Ave.	—	L	48(1)	Double-deck, left-hand drive.
8/1920	703-707	5	Fifth Ave.	—	Fifth Ave.	—	L	48(1)	Double-deck, left-hand drive.
3/1921	708	1	Fifth Ave.	—	Fifth Ave.	—	L	48(1)	Double-deck, left-hand drive.
4/1921-8/1921	710-751	42	Fifth Ave.	—	Fifth Ave.	—	L	48(1)	Double-deck, left-hand drive.
4/1922-7/1922	101-110	10	Fifth Ave.	—	Fifth Ave.	—	J	27	
10/1922	709	1	Fifth Ave.	—	Fifth Ave.	—	L	48(1)	Double-deck, left-hand drive.
12/1922	752-754	3	Fifth Ave.	—	Fifth Ave.	—	L	48(1)	Double-deck, left-hand drive.
3/1923-6/1923	111-121	11	Fifth Ave.	—	Fifth Ave.	—	J	27	
7/1923	801-836	36	Detroit Motorbus	—	Fifth Ave.	—	—	60	
10/1923-12/1923	122-153	32	Fifth Ave.	—	Fifth Ave.	—	J	27	
10/1923	201	1	—	—	Safeway	—	—	29	
3/1924	154-165	12	Fifth Ave.	—	Fifth Ave.	—	J	27	
4/1924-5/1924	901-940	40	Yellow Coach	—	Yellow Coach	—	—	—	Some converted to 29-seat single-deck.
6/1924	166-167	2	Fifth Ave.	—	Fifth Ave.	—	J	27	
5/1924-6/1924	202-219	18	—	—	Safeway	—	—	29	
5/1924	601-637	37	Detroit Motorbus	—	Safeway	—	—	60(2)	
7/1925-10/1925	301-333	33	Gilbralter	—	Fifth Ave.	—	J	27(2)	
10/1925-3/1926	401-480	80	Gilbralter	—	Safeway	—	—	27	60 leased by DSR.
8/1928-10/1928	2001-2024	24	Fitzjohn	(3)	Studabaker	(4)	Body-D, Chassis-75Jr.12(5)		
6/1929	1001-1032	32	Twin Coach	—	Twin Coach	—	40		Purchased by DSR in 1934.

MISC COACHES LISTED 4/30/1926

RECEIVED	COACH NUMBERS	NUMBER COACHES	BODY BUILDERS	SERIAL NUMBER	CHASSIS BUILDER	SERIAL NUMBER	MODEL	SEATS	NOTES
1925	755(801)	1	Yellow Coach	—	Yellow Coach	—	—	—	Demo
9/1925	6	1	—	—	Reo	—	—	—(6)	
4/1925	4-5	2	—	—	United	—	—	—(6)	

MISC COACHES LISTED 7/1/1931

1, 3, 4, 6, 7, 8, 9, 10 (6)

(1) Originally had open upper deck which was semi-enclosed, also seating was increased to 52. By 1931 eight had been rebuilt into 28-passenger single-deck buses—701, 712, 715, 720, 726, 740, 741, 753.

(2) When DMC found the 800-836 chassis unable to handle the weight of their bodies they had to rebuild them within two years. Taking the 36 bodies and obtaining an additional one from Gilbralter, they were placed on Safeway chassis and became numbers 601-637. Taking 33 chassis (the disposition of the other three is unknown) they were placed under bodies built by Auto Body Co. and numbered 301-333. During 1927, coach 607 was equipped with two Dobler Steam motors for testing.

(3) Date received	Fitzjohn serial numbers	(4) Studabaker serial numbers
8/28	SD80-SD 91	3250938, 3250997, 3250926, 3250937, 3250931, 3250996, 3250995, 3250999, 3251001, 3250998, 3251002, 3251000
9/28	SD 95 (demo)	3251083
10/28	SD 99-SD 100	3251136, 3251161
10/28	SD 102-SD 116	3251150, 3251160, 3251162, 3251137, 3251135
10/28	SD 109-SD 112	3251134, 3251139, 3251163, 3251138

(5) Purchased to compete with the jitneys, later most rebuilt to seat 21, all converted except 2014, 2017, 2018, 2019.

(6) After 1925 Detroit Motorbus took over several small suburban companies to obtain their routes. It appears that few of their buses were retained; these were all we found listed.

LAKE SHORE COACH LINES ROSTER

RECEIVED	COACH NUMBERS	NUMBER COACHES	BODY BUILDERS	SERIAL NUMBER	CHASSIS BUILDER	SERIAL NUMBER	MODEL	SEATS	NOTES
THE FOLLOWING 27 COACHES RECEIVED FROM DETROIT MOTORBUS CO. IN 1932:									
1932	100 series	27	Fifth Ave.	—	Fifth Ave.	—	J	25	Built 1922-23.
1934	61-67	7	Yellow Coach	—	Yellow Coach	040-046	V-F-652	29	Numbers not consecutive.
1934	68	1	Yellow Coach	—	Yellow Coach	—	Z-AAG-337	33	Built 1929.
1935	69	1	Yellow Coach	—	Yellow Coach	143140	W-G-366	20	Built 1930.
1935	71-74	4	Yellow Coach	—	Yellow Coach	092-095	716	23	
1936	201-202	2	Yellow Coach	—	Yellow Coach	391-392	728	34	
12/1936	203-204	2	Yellow Coach	—	Yellow Coach	743-744	728	34	
—	80 & 90 series	—	Union City Body Co.	—	Ford	—	70	—	
—	50 & 100 series	—	Union City Body Co.	—	Ford	—	09B	—	

RECEIVED	COACH NUMBERS	NUMBER COACHES	COACH BUILDERS	SERIAL NUMBER	MODEL	SEATS	NOTES
1946	301-304	4	GMC	091-094	TD-3609	—	
1946	305-310	6	GMC	191-196	TD-3609	—	
1948	311-320	10	GMC	1024-1033	THD-3610	36	
1948	321-320	2	GMC	1609-1610	TDH-3610	36	
1949	323	1	GMC	222	TDH-3612	36	
1950	324-333	10	GMC	213-222	TGH-3101	—	
1951	334-338	5	GMC	486-490	TGH-3101	—	
1951	339-340	2	GMC	505-506	TGH-3101	—	
2/1953	401-406	6	GMC	2373-2378	TDH-4509	45	
9/1954	407-412	6	GMC	657-662	TDH-4512	45	
1955	501-508(1)	8	GMC	1360-1367	TDH-5105	53	
1955	509	1	GMC	616	TDH-5105	53	
5/1959	413-418	6	GMC	3178-3183	TDH-4512	45	
1960	501-504(2)	4	GMC	710-713	TDH-5301	53	
1960	505-508(2)	4	GMC	779-782	TDH-5301	53	
1960	510	1	GMC	783	TDH-5301	53	
1960	419-424	6	GMC	141-146	TDH-4517	45	
1963	511-516	6	GMC	1087-1092	TDH-5303	53	
1964	517	1	GMC	2090	TDH-5303	53	
1964	518-521(1)	4	GMC	069-072	TDH-3501	35	
1965	518-520(2)	3	GMC	3531-3533	TDH-5303	51	
1965	425-429	5	GMC	933-937	TDH-4519	45	
1967	521	1	GMC	5954	TDH-5303	51	
1967	522-526	5	GMC	5955-5959	TDH-5303	51	

On 9/1/71 Lake Shore Coach Lines was taken over by SEMTA.

DEARBORN BUS COMPANIES

RECEIVED	COACH NUMBERS	NUMBER COACHES	BODY BUILDERS	SERIAL NUMBER	CHASSIS BUILDER	SERIAL NUMBER	MODEL	SEATS	NOTES
_____ DEARBORN COACH COMPANY									
THE FOLLOWING 48 COACHES RECEIVED FROM DETROIT MOTORBUS CO. IN 1932:									
1932	110-167	10	Fifth Ave.	—	Fifth Ave.	—	J	25	Built 1922-24.
1932	201-219	18	—	—	Safeway	—	—	29	Built 1923-24. Did not receive 206.
1932	438-480	20	—	—	Safeway	—	—	27/29	Built 1925-26.
By 1934	501-502	2	—	—	Ford	—	—	21	
4/1936	—	3	Fitzjohn	6056	Ford	BB18-2554411	35-Z	23	
				6057		BB18-2639400			
				6072		BB18-2750676			
6/1936	—	1	Fitzjohn	6132	Ford	BB18-3294631	35-Z	23	
8/1936-7/1937	301-309?	9	Garwood	—	—	—	C	24	Aerocoach states Dearborn Coach had 9—photo exists of 302. Had Ford motor.
10/1936	—	1	Fitzjohn	6133	Ford	BB18-3299807	35-Z	21	
2/1937	—	1	Fitzjohn	6363	Ford	BB18-3471197	35-Z	24	
4/1937	—	1	Fitzjohn	6416	Ford	—	35-Z	24	
5/1937	—	2	Fitzjohn	6430	Ford	BB18-3734075	35-Z	24	
				6431	Ford	BB18-3734067			
6/1937	—	2	Fitzjohn	6432	Ford	BB18-3734068	35-Z	24	
				6433	Ford	BB18-3740508			
10/1937	—	1	Fitzjohn	6448	Ford	BB18-4310024	35-Z	24	
11/1937	—	2	Fitzjohn	6486	Ford	BB18-4129452	35-Z	24	
				6487		BB18-4162430			
1/1938	—	2	Fitzjohn	6488	Ford	BB18-4369349	35-Z	24	
				6489		BB18-4385355			
12/1938	—	3	Fitzjohn	6515	Ford	BB18-4393554	35-Z	24	
				6516		BB18-4393503			
				6517		BB18-444294			
—	700 series	—	—	—	Ford	—	Type 70	—	
2/1943 4/1944	800-832	32	Union City Body Co.	—	Ford	Known numbers: 559826, 559838, 534100, 553085, 570182-570187, 570274-570279, 577677-577685, 559992.	29B	—	
1947	900 series	49	Union City Body Co	—	Ford	—	79B	29	

215

RECEIVED	COACH NUMBERS	NUMBER COACHES	COACH BUILDERS	SERIAL NUMBER	MODEL	SEATS	NOTES
10/1947	101-108	8	GMC	824-831	TDH-3610	36	
1/1948	109-110	2	GMC	1040-1041	TDH-3610	36	

INTERTOWN SUBURBAN LINES (name change only)

RECEIVED	COACH NUMBERS	NUMBER COACHES	COACH BUILDERS	SERIAL NUMBER	MODEL	SEATS	NOTES
1951	111-120	10	GMC	1971-1980	TDH-4509	45	
1952	121-125	5	GMC	2338-2342	TDH-4509	45	
8/1953	126-135	10	GMC	118-127	TDH-4512	45	
4/1954	136-138	3	GMC	433-435	TDH-4512	45	
6/1954	139-141	3	GMC	581-583	TDH-4512	45	
9/1954	142-145	4	GMC	596-599	TDH-4512	45	
9/1954	151-160	10	GMC	260-269	TDH-3714	37	
1955	161-162(1)	2	GMC	367-368	TDH-3714	37	
1955	163-170	8	GMC	401-408	TDH-3714	37	
2/1955	158-162(2)	5	GMC	918-922	TDH-4512	45	
1/1956	171-180	10	GMC	1275-1284	TDH-4512	45	
8/1956	181-190	10	GMC	1766-1775	TDH-4512	45	
8/1956	191-200	10	GMC	1752-1761	TDH-4512	45	
2/1957	201-210	10	GMC	2057-2066	TDH-4512	45	
1960	2010-2011	2	GMC	476-477	TDH-4517	45	
1960	2013-2017	5	GMC	1544-1548	TDH-5301	52	To Great Lakes Transit.
1961	2125-2127	3	GMC	1018-1020	TDH-4517	45	2125-2126 to South Coast Transit Corp.
1961	2128-2129	2	GMC	1029-1030	TDH-5301	52	

METROPOLITAN TRANSIT INC.

RECEIVED	COACH NUMBERS	NUMBER COACHES	COACH BUILDERS	SERIAL NUMBER	MODEL	SEATS	NOTES
1962	1-2	2	GMC	3449, 3638	TDH-5301	52	
1963	3-8	6	GMC	473-478	TDH-5303	52	
1964	9-13	5	GMC	1689-1693	TDH-5303	52	
1964	2012-2013	2	GMC	332-333	TDH-4519	45	
1965	2014-2015	2	GMC	775-776	TDH-4519	45	
1965	2016-2017	2	GMC	901-902	TDH-4519	45	
1965	14-18	2	GMC	3145-3149	TDH-5303	52	
1966	19-23	5	GMC	4193-4197	TDH-5303	52	
1967	24-28	5	GMC	5960-5964	TDH-5303	52	
1967	101-102	2	GMC	892-893	SDM-5302	49	
1967	2018-2019	2	GMC	1625-1626	TDH-4519	45	
1968	29-36	8	GMC	184-191	T6H-5305	52	
1969	2020-2021	2	GMC	221-222	kT6H-4521	45	
1972	37-46	10	GMC	330-339	T8H-5307A	41	Leased to Metropolitan by SEMTA.
1974	103-105	3	GMC	1378, 1387, 1393	PD-4106	41	Built 1962; purchased 5/20/74 for Metropolitan by SEMTA.

1/1/74 SEMTA took over Metropolitan Transit Inc.

SEMTA Coach No. 7923L, a G.M. RTS, is shown here in a publicity photo.
Courtesy Motor Bus Society Library, Inc.

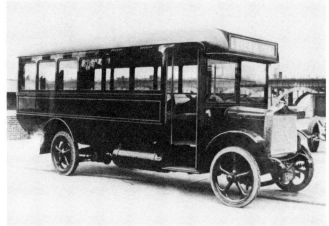

This company photo of No. 801 was taken by the gate to Water Works Park in Detroit.

Courtesy Motor Bus Society Library, Inc.

Above right: This 1924 photo of No. 135 was taken in New York, showing its original appearance as shipped to Detroit.

Courtesy Motor Bus Society Library, Inc.

Safeway coach 456 at the DSR's main shops in Highland Park on January 9, 1932. The DSR leased 60 of these coaches until the mid-1930s.

Manning Brothers Historical Collection

In 1929 the DMC purchased 32 of these Twin model 40 coaches for its heavy routes. Later, the DSR purchased all 32, renumbering them 319-350.

Schramm Collection

IMPORTANT DATES

1836

Spring   Detroit & St. Joseph Railroad starts construction.[9]

Fall   Erie & Kalamazoo opens service from Port Lawrence (Toledo) to Adrian.[11]

1837

June 20   Erie & Kalamazoo receives a Baldwin locomotive. It goes into operation within days to become the Midwest's first steam locomotive in revenue service.[38]

1838

Jan.   Michigan Central (ex-Detroit & St. Joseph) opens service from Detroit to Dearbornville (Dearborn).[11]

1839

Oct. 17   Service to Ann Arbor begins.[37]

1841

Dec. 29   Mich. Central opens to Jackson.[37]

1843

Sept. 25   Mich. Southern opens to Hillsdale.[37]

1846

Feb. 2   Mich. Central reaches Kalamazoo.[37]

March 28   State places on sale both the Central and Southern.[11]

1849

April 23   Mich. Central opens to New Buffalo with boat connections to Chicago.[11]

May 28   Mich. Central's first steamboat, *May Flower*, sets sail for Buffalo.[7]

1852

Jan. 9   Mich. Southern reaches LaPorte, Indiana.[12]

Feb. 20   Mich. Southern's Buffalo & Mississippi Rail Road complete from Michigan City to Chicago. Passengers and freight transfer to LaPorte by stage.[13]

May 21   Mich. Central opens *thru* service Detroit to Chicago.[13]

May 22   Mich. Southern opens *thru* service Toledo to Chicago.[37]

1863

Aug. 4   Detroit's first horse-drawn streetcar began revenue service on Jefferson Avenue to Elmwood Avenue. Extended to city limits (Mt. Elliott) October 1, 1863.[1]

1886

June 9   Official opening of Van Depoele electric line from Windsor to Walkerville, Ontario, Canada.[7]

Sept. 1   Detroit's first electric line started on Dix Ave. (Vernor Highway), also a Van Depoele system.[5]

1890

Sept. 30   Ann Arbor Street Railway began operation.[39]

1891

Jan. 9   Ann Arbor & Ypsilanti Street Railway began scheduled service with a small steam motor from Ypsilanti to Wells St., Ann Arbor city limits. First official trip Jan. 3.[10]

1892

June 1   Two Healy Motors began regular service operating from the River Rouge Bridge on West Jefferson to Wyandotte (first trip May 31).[6]

Nov. 24   Healy motors were replaced by electric cars between Detroit and Wyandotte, after trial run on Nov. 19 (area's first electric interurban operation).[25]

1895

July 14   Official opening of Rapid Railway from Detroit (city limits) to Mt. Clemens (first trip June 30).[11]

Aug. 21   Michigan Ave. line electrified to Livernois (city limits).[12]

Oct. 1   Pontiac to Sylvan Lake began operations.[20]

1896

Feb. 8   The Oakland Railway began operating from downtown Detroit to Royal Oak.[5]

Nov. 26   Regular electric service between Ypsilanti and Ann Arbor started. Cars could now go into downtown where steam had been prohibited. (Nov. 24 was scheduled first day, but the dynamo burned out.

1897

Aug. 29   The "Lusk Bill" became effective, which allowed the hauling of freight at night without consent of local authorities.[9]

Dec. 24   The first car operated by the Detroit, Ypsilanti & Ann Arbor Railway arrived in Dearborn from Detroit.[5]

1898

June 12   Regular service began on the Detroit, Ypsilanti & Ann Arbor Railway.[8]

June 30   The Grand River Electric Railway began operating from Detroit to Rose Hill (approximately Schoolcraft).[12]

July 4   First trip on Detroit & River St. Clair Railway to Algonac.[9]

Sept. 28   The cars of the Detroit, Lake Shore & Mt. Clemens Railway began operating from Woodward and Jefferson (trial run Aug. 8).[12]

1899

Feb. 14   First car operated from Wayne to Plymouth. Regular service started Feb. 18.[17]

Sept. 2   Line from Ypsilanti to Saline began operation.[13]

Sept. 27   The first car of the Detroit, Rochester, Romeo & Lake Orion Railway to reach the Rochester bridge.[11]

Nov. 11   Detroit, Plymouth & Northville Railway opened to Northville.[11]

1900

May 28   The line from Farmington Junction to Sylvan Lake was opened.[20]

Aug. 2   Michigan Traction started operations from Battle Creek to Kalamazoo.[10]

Sept. 27 Boland incorporates Jackson & Suburban Traction which included Jackson City lines and Jackson to Grass Lake & Wolf Lake.[11]

Nov. 10   The Detoit, Utica & Romeo Railway reached Center Line.[33]

Dec. 31   The Detroit United Railway was incorporated.[1]

1901

Jan. 23   The Detroit, Ypsilanti, Ann Arbor & Jackson Railway was incorporated to take over both the Detroit, Ypsilanti & Ann Arbor Railway plus the Ypsilanti & Saline Electric Railway, and to extend the line to Jackson.[1]

Feb. 20   The DUR took over the Wyandotte & Detroit River Railway.[1]

April 6   Detroit Council passed an ordinance requiring a depot for electric freight.[1]

May 1   The Detroit & Northwestern Railway was conveyed to the DUR.[1]

June 1   The Detroit & Pontiac Railway was conveyed to the DUR.[1]

June 29   The "Boland" line from Jackson to Grass Lake formally opened.[7]

July 1   DUR took over joint operation of Rapid Railway.[15]

July 13   The first steam train operated from Flint to Goodrich on what was later the DUR electric line.[16]

Aug. 1   The Detroit & Flint Railway gave a deed for all its property to the DUR.[1]

Aug. 22   The first car of the DYAA&J made a trip to Chelsea and back to Ann Arbor.[7]

Aug. 31   The DUR acquired the Sandwich, Windsor & Amherstberg Railway (SW&A) in Canada.[1]

Sept. 16 The first electric car arrived in Flint.[16]

Sept. 30 Jackson & Ann Arbor Railway incorporated.[1]

Oct. 14   Scheduled service began from Grand Rapids to Holland.[30]

Dec. 8   First car of DYAA&J reached Grass Lake.[7]

Dec. 23   E. W. Moore and friends made first trip from Cleveland to Detroit by electric car. Regular service operated December 1901 to January 1902, at which time the Detroit & Toledo Shore Line went bankrupt.[9]

1902

Jan. 18   The first car from Ann Arbor arrived in Jackson.[12]

Feb. 3   Lansing, St. Johns & St. Louis Railway began operations from Lansing to St. Johns with steam. On 11/14/03 electric operations began.[34]

Feb. 5   Everett-Moore syndicate went into bankruptcy.[1]

1903

June 24   Jackson & Battle Creek Traction began operations.[35]

1904

March 26 Lansing & Suburban Traction Railway purchased Lansing, St. John & St. Louis Railway.[7]

July 19   Grand Rapids, Holland & Chicago Rwy. was incorporated. On 8/1/04 takes over Holland & Lake Michigan Rwy.[11]

1906

March 1   The DUR took over control of Detroit, Monroe & Toledo Railway.[1]

March 31 Michigan United Railway filed for incorporation.[11]

May 1   MUR took over Michigan Traction including Michigan Traction Extension, Jackson & Battle Creek Traction Co. and Lansing & Suburban Traction Co.[11]

Sept. 5   Jackson, Ann Arbor & Detroit Railway incorporated and acquired the Jackson & Ann Arbor Railway and Detroit, Plymouth & Northville Railway.[1]

1907

Jan. 14   The Detroit, Jackson & Chicago incorporated to operate DUR properties Detroit to Jackson and Wayne to Northville.[1]

Feb. 1   The DYAA&J conveyed its property to DJ&C.[1]

May 9   MUR took over Jackson Consolidated Traction Co.[11]

July 19   The JAA&D conveyed its property to the DJ&C.[1]

1909

Sept. 23 Line from Lansing to Leslie opened followed by completion to Jackson 11/6/09.[36]

1911

Dec. 27   Michigan United Traction incorporated.[11]

1914

July 8   The DUR's Detroit, Almont & Northern Railway extension from Romeo to Almont opened.[1]

1915

May 17   Service between both Kalamazoo and Battle Creek to Grand Rapids begins.[37]

July 1   The DUR's Detroit interurban terminal at Bates and Jefferson opened.[1]

Aug. 20   The extension from Almont to Imlay City opened.[1]

1919

Dec.   The Ontario Hydro-Electric Power Commission allowed to purchase the SW&A from the DUR. The agreement was validated during election. But take-over occurred April 1, 1920.[31]

1920

April 5   Voters approved a $15 million bond issue to begin construction of Municipal Operation (MO) in Detroit.[3]

June 11   Detroit Motorbus starts first bus line on Jefferson using double-deck buses.[21]

1921

Feb. 1   First MO cars began operating on two Detroit city lines.[3]

Dec. 5   Stephenson line service is extended to Royal Oak.[1]

Dec. 15	DUR and DSR start joint operation on the Trumbull car line.[3]

1922

May 15	The city of Detroit purchases the DUR's lines within the city.[3]

1923

June 19	Inbound Shore Line interurbans turned at Detroit's east city limits (Wayburn loop), no longer going to the downtown terminal.[3]

1924

Sept. 14	The Peoples Motor Coach Co. incorporated by the DUR to begin bus operations.[1]
Oct. 1	Peoples Motor Coach began operation from Detroit to Wyandotte, Trenton and Grosse Ile.[1]

1925

Feb. 1	DUR replaced streetcars with buses in Ann Arbor.[1]
March 10	The court appointed receivers for the DUR on petition filed by Yellow Coach Co. (GMC).[1]
June 27	Southern Michigan Transportation incorporated to operate buses between Kalamazoo and Jackson and from Jackson to Lansing.[27]
July 10	Rapid Transportation Co. incorporated to operate buses from Bay City to Flint.[27]
Sept. 27	Rail service between Ypsilanti and Saline abandoned, replaced by buses 10/15/25.[7]

1926

June 30	Interurban service between Detroit and Farmington on Grand River abandoned and replaced by buses 7/1/26.[32]
Nov. 15	Portion of line from Jenison to Holland abandoned, portion from Jenison to Grand Rapids operated until 6/25/32.[30]

1927

April 8	Franchise runs from Wayne to Northville, to Farmington, to Redford and from Farmington Junction to Orchard Lake abandoned.[32]
May 25	Line from Wyandotte to Trenton abandoned for new super highway.[25]
June 21	The line from St. Clair Shores to Mt. Clemens abandoned.[18]
July 5	Line from Imlay City to Romeo abandoned.[19]

1928

April 1	DJ&C separates from DUR to be operated by Michigan Electric Railway.[1]
May 1	Grosse Pointe Village would not allow DUR cars to operate into village, ending service on Shore Line.[22]
Aug. 6	Western Division abandoned (Kalamazoo to Grand Rapids & Battle Creek to Allegan).[11]
Aug. 18	Detroit to Wyandotte rail line abandoned (DSR operates the portion to Penn wye until 1/18/31).[3]
Sept. 12	Sale of DUR takes place. New company is Eastern Michigan System. Officially the sale was confirmed on 9/26.[3]
Oct. 5	MPUC approved name change of all companies operated by Peoples Motor Coach to Eastern Michigan Motorbuses.[26]

Nov. 30	Jackson-Battle Creek and Kalamazoo-Battle Creek lines abandoned.[31]

1929

May	Southern Michigan Transportation took over the Rapid Transportation Co.[27]
May 16	Line between Lansing and St. John also Lansing and Owosso abandoned.[31]
May 18	Line between Lansing and Jackson abandoned.[31]
Sept. 4	Detroit, Jackson & Chicago Railway abandoned passenger operations.[2]

1930

Jan. 13	Rapid Railway line from Detroit to Port Huron via Mt. Clemens abandoned. DSR operated to Mt. Clemens until 1/11/31, after which a single daily run made to protect franchise.[2]

1931

April 25	Pontiac and Flint Divisions abandoned (City operations in both cities continued).[2]
June 18	Eastern Michigan-Toledo Railroad went into receivership.[28]
Nov. 7	Eastern Michigan Railways & Motorbuses went into receivership.[28]

1932

Jan. 1	Detroit Motorbus lost right to operate in city of Detroit. Two new companies emerged: Lake Shore Coach lines in Grosse Pointe and Dearborn Coach in that area.[3]
Oct. 5	Last car operated on Detroit to Toledo line. Last service to Detroit 10/4/32.[6]

1934

May 31	The last interurban car operated on the Stephenson line.[29]
Aug. 31	Receivership for Eastern Michigan Motorbuses ended.[27]

1935

Jan. 31	Eastern Michigan Motorbuses took over Southern Michigan Transportation Co.[27]

1938

Aug. 5	Eastern Michigan Transportation Corp. was incorporated by bondholders of Eastern Michigan Railways.[27]

1941

April 1	Greyhound took over Eastern Michigan Motorbuses.[27]
June 11	Greyhound reorganized forming Great Lakes Greyhound Lines.[23]

1956

April 8	DSR operated last streetcar in Detroit on Woodward Ave.[3]

1958

Feb.	Greyhound sold all the area suburban lines to Great Lakes Transit.[21]

1967

July 10	Southeastern Michigan Transportation Authority established by the Michigan State Legislature, Public Act 204.[21]

1971

Sept. 1	Lake Shore Coach Lines was taken over by SEMTA.[21]

1973
July 2   Pontiac Municipal Transit taken over by SEMTA.[21]

1974
Jan. 1   Metropolitan Transit was taken over by SEMTA (operated in Dearborn area).[21]

April 1   Great Lakes Transit taken over by SEMTA.[21]

1975
March 20 Martin Lines taken over by SEMTA (operated in Woodward corridor).[21]

Sources

1. Detroit United Railway files
2. Eastern Michigan System files
3. Detroit-Department of Street Railways (DSR)
4. *History of Detroit and Michigan*, by Silas Farmer
5. The *Detroit News* (originally *Evening News*)
6. *So Proudly We Record* (History of Wyandotte)
7. The *Detroit Free Press*
8. The *Ann Arbor Argus*
9. The *Detroit Journal* (absorbed by *News* 7/21/22)
10. Beal in *Michigan Pioneer History*
11. *Poor's Manual* various years
12. *Detroit Tribune*
13. The *Ann Arbor-Argus-Democrat*
14. *Rochester Era*
15. Jenks Papers (Burton Historical Collection)
16. *To-Day* Detroit paper
17. The *Northville Record*
18. *Mt. Clemens Monitor*
19. *Port Huron Times Herald*
20. *Pontiac Press*
21. Detroit Motorbus files
22. *Flint Daily Journal*
23. Dept. of State Files (Michigan)
24. Southeastern Michigan Transportation Authority
25. *Wyandotte Herald*
26. Michigan Public Utilities Commission papers
27. *Bus Transportation* various issues
28. *Moody's Public Utilities* various years
29. *Royal Oak Tribune*
30. *Interurban Era in Holland*, by Donald L. van Reken
31. *Garden Gateway to Canada* (History of Windsor)
32. *Plymouth Mail*
33. *Utica Sentinel*
34. The *Lansing State Journal*
35. *Jackson Daily Citizen*
36. *Jackson Patriot*
37. Annual Reports of Commissioners of Railroads
38. *Toledo Blade*
39. *Ann Arbor Democrat*
40. A. R. Lenderink, "Interurban Railway in Kalamazoo County," in *Michigan History* (March 1959)
41. *All Aboard* by Willis Dunbar
42. LaPorte, Indiana, newspapers
43. *Chicago Journal*
44. CERA Bulletin #103

CITY STREETCAR SYSTEMS IN MICHIGAN

Lower Peninsula

CITY	HORSECAR	ELECTRIC	MILES	ABANDONED
Adrian	—	1889	4	1924
Ann Arbor	—	1980	6	1925
Battle Creek	1883	1893	15	1932
Bay City	1865	1887	14	1921
Benton Harbor & St. Joseph	1888	1892	12	1935
Cheboygan	1893	—	3	1898
Detroit	1863	1892	(a)	1956
Detroit (suburbs)	—	1886	(b)	(c)
Fenton	1891	—	2	1915
Flint	—	1901	41	1936
Grand Haven	—	1902(d)	2	1928
Grand Rapids	1864(e)	1891	68	1935
Grand Rapids & Jenison	—	1927	8	1932
Holland	—	1899(d)	6	1926
Jackson	1886	1891	16	1936
Kalamazoo	1885	1893	16	1932
Lansing	1885	1890	17	1933
Manistee	—	1892	10	1921
Monroe	—	1917	2	1919
Mt. Clemens	1890	1895	3	1930
Muskegon	1882(f)	1890	13	1929
Owosso & Corunna	?	1895	5	1926
Pontiac	—	1895	14	1931
Port Huron	1860	1886	12	1930
Saginaw	—	1890	21	1931
Ypsilanti	1896(g)	1896	1	1917

Upper Peninsula

CITY	HORSECAR	ELECTRIC	MILES	ABANDONED
Escanaba	—	1892	20	1932
Houghton Cty	—	1900	32	1932
Iron River	—	1913	6	1921
Ironwood & Hurley	—	1910	12	1932
Ishpeming & Negaunee	—	1893	5	1927
Marquette	—	1891	6	1935
Menominee & Marinette	1889	1890	18	1928
S. S. Marie	—	1888	8	1931

(a) Maximum city trackage—1934 a high of 466.66 miles (included leased track to Royal Oak).
(b) Two systems: Woodward Ave. & Dix Ave. 3.25 miles.
(c) Woodward Ave. became part of city line and Dix Ave converted to horsecar line.
(d) Seasonal operation
(e) Also had cable cars
(f) Mule operation
(g) Steam operation (part of Ypsi-Ann 1891)

INDEX